D0443977

OUTRAGE, INC.

OUTRAGE, INC.

How the Liberal Mob Ruined Science,
Journalism, and Hollywood

DEREK HUNTER

An Imprint of HarperCollins*Publishers*

OUTRAGE, INC. Copyright © 2018 by Derek Hunter. All rights reserved. Printed in the United States of America. No part of this book may be used or reproduced in any manner whatsoever without written permission except in the case of brief quotations embodied in critical articles and reviews. For information, address HarperCollins Publishers, 195 Broadway, New York, NY 10007.

HarperCollins books may be purchased for educational, business, or sales promotional use. For information, please email the Special Markets Department at SPsales@harpercollins.com.

Broadside Books™ and the Broadside logo are trademarks of HarperCollins Publishers.

FIRST EDITION

Library of Congress Cataloging-in-Publication Data has been applied for.

ISBN 978-0-06-283552-9

18 19 20 21 22   LSC   10 9 8 7 6 5 4 3 2 1

Contents

Introduction

On inauguration day for President Donald Trump, the professional demonstrator class took to the streets of the nation's capital to express their deeply held belief that smashing store windows and burning cars was the best way to advance the cause of justice. Justice for what was never explained. But the next day, again in the name of justice, they broke out their crocheted "pussy hats" and chanted dried-up slogans in the Women's March because, apparently, Trump had a secret plan to ban women, or something. Who knew that the only thing denying the masses justice was the lack of burning limos and some yarn?

Those liberal rage protests were made-for-TV events, perfect for media still in shock that all their hard work to elect Hillary Clinton had been rejected by residents of swing states they'd universally assumed were in the bag for her. Decades of in-kind donations in the form of favorable and soft-pedaled coverage not only hadn't paid off, they'd backfired.

Tears flowed, and resolve hardened. The great unshowered drum circle of animosity had to be kept rolling for the liberal cause, harnessed under the banner of "the resistance." But unlike real heroes, whose lives were on the line when they stood up to tyranny under that name, these "fighters" were facing off with shadows cast by their own imaginations. And it worked.

Angry thousands took to the streets, demanding action, or inaction, or something. Their demands weren't particularly clear, but they were serious, damn it, because they were under assault, or something.

Three months later, it was the March for Science. Donald Trump, still imbued with that "new president smell," was a threat somehow.

The *New York Times* headline said it—"Scientists, Feeling Under Siege, March Against Trump Policies"[1]—so it must be true: scientists were "under siege," and were becoming an army of Steven Seagals.

But how? What had President Trump done in ninety days to drive people into the streets, to make them feel "under siege," as the *Times* put it? Nothing, really. He'd called human-caused climate change a "hoax" created to harm US manufacturing during the campaign, which is hardly a fringe opinion, but as far as any policy action went, he hadn't even pulled the United States out of the symbolic Paris Agreement yet.

The *Times* said that the participating scientists were "abandoning a tradition of keeping the sciences out of politics and calling on the public to stand up for scientific enterprise."[2]

But is there a "tradition of keeping the sciences out of politics" anymore? From abortion to nuclear power, politics is in everything now, so why would anyone expect the March for Science to be any different?

A simple check of the march's sponsors on its website would have revealed a veritable who's who of liberal activist groups and organizations dependent, to one degree or another, on government "investment" in their industries, mostly climate change. Many of them oppose nuclear power, despite its being the cleanest power source available. And what does the United Auto Workers union have to do with science?

This continuation of the inauguration day riots and the Women's March, this protest "for science" was populated by gluten-free, juice-cleansing progressives who don't vaccinate their children, yet the media ignored the "Star Wars cantina" of liberals and organizations in their reporting and simply went with the "nonpartisan" label. But declaring something nonpartisan doesn't make it so, or no one in Washington, DC, would be partisan. By contrast, the annual March for Life is rightly labeled as "conservative" by the media because it is, in fact, organized by conservatives.

There's nothing wrong with liberals organizing a liberal march for a liberal cause; that part is fundamentally American. And there's nothing surprising about march organizers attempting to hide their political agenda in the hope of broadening their appeal. The problem enters when the referees—journalists—play along.

It could be chalked up to laziness; simply copying and pasting a group's press release is a lot easier than looking into who the people are, which seems dangerously close to work. While journalists are known for their laziness, they're also known for their liberal bias. That's what was at play with coverage of the March for Science and pretty much every other march since Donald Trump was elected president.

But why did science—the pursuit of truth—become political? Because there's power in it—the power to impact policy and federal and state law. With that power comes money in the form of government grants and donations from wealthy benefactors who, oftentimes, stand to make their personal fortunes even larger if government forces Americans to use their products and services under the banner of "green energy."

Former vice president Al Gore didn't amass a net worth of more than $200 million while hosting teleconferences from his solar-powered bunker in the woods and encouraging people to ride their bikes to work. He made it while flying in private jets to exotic locations around the world to chastise the average person driving a pickup truck to a job site about how he needs to lower his "carbon footprint."

The March for Science is a prime example of what has happened to journalists—they've set aside skepticism and the documenting of events and exchanged them for "pussy hats" and a seat in the drum circle.

The worst thing ever to happen to journalism wasn't social media or cable news, though both played their part in its demise; it was Watergate.

The most celebrated moment in journalistic history (celebrated again at the 2017 White House Correspondents' Dinner), it created the concept of the reporter as celebrity. Bob Woodward and Carl Bernstein made an untold fortune, were played in a movie by Robert Redford and Dustin Hoffman, were showered with awards, and sent many journalists running down the path of fame rather than truth. And fame is the only thing heroin gets addicted to.

The thing was, Woodward and Bernstein were real journalists. They reported a real story of corruption, worked sources, uncovered information, checked their facts, and got the story right. In other words, they earned their accolades.

Today, too many journalists aren't interested in doing the work, they just want the rewards. For a journalist or pundit to achieve some level of fame, all he or she has to do is get on TV. And the bar for entry for that has been lowered to the point that you'd need a shovel to get under it.

What once required sources, digging, and investigation now consists of information simply given to reporters by partisans to harm their opponents and rumors reported with little to no verification—a game of telephone with second- and thirdhand information whispered by anonymous sources whose motives and truthfulness go unquestioned if the information is juicy enough.

Add in the immediacy of the Internet age—report the story first, check the facts later—and you have a profession where verification is for suckers. Twitter followers, Facebook fans, page views, and TV hits are the hard currency of journalism. Impartiality is as quaint a notion as going steady or waiting until marriage is in the time of Tinder.

The truth about journalism is that it stopped being about truth a long time ago. All the 2016 election did was free reporters from the last vestiges of an antiquated notion of impartiality.

Edward R. Murrow, Walter Cronkite, Tom Brokaw, Peter Jennings, and Dan Rather all had their biases, but there was nothing to contrast them against to expose just how pronounced they were. Fox News changed that, and the new media of the Internet gave new avenues for stories to reach the public.

What once was left of center is now "Mao was a corporate sell-out" crazy, and proudly so. Journalists are a few years away from wearing all-black Antifa uniforms and covering the Democratic National Convention as delegates.

Until journalists fully remove their masks, it's important to know that what you're seeing is what they want you to see—stories they deem newsworthy, presented in a way most favorable to their sensitivities. Media bias is more than just how a story is reported, it's which stories are reported. The power to ignore, to pick and choose, is the most pernicious power journalists have, and they exercise it regularly.

That's why they've always hated Rush Limbaugh, it's why they hate Fox, it's why they hate conservative news websites—they allow the public to see what's on the cutting room floor, the stories and the opinions they didn't want you to see.

This exposure is changing journalism. Some news outlets still have investigation teams and do deep dives into important issues, but they're becoming rarer than unicorns. Everyone else has realized that they can attract as many eyeballs with quick, drive-by stories with deeply partisan headlines. It's clickbait; sensational reporting that makes the *Weekly World News* seem like the Pentagon Papers.

We've entered a new era of political bias and near-uniform group-think. In the wake of the riots in Ferguson, Missouri, and the rise of #BlackLivesMatter, the Left decided that racism is rampant in America and its most pressing problem. Common sense and hard data showed otherwise, but journalists weren't about to let the facts stand in the way of a good narrative. Taking issue with any part of that narrative suddenly made you a hatemonger whose opinions should not be heard. That may be a lot of things, but what it is decidedly not is journalism.

———————

This is a book about what happens when one political faction claims exclusive domain over the truth and works to prevent any further discussion on the concept. Since the media have long had a liberal bias, that's been easy to miss or misunderstand. However, when you look at the virtual industry created to churn up outrage, it becomes clear that conservatives have been elbowed out of journalism—and science and pop culture. Under the guise of saving these institutions, making them "more progressive," they have actually destroyed them.

To "save" journalism from conservatives, newspapers stopped printing "all the news that's fit to print," changing to "the truth is more important now than ever," as the *New York Times'* motto now says. To save science from conservatives, the media lowered the bar for deciding what's true. To save pop culture from conservatives, they made entertainment that didn't entertain anyone.

We tend to talk about liberal bias as a frustration, an annoyance we've learned to live with, a distracting background noise conservatives have to tune out. The problem with this is that it's accepting defeat. And defeat on this issue is a major loss on the wider issue of what kind of country we will have.

We now live in a country where liberals don't just get to frame the debate, they are trying to decide what the facts are and who is allowed in on the discussion. To defeat this subtle, fascistic purge from the public square, you have to know how to recognize it; you can't fight what you can't see. We need a guide to recognizing the danger of letting this process continue unchallenged before it lays total claim to the capital "T" truth and successfully runs conservatives out of public life.

———————

You can see the blending of pop culture and journalism in the way the media report on the favorites of the East Coast elites. You'd think that entertainment is just that: entertainment. You'd be wrong. Everything has been weaponized in this battle. As Andrew Breitbart said, "Politics is downstream from culture."

Judging solely by the media attention it got, you'd think *The Daily Show* when the vaunted Jon Stewart was host was one of the most watched shows of the twenty-first century. You would be wrong—it rarely made the top 100 rated shows of the week. Yes, you read that right. *The Daily Show,* even with Stewart as host, routinely garnered fewer viewers than reruns of *Family Guy* on the Cartoon Network. Yet when Stewart spoke, the media listened—even though the people didn't.

The power of the media is both the power to create and the power to destroy. For every media-created sensation, there is someone whose life was obliterated by the hashtag mafia.

From an anonymous public relations professional who had her life turned upside down over a joke tweet to an employee at a charity being fired because the media decided a picture of a woman they'd never heard of before was newsworthy, slow news days and the faux-outrage culture have a string of bodies behind them.

And that's the problem: outrage fuels page views, and page views equal money.

Journalists like to act like they're above the fray, interested only in the self-imposed nobility of their profession, yet they happily dive into the dirt when outrage can be stoked to create a story. If it offends liberals, it leads.

TMZ and *People* magazine are expected to be fluff, *Time* is expected to be news. You'd be hard pressed to spot the difference between them now.

All this while journalists shower themselves with more awards than Hollywood does.

What these liberals can't understand is that flyover country is content to put in an honest day's work for enough money to keep their families fed, housed, and clothed. Unlike liberals, when they see a successful person with a big house and a nice car, they don't turn to their kids and lecture them on how it's unfair that someone has more than they do; they tell them that they, too, can have those things if they work for them.

That there's a large swath of the country content with the ability to afford beer and have their weekends free for hanging out with friends on a lake or a road trip to an amusement park is anathema to the average liberal journalist. On the Upper West Side of Manhattan or in the power circles of DC, you'd be institutionalized for even joking about such things.

Every election cycle, the liberals emerge from their cocoons, grab their media credentials, and set off to visit flyoverland to cover political races the way an elementary school takes a field trip to a zoo.

They file stories from diners, then run back to the safety of their hives—and, after a good delousing and Silkwood shower, regale their colleagues with tales of slumming it and set back out on their quest to change the world.

None of this is lost on their audience. But their audience is lost because of this.

Speaking of alienating audiences, no group has been more eager to embrace any liberal cause or agenda item than Hollywood. Actors, producers, and movie executives proudly paint themselves as champions of the average American—from their walled-off mansions in their double-gated communities.

Agenda-driven movies are churned out regularly, picturing an evil corporation planning to poison a small town or a corrupt billionaire willing to risk it all on some illegal scam to win a little more.

Most of these movies and shows aren't produced with profit in mind; they have a message they want to convey. Only audiences don't show up to hear it.

Hollywood excels at presenting the rare as the norm in the name of a liberal agenda. The percentage of transgender characters on TV, for example, exceeds any reasonable estimate of the percentage in the population at large by a factor of at least ten.

But such character choices and casting decisions mean free and favorable press for a project and many times the showering of the main currency in Hollywood (after huge piles of cash and hookers): awards.

Entertainment, like sports, serves a purpose: an escape from the stresses of everyday life. But escape isn't allowed anymore; everything is political because, to many, politics is everything.

Hollywood is littered with high school dropouts with net worths larger than some third-world countries' GDP who gleefully lecture Americans on their need to live differently, to "shrink their carbon footprint," while doing body shots off the flavor-of-the-month Victoria's Secret model on their party yacht. Nothing against Victoria's Secret models or party yachts—the world would be a happier place if there were more of both—but the American people are tiring of lectures on how people who don't live in New York or Los Angeles should live by millionaires whose only interaction with the rest of the country is when their private jets discharge their chemical toilets on them from 25,000 feet.

That might be why movies had the lowest attendance in twenty years in 2017;[3] if the public wants to be preached to, they'll go to church, not the theater.

Holding your audience in contempt, it turns out, is not a smart business model.

But politics, if you'll excuse the expression, trumps everything. Especially in the age of Trump.

Together, journalism, science, and Hollywood form the legs of a stool of manipulation; an unholy trinity of propaganda to herd the masses into a corral of contentment. With institutions of higher learning churning out a new batch of self-entitled delicate little flowers ready to be offended, it couldn't have gone more smoothly if it had been planned by the Democratic Party itself.

But a little thing called Fox News came along, followed by the Internet. With them came the free flow of information that marked the beginning of the end for the old monopolies.

People are learning that they've been shown the world through a small window and now have access to a panoramic view of things. The old order is dangling off a cliff, scrambling to keep its last few fingers of grip on the way things will soon used to be.

This book is not about any one event or any particular series of events; it's about exposing the liberal anger industry that has created systemic bias and subtle indoctrination designed to manipulate an unsuspecting public. Because an angry person tends not to think logically, and logic is the kryptonite of modern liberalism.

It's about how these once great and important institutions have become a complete mockery of what they once were, of what they purport to still be. It's about standards and how those who hold others to them don't come close to meeting them themselves. It's about how, were it not for double standards, liberals would have no standards at all.

It is . . . an outrage.

OUTRAGE, INC.

Chapter 1

The Crazy Factory

There's an amazing phenomenon that occurs in some human beings when things are going well—they actively seek something to be upset about. This is a distinctly first-world problem.

School systems across the country will dispatch a SWAT team to the cafeteria should any student dare bring a peanut butter and jelly sandwich, with or without the crust cut off, because many of the delicate little flower children could go into anaphylactic shock from their peanut allergy. In the third world, where starvation reigns, peanut allergies are virtually nonexistent.

When Anderson Cooper of *60 Minutes* went to Niger to report on the devastating malnutrition of children in that country and the revolutionary vitamin-enriched peanut butter–based product called Plumpy'Nut, he asked the head of Doctors Without Borders about the scourge of peanut allergies sweeping the developed world. "We just don't see it," Dr. Susan Shepherd responded. "In developing countries food allergy is not nearly the problem that it is in industrialized countries."[1]

While the peanut is revolutionizing famine relief and saving lives, it's being banned in schools across the United States as if it were a weapon of mass destruction.

Is there something uniquely unhealthy or deficient about the biological makeup of children in the richest country on the planet? Or is there something different, something sociological, at work?

A mere century ago, and for all of human existence, almost everyone's daily lives revolved around one simple goal: not dying.

You'd get up in the morning, work all day to gather enough food to keep yourself and your family alive, hope you didn't hurt yourself in that process, and go to bed with the need to repeat the pattern again tomorrow. A broken limb could mean hunger; a simple cut could lead to an infection that caused death. And there was always the possibility of flu taking you out, or a drought, or insects, or simply a stranger coming along and killing you. Life was a daily struggle for literal survival for most of human existence.

Around the time of the Industrial Revolution and the years that followed, life changed dramatically. What was backbreaking work became mechanized, saving effort and lives. Simple diseases such as tetanus were defeated. Instead of meaning death, they could now be beaten with a quick shot from a doctor, freeing people to go about their day.

But something in our reptilian brains won't let us accept how good we have it, how safe we are. We seek out threats, create problems, because it's easier to blame something external for our difficulties than it is to accept blame for our bad decisions or realize that, for lack of a better phrase, "shit happens."

You'd think a generation raised in the 1970s with that bumper sticker on the back of so many station wagons would have come to terms with that fact, but there's too much political gain to be made from laying responsibility on others that the social sciences have evolved into excuse-manufacturing machines for failures.

Nothing exemplifies this psychobabble of pop psychology like the concepts of "microaggressions" and "privilege." They're like a blanket absolution from the pope to all Catholics—they're your cosmic "get out of jail free" card.

For the uninitiated, meaning the sane, a microaggression is defined by Merriam-Webster as "a comment or action that subtly and often unconsciously or unintentionally expresses a prejudiced attitude toward a member of a marginalized group (such as a racial minority)."[2]

To put that into plain English, a microaggression is a "transgression" or "insensitivity," usually racial or gender-based, so minute that it's possible that neither the offender nor the offended realize it or recognize it as such at the time. It's really the concept of third-party offense that is now treated as a rational assault of some kind. And also a new level of insanity in a time when there are very few overt or covert offenses to crusade against.

In short, it's a way to manufacture outrage in a time with few outrages. Therefore, it is a "legitimate" field to be studied.

One such example of those studies is the National Science Foundation's awarding of a $548,459 grant to the University of Michigan to look at "Microaggressions in Engineering Student Teams: Effects on Learning, Performance, and Persistence." The thesis is that evil urinal users make women so uncomfortable that they are literally chasing them out of the field of engineering. The abstract reads, in part:

> *This early stage research project will identify specific behavioral manifestations of gender stereotypes—microaggressions—and their cumulative effect on learning, performance, and persistence in introductory engineering course teamwork. Such microaggressions may cause the climate of the team to become less welcoming to women. The proposed research unites two areas of strong research interest (social science research on gender stereotypes and engineering education on teamwork and climate) to advance understanding of women's underrepresentation in engineering as compared to men.[3]*

Why is it important that "science" discover why men are more interested in a particular field of study than women and not vice versa (which is a question rarely asked)? The truth is, it is not. Men and women are different. That didn't used to be a controversial statement to make. But now saying it could land you in a reeducation gulag or get you exiled from your profession.

Exile was the punishment for Tim Hunt, Nobel laureate in physiology or medicine in 2001, when he made a joke about women in a laboratory setting in 2015. He told a conference, "Let me tell you about my trouble with girls. Three things happen when they are in the lab. You fall in love with them, they fall in love with you, and when you criticize them, they cry."

The seventy-two-year-old was clearly joking, but joking and micro-aggressing are the same thing—all parts of privilege; in this case, the most pernicious form of privilege the world has ever known: white privilege.

Time magazine pounced with a piece soaked in bias entitled "A Nobel Scientist Just Made a Breathtakingly Sexist Speech at International Conference." Soon every major news outlet was on the case with a similar story dripping with outrage and contempt.

Caving in to the mob, Hunt's employer relieved him of his teaching post at University College London and he became the object of ridicule and scorn across the media and academia. All over a joke.

Microaggressions are all the rage now in the social scientists' scramble to create more victims. The National Science Foundation doled out another grant for $229,061 to the University of Georgia for "Exploring Racial Microaggression in Science Education."[4]

The quarter of a million taxpayer dollars were awarded for the university to

> *examine ways to broaden participation in STEM for science education faculty of African ancestry and science education Latino/a faculty. Research shows that science and science education faculty and students from these populations regularly face intentional and unintentional acts of racial microaggressions that often negatively impact whether they remain in the STEM pipeline. Since many of these acts of racial microaggression come from administrators, colleagues, and peers, this project will serve as an important step in directly addressing this issue. The research will (a) identify actions or activities that might be precursors of or lead to microaggressions; (b) seek to better understand why the microaggressors might be aware or unaware of their acts; and (c) collect data about approaches and policies that have been used by colleagues and administrators to minimize racial microaggressions.[5]*

Again, a third-party observer will be at the ready to be offended should anything offensive slip past the actual participants, and to reeducate any and all parties, should they require it.

The abstract continues, "The Critical Race Theory will be used as the lens to frame the study."[6]

Again, for normal people who aren't obsessed with or haven't figured out how to monetize victimhood, here is how the UCLA School of Public Affairs defines critical race theory:

> CRT recognizes that racism is engrained in the fabric and system of the American society. The individual racist need not exist to note that institutional racism is pervasive in the dominant culture. This is the analytical lens that CRT uses in examining existing power structures. CRT identifies that these power structures are based on white privilege and white supremacy, which perpetuates the marginalization of people of color. CRT also rejects the traditions of liberalism and meritocracy. Legal discourse says that the law is neutral and colorblind, however, CRT challenges this legal "truth" by examining liberalism and meritocracy as a vehicle for self-interest, power, and privilege. CRT also recognizes that liberalism and meritocracy are often stories heard from those with wealth, power, and privilege. These stories paint a false picture of meritocracy; everyone who works hard can attain wealth, power, and privilege while ignoring the systemic inequalities that institutional racism provides.[7]

In short, everyone is racist, everything is racist, you're a racist even if you're not racist, because of racism. Or something.

You can't escape. You're guilty of something, nebulously defined, that you can't help but commit because the "system" in which you live is built on it.

Similar theories can be found to explain gender, sexual orientation, class, religion (not Christianity), age, and nearly every other way human beings can be subdivided. And the government is using our tax dollars to study all of it.

It's called "intersectionality," which is a made-up term to "describe overlapping or intersecting social identities and related systems of oppression, domination, or discrimination. Intersectionality is the idea that multiple identities intersect to create a whole that is different from the component identities. These identities that can intersect include gender, race, social class, ethnicity, nationality, sexual orientation, religion, age, mental disability, physical disability, mental illness, and physical illness as well as other forms of identity."[8] These characteristics create a hierarchy in victimhood.

The concept of intersectionality allows literally anything to be blamed on someone else. Didn't get a job you wanted? Intersectionality has you covered—it was because you're X, Y, or Z. Got pulled over for speeding? Same rules apply.

There is nothing for which blame can't be attributed to an external force or entity under the umbrella of intersectionality.

The only question is: When will we have done enough to remedy every potential victim's complaints?

———————————

What's wrong with encouraging women who are interested in becoming scientists to feel more comfortable in graduate programs? Nothing, if that were the point here. But it's not. Instead, we're seeing a dynamic that will come into play throughout the book. Many academic disciplines pushed out their most conservative members over time. Then they pushed out the conservatives who were left. Then they pushed out the conservative moderates who were left. They always want the most conservative third of their colleagues intimidated, quieted, and expelled, no matter how liberal that third might be.

That ongoing purge is spreading out from US universities, and it's moving through journalism, science, and pop culture, politicizing and thereby destroying all of them. It's worth seeing what the rot has done to our colleges, because that's where everything else flows from.

There is no quarter for anyone looking for sanity in modern

times. Common sense, as the saying goes, is not all that common—and it's becoming less common every year. For all the indoctrinating and brainwashing the media and Hollywood do, they are pikers compared to the numbers of delicate participation trophy-stockpiling zombies the crazy factories are churning out annually.

Growing up, you probably saw a few movies about what college life was like or could be like. They involved parties, road trips, some douchebag with a popped collar and a BMW trying to steal someone's girlfriend, and all manner of other things that made the idea of burying your future in student loan debt worth it. In reality, college is now a series of grievance filings and protest marches over everything. To echo Marlon Brando in *The Wild Ones*, when asked what students are protesting against, their answer is pretty much "Whaddya got?"

Colleges have transformed from oases of ideas and questions to reenactments of East Berlin at the height of the Cold War. Paranoia reigns, and radical left-wing politics and outrage are the currency of the realm.

Other than Bitcoin and the Apple stock price, few things have increased at the rate of college tuition. In the 1987–88 school year, the average annual cost of a four-year private school was $15,160; that increased to $34,740 in 2017–18.[9] From a percentage standpoint, public four-year schools saw a higher average increase over the same period, going from $3,190 to $9,970.[10]

For that "investment," four-year institutions graduate, on average, only 54.8 percent of students after six years.[11] Though slightly higher than .500 is likely a good enough winning percentage to get you into the NFL playoffs, it's less than optimal when the flip side is sleeping in your parents' basement with crushing debt.

Considering that the average college graduate in 2015 had $30,100 in loan debt upon graduation,[12] which doesn't count people who borrowed thousands or tens of thousands of dollars and didn't graduate, you can see why some students could be upset.

What they should be upset about is the poor quality of what they're learning even if they do graduate.

With the possible exception of an online university or two, campuses from coast to coast have become petri dishes of progressive politics, the reeducation camps of the American Left charging a fortune per credit hour.

It'd be slightly less bad if these institutions were funded privately, but most are getting a cut of your paycheck, which means there's a drop of your sweat equity in every drum circle, every storming of a speech, and every list of demands these entitled wannabe activists hand-deliver to an overpaid administrator who is all too willing to capitulate.

You have to wonder what the kids are learning and what classes they are taking to have so much free time on their hands. The answer is as horrifying as it is hilarious.

These are real classes that have been offered at various times at major universities:

Massachusetts Institute of Technology: Topics in Comparative Media: American Pro Wrestling

Course description: This class will explore the cultural history and media industry surrounding the masculine drama of professional wrestling. Beginning with wrestling's roots in sport and carnival, the class examines how new technologies and changes in the television industry led to evolution for pro wrestling style and promotion and how shifts in wrestling characters demonstrate changes in the depiction of American masculinity. The class will move chronologically in an examination of how wrestling characters and performances have changed, focusing particularly on the 1950s to the present. Students may have previous knowledge of wrestling but are not required to, nor are they required to be a fan (although it is certainly not discouraged, either).[13]

Oberlin College: How to Win a Beauty Pageant: Race, Gender, Culture, and US National Identity

This course examines US beauty pageants from the 1920s to the present. Our aim will be to analyze pageantry as a unique site for the interplay of race, gender, class, sexuality, and nation. We will learn about cultural studies methodology, including close reading, cultural history, critical discourse analysis, and ethnography, and use those methods to understand the changing identity of the US over time. This course includes a field visit to a pageant in Ohio.[14]

University of Pennsylvania: Wasting Time on the Internet: Live without dead time.—Situationist graffiti, Paris, May 1968

We spend our lives in front of screens, mostly wasting time: checking social media, watching cat videos, chatting, and shopping. What if these activities—clicking, SMSing, status-updating, and random surfing—were used as raw material for creating compelling and emotional works of literature? Could we reconstruct our autobiography using only Facebook? Could we write a great novella by plundering our Twitter feed? Could we reframe the internet as the greatest poem ever written? Using our laptops and a wifi connection as our only materials, this class will focus on the alchemical recuperation of aimless surfing into substantial works of literature. Students will be required to stare at the screen for three hours, only interacting through chat rooms, bots, social media and listservs. To bolster our practice, we'll explore the long history of the recuperation of boredom and time-wasting through critical texts about affect theory, ASMR, situationism and everyday life by thinkers such as Guy Debord, Mary Kelly Erving Goffman, Betty Friedan, Raymond Williams, John Cage, Georges Perec, Michel de Certeau, Henri Lefebvre, Trin Minh-ha, Stuart Hall, Sianne Ngai, Siegfried Kracauer and others. Distraction, multi-tasking, and aimless drifting is mandatory.[15]

Cornell University: Tree Climbing: Whether you are a rain forest canopy researcher, an arborist, or just a kid at heart, everyone loves to climb trees. Recall the excitement and your sense of adventure when you first crawled into the branches to look inside a bird's nest. Then you swung from limb to limb without a thought of ropes and harnesses. But what about that big tree down the street you always wanted to climb, but couldn't reach the first branch? Cornell Outdoor Education's Tree Climbing course will teach you how to get up into the canopy of any tree, to move around, even to climb from one tree to another without touching the ground. This course will teach you how to use ropes and technical climbing gear to reach the top of any tree, to move around, and even to climb from tree to tree without returning to the ground. All equipment is included in the course fee.[16]

What parents wouldn't be proud to pay Ivy League prices for their child to learn to climb a tree?

If they were only climbing a tree, it might not be that awful. It'd be a waste of time and money, but at least it would be only a wasted class or two that are little more than a distraction but count toward an overall credit total, so little damage done. That, however, is not where the damage institutions of higher education are fomenting either begins or ends. On the slightly more innocuous "waste" side of the equation sit gender and ethnic studies.

While the idea of majoring in bisexual polar bear studies might be appealing to people who want to piss off their parents, it's not exactly an "in demand" career path. Aside from being qualified to teach others these worthless topics, there aren't exactly a lot of jobs out there for people who've majored in "an interdisciplinary field that focuses on the complex interaction of gender with other identity markers such as race, ethnicity, sexuality, nation, and religion," as UCLA describes its Department of Gender Studies.[17]

These "grievance studies" fields train still-forming minds to seek and find injustices, real or imagined. The obsession with the superficial—skin color, how people go to the bathroom, who they sleep with, their religion—becomes all-consuming because, they are taught, oppression is all around and must be destroyed.

These social justice warriors (which can't really be that far off as an optional major, or at least minor, for students, probably at Smith College or UC Berkeley) learn everything there is to know about something no one cares about. They're well versed on who was the first of each configuration of human being to accomplish something without ever realizing that the accomplishment itself doesn't need the qualifier.

There are 7 billion people on the planet; only a handful have ever flown on a space shuttle. Therefore, flying on the space shuttle is an amazing accomplishment in and of itself. Yet leftist professors and students look not at the accomplishment itself as something worthy of celebration but at the race of the person.

Guion Bluford was the first African American to go into space and to fly on a space shuttle.[8] He did so in 1983, in the early years of the program. Bluford is not remarkable because he's a black guy who went to space or flew on the space shuttle; he's remarkable because he went into space. You haven't flown on a space shuttle, have you? See?

But to say that in 2018 is the modern equivalent of burning a cross on someone's front lawn to social justice warriors (SJWs).

To focus on a person's race for an accomplishment is to cheapen the accomplishment. "See, even a (whatever type of person) can do this" is the mentality. Well, why wouldn't every type of person be able to do that? Why is it extra special that one person did it? SJWs don't realize it, but the patronizing attitude of "You can do it, too" toward various configurations of people implies that they believe it is special that the others did it, as if they or the world didn't think they could.

This mentality stems from college grievance majors. Many programs started decades ago, when there were real problems to be addressed. Ironically, as the problems were solved, instead of terminating the courses or refocusing them as historical studies, the departments grew even larger and more powerful. So they needed to create new problems.

That universities would choose to offer degrees in gender or ethnic studies is a testament to the influence of liberals on education. You'd have better luck finding a thriving video store that rented exclusively Betamax tapes than you would finding demand in the private sector for someone with a degree in "queer studies."

Social sciences and the humanities, the umbrella under which the various gender and ethnic studies fall, rank second and sixth in the majors with the highest unemployment rates, respectively.[19] Combined, which they really should be, they'd win by a mile. (First is architecture, which makes more sense if you try to think of a successful architect beyond Frank Lloyd Wright and Mike Brady.)

You'd be better served by setting a huge pile of cash on fire than pursuing a degree in these fields—at least you'd get some warmth out of the deal. Though this may be temporary, you'd happily trade temporary for the permanence of student loans, from which even personal bankruptcy can't spare students.

Emboldened by the ability to obtain a gold-embossed certificate declaring them an expert in grievance studies, SJWs set out to find and correct the "rampant problems" of racism, sexism, homophobia, Islamophobia, transphobia . . . pretty much everything this side of triskaidekaphobia, because who are you to judge numbers?

One of the issues for these soldiers in an army of generals is that when they go looking for problems to solve, they don't find them; they can't find them. Yes, they do exist; in a nation of 330 million people there are going to be bigoted people, but they're far from the norm. They're the half teaspoon of salt in the chocolate chip cookie dough—you don't even know it's there.

Thanks to the liberal mob—empowered, emboldened, and encouraged by professors and administrators who should know better (and do, but their jobs have to be justified)—college campuses have become hotbeds of protests against phantoms and ghosts. And worse, hoaxes.

The spike in fake "hate crimes" is a result of whipping students into a frenzy over the prospect of those things existing on campus.

When fired-up SJWs can't find what they've been told is prevalent, they create it themselves to "draw attention" to the problem.

Evergreen State College in Washington spent most of 2017 under siege, not by some outside set of rabble-rousers, but by its own student body. The tiny liberal college committed the unforgivable sin of employing someone who dared disagree with an angry liberal mob demanding, of all things, segregation.

No, these weren't Klansmen in America's Northwest suddenly mobilizing out of thin air to declare that the races should not mix, these were rabid left-wingers who wanted all white students to leave campus for a day because they were white. Unless the dictionary has been rewritten, this is the very definition of segregation by race.

Local media called this discrimination "a campuswide equity proposal."[20]

"A day of absence" is part of a traditional liberal activism two-day workshop at Evergreen, described as "a day for community building around identity groups. We achieve this by voluntary identity group gatherings. People who would like to participate in Day of Absence are free to choose which identity group gathering to attend."[21]

According to the school, the "day of absence" offers two options for students: "One gathering is designed to explore race in ways that support our students, staff, and faculty of color. The other gathering is designed for people who want to be allies in anti-racism work. We invite everyone to attend the program of their choice, wherever they feel most comfortable."[22]

In 2017, it seems, for some students to "feel most comfortable" required all white people to leave campus for the day, or, to put it another, and the most obvious, way, total and complete segregation.

When a liberal professor questioned the college's decision to send non-minority students off campus for an "allies" meeting, rather than have everyone on campus for a discussion, all hell broke loose.

Biology professor Bret Weinstein sent an email to protest the idea. "There is a huge difference between a group or coalition deciding to voluntarily absent themselves from a shared space in order to highlight their vital and under-appreciated roles," he wrote, "and a group or coalition encouraging another group to go away. The first is a forceful call to consciousness which is, of course, crippling to the logic of oppression. The second is a show of force, an act of oppression in and of itself." Weinstein made clear that he was protesting this segregation and expulsion idea, adding, "On a college campus, one's right to speak—or to be—must never be based on skin color." He then offered to host an event on campus where students were invited to have a civil discussion on racism, as long as they "attend with an open mind, and a willingness to act in good faith."[23]

In 2017, college campuses are where those things go to die . . .

Weinstein was attacked by student activists as a racist. This lifelong progressive was described by the liberal *Seattle Times* as someone who took a "stand against an equity event."[24] After a prolonged siege, he and his wife, who was also on the school's faculty, were driven out, forced to resign. They sued the school, ultimately settling their claim for $500,000.[25]

The key takeaway here is that students and faculty always want to expel the most conservative people, *even when the most conservative people left are incredibly liberal.*

The president of Evergreen, George S. Bridges, penned an op-ed in the *Seattle Times*, declaring, "In a divided country, our campus will remain united."[26] But it was his university that was coming apart.

To appease the small number of vocal activists, who'd been disrupting classes and campus life, Bridges relieved them of their homework—or, in other words, absolved them from the duties that had brought them to campus in the first place.[27] He also acquiesced to their demands, which included:

The start of mandatory diversity and cultural sensitivity training for all faculty members

The creation of an equity/multicultural center

The hiring of a vice president or vice provost who will focus on equity and diversity issues

Adoption of a new policy where every official event at the college will start with an acknowledgment that Evergreen State is on land stolen from Native Americans[28]

If the "acknowledgment that Evergreen State is on land stolen from Native Americans" doesn't solve everyone's problems, nothing will. . . .

Bridges's capitulation did stop the protests. However, enrollment dropped nearly 6 percent in the aftermath, which led to a hiring freeze due to the lost revenue.[29] Layoffs followed to close the $2.1 million budget shortfall.[30]

All this because a left-wing professor thought the idea of segregation was not a good one. Who wouldn't want to spend upwards of $24,000 per year to send their child to Evergreen? The greatest lessons the school teaches now are how not to act and how not to lead. Seems as though a prison documentary could instill the same lessons for the cost of a Netflix subscription.

But Evergreen isn't an anomaly, it's both a reflection of our times and a harbinger of things to come. When the Left can't find a big scandal, it'll blow up a little one. If it can't find a little scandal, it'll invent one.

The fetishization of victimhood has led to a series of high-profile claims emanating from college campuses that were widely reported but turned out to be frauds. Among them:

> A Halloween party at a Yale University frat house was rocked by charges of racism, with a "victim" telling the *Washington Post* that people at the door had told her that "white girls only" would be let in.[31] It turned out to be a lie. After the

president of the fraternity left the school because of the negative publicity, an investigation by Yale found that there was no truth to the story the *Post* had run unquestioningly.[32]

› Haakon Gisvold attended a fraternity party at the University of North Dakota until, he alleged, he was choked, stripped, and kicked out because he's gay. The only problem was that it didn't happen. He made the whole thing up. The Huffington Post ran with the original story but deleted, rather than correcting, it after the hoax was exposed. Even though police demanded that Gisvold face charges for filing a false report, prosecutors declined.[33]

› Kean University in New Jersey was rocked when, in 2015, black students and faculty received threats to "kill every black male and female at kean university." After the outrage that ensued, it was discovered that a black activist named Kayla-Simone McKelvey created the fake Twitter account, sent the threats, then showed them to other students at an anti-racism rally she was attending as if she'd discovered the messages.[34] One student, at the height of the threats, tweeted, "HOW MUCH MORE DIRECT EVIDENCE DO YOU NEED? RACISM IS REAL, THIS IS A THREAT! ACT NOW!"[35] Police did act, arresting McKelvey, and she was sentenced to ninety days in jail.[36]

These are but a few of the hundreds of examples of frauds and hoaxes perpetrated on college campuses in the last few years, each of which spawned protests and demands of administrators to "do something" about the scourge of bigotry. There have been no large-scale demonstrations calling for addressing the scourge of false claims of discrimination.

Ground zero for the new "Everyone is guilty, no evidence necessary" college experience is the University of Missouri.

At the height of the #BlackLivesMatter movement, students at the Mizzou jumped in with both feet. Ferguson, Missouri, was not far away, so the heat from the Michael Brown lie of "Hands up, don't shoot" was acutely felt on campus. From there, the marches and protests on campus grew into a self-sustaining outrage machine.

The president of student government, Payton Head, took to his Facebook page in late 2014 to claim that the school was a bastion of racism, homophobia, and transphobia because, he alleged, "people riding in the back of a pickup truck screamed racial slurs at him."[37] On a busy campus, there were no witnesses to the incident.

Not having any evidence of or witnesses to an event that happens to fit exactly the liberal narrative is no requirement for outrage—the charge is enough. Protests erupted, and the university's chancellor issued a statement condemning the "attack." The condemnation was, as always, not enough.

The protests continued, and although they never involved anywhere near a majority of students, they grew to include faculty. Unsurprisingly, the fact that liberal institutions employ a lot of liberals is as shocking as Oprah Winfrey making the cover of this month's O, The Oprah Magazine.

School was disrupted. Classes were canceled. Eventually, calm-ish was restored. But it took months.

Press reports on the deterioration of campus life were not about the new chaos of campus life; they were sympathetic to the protests. But the truth, especially when presented via the contrast of proud progressives making sweeping declarations and condemnations, always comes through.

Rather than leading and demanding order and compliance with laws and campus regulations, Mizzou president Tom Wolfe capitulated and acquiesced. Ultimately, the disorder cost him his job when members of the school's football team threatened to refuse to play unless he quit and were backed up by their coach. Rather than firing the coach and inviting any athlete who refused to fulfill his end of the bargain to give up his athletic scholarship, Wolfe resigned. The school's chancellor soon followed.[38]

But no amount of capitulation was ever going to be enough—you can't plug a black hole with appeasement. The protests continued, even escalating. They eventually led to the firing of two professors who made physical threats against students, including Melissa Click, who was filmed calling for some "muscle" to remove a student journalist covering the protests.[39] Head was eventually caught spreading a false story about the KKK roaming around campus, the very concept of which is laughable, and had to apologize.[40]

The whole ordeal went well for no one. But although Click was eventually hired by Gonzaga University in the state of Washington (liberals always take care of their own),[41] her former employer has hit some difficult times.

In the aftermath of the sustained protests and the accompanying attention, the University of Missouri suffered a major decline in enrollment of 12.9 percent.[42] The situation deteriorated to the point that the school closed four dormitories because it didn't have enough students to fill them.[43]

While the progressive mob was popular with the media and like-minded liberals, the American people wanted nothing to do with them. Fired professors may "fail up" to new positions, but the name of the University of Missouri is associated with the chaos of that time and is still suffering the repercussions of capitulation.

Missouri may be the worst, most blaring example of how progressive politics can ruin a school, but it is hardly the only one. From coast to coast, left-wing protests shut down speeches not only by conservatives but by anyone deemed not sufficiently liberal.

The concept of "free speech zones" and "safe spaces"—areas on campus where students traumatized by not getting their way, for example, by the school allowing a speech by someone they disapprove of or the election of Donald Trump, have access to coloring books and Play-Doh to "help them deal with the stress" of someone "existing wrong"—are commonplace.[44]

But no amount of coddling or children's toys will ever be enough, nor will they prepare an adult to be an adult. Yet these crutches are the new normal at institutions of higher learning. Smoking a joint or drinking a beer has been replaced by puppy therapy.

And all this on the taxpayer dime, as universities, both public and private, have more than doubled their tuition costs since 1998.[45]

So crippling debt, an atmosphere of paranoia, and constant harassment are now the staples of college life. If a graduate manages to find a job, he or she has the next thirty years to pay off the privilege of surviving it all.

If *Animal House* were made today, it would be considered a hate crime, and there'd be plenty of faculty and staff ready, willing, and able to report it.

The current belief is that at the end of this insanity, students will head out into the real world and there be forced to get over themselves. The problem with that narrative is that other areas of American life are destroying themselves with ideological purges and radicalized mobs, too. There's always a plan B, a career parachute of sorts: when their lack of marketable skills and practical knowledge confronts them in a way they can't drum-circle their way around, the leaders of this nonsense know they can always get jobs as journalists.

Chapter 2

Who Checks the Fact-Checkers?

Amid the drumbeat of "fake news" and righteous indignation from behind media credentials, there lives an incredible arrogance based on nothing but a job title: journalist.

A good rule of thumb in life is always to be wary of anyone who appoints himself an arbiter of truth. Truth isn't really in need of a referee; one need only point it out, and there it is. Yet a trend exists in media to assign someone to be the minister of truth—the decider of what is and is not in the world of politics.

This trend took off thanks to PolitiFact. Founded in 2007 by the *Tampa Bay Times*, it's a fact-checking website so interested in the truth that it has a capitalized "Fact" right there in its name. But, as with everything else in politics and media, there's a lot more than meets the eye.

Fact-checkers such as PolitiFact are not fact-checkers at all. Some of their "checks" are simply wrong; others are subjective; still others spun so wildly they make Tweak on *South Park* seem cool, calm, and collected.

It's not just PolitiFact. Since the website won a Pulitzer Prize in 2009, many other news organizations have entered the fray, most notably CNN and the *Washington Post*.

But no matter how many outlets join the game, it's still rigged.

Sometimes politicians make statements that are undoubtedly false; it's a part of the game. In many cases the American people don't want to hear the truth. Who wants to hear that Social Security and Medicare are going to have to change or that $20 trillion in debt isn't such a hot idea? By the time the feces hit the fan, the people who should be paying attention to such dire realities will be dead anyway. And there's golf to be played.

But other lies aren't lies at all. They're nuance. And fact-checking nuance is as pointless as arguing with your kids about how good broccoli tastes so they will eat it.

The supposed point of fact-checkers is to give liberal reporters in a liberal newsroom the chance to attack conservatives under the guise of reporting. Fact-checkers are supposed to be arbiters of fairness, restoring the credibility of journalism everywhere, but instead they are destroying it.

The "Lie of the Year" for 2012, awarded by PolitiFact, was not the Democratic Party super PAC ad that accused Republican presidential nominee Mitt Romney of being somehow responsible for a woman's death from cancer; that didn't rate. So what did? A Romney campaign ad about where Jeeps would be made.

Don't feel bad if you don't remember it; no one does. And no one should. Given all the bullshit flung in a presidential campaign that didn't even turn out to be close, one ad—which was nowhere near LBJ's "Daisy" nuclear bomb ad—is insignificant. But PolitiFact declared it to be "brazenly false."[1]

What was its case? Well:

PolitiFact has selected Romney's claim that Barack Obama "sold Chrysler to Italians who are going to build Jeeps in China" at the cost of American jobs as the 2012 Lie of the Year.[2]

Notice the quotation marks, where they start and end. That will come into play in a minute.

PolitiFact reported that the "lie" started with a piece by Paul Bedard of the *Washington Examiner*, in which he reported Chrysler, which produces Jeeps, was "now considering cutting costs by shifting production of all Jeeps to China."[3] Later that day, Republican presidential candidate Mitt Romney repeated the report to an audience in Ohio. It turned out that the Bedard report was inaccurate in its use of the word "all."

After his speech, journalists clamored to get the Romney campaign to admit it had lied by repeating the mistaken news report. The Romney campaign took the issue and ran with it in an accurate form.

The facts were that Chrysler had received bailout money from the Obama administration to stay alive, then was sold to the Italian automaker Fiat. Jeeps had been manufactured in China, but production had been stopped in 2009. Now Fiat was indeed considering restarting production there, rather than shipping American-made Jeeps to China.

It is that fact that the Romney campaign decided to highlight in a campaign ad. And it was that fact that was declared to be its "Lie of the Year."

Again, PolitiFact wrote:

PolitiFact has selected Romney's claim that Barack Obama "sold Chrysler to Italians who are going to build Jeeps in China" at the cost of American jobs as the 2012 Lie of the Year.[4]

What was in the ad that set off the bells and whistles at PolitiFact? PolitiFact continued:

"Who will do more for the auto industry? Not Barack Obama," the ad began, adding, "Obama took GM and Chrysler into bankruptcy and sold Chrysler to Italians who are going to build Jeeps in China. Mitt Romney will fight for every American job."

You probably don't remember that ad because no one remembers an ad from past political campaigns. But the above sentence is absolutely all that PolitiFact had to say about its declaration.

What about the ad, not the statement on the campaign trail, was a lie? Nothing.

On January 17, 2013, just one month after PolitiFact declared the concept of Fiat-Chrysler manufacturing some Jeeps in China the "Lie of the Year," Reuters ran a story entitled "Fiat Sees at Least 100,000 Jeeps Made in China by 2014." It reported, "'We expect production of around 100,000 Jeeps per year which is expandable to 200,000,' [Sergio] Marchionne, who is also CEO of Chrysler, said on the sidelines of a conference, adding production could start in 18 months."[5]

PolitiFact quoted the "false" ad as saying that the new owners of the company "are going to build Jeeps in China," yet a month later the company announced it was going to start building Jeeps in China rather than assembling them in the United States and shipping them overseas.

Bedard was mostly right, though Jeep production continued in the United States. Romney's ad was absolutely right.

PolitiFact argued, "When pinned down with questions on the ad, the Romney team either dodged or defended the ad as literally accurate." Because the ad *was* "literally accurate." If PolitiFact wasn't checking the literal accuracy of the ad, what the hell was it checking?

Well, it turns out that PolitiFact tipped its hand early on in the piece:

> *It's not that President Obama and his campaign team were above falsehoods, either. Their TV ads distorted Romney's positions on abortion and immigration* **to make them seem more extreme than they actually were.** *A pro-Obama super PAC even created an ad suggesting Romney was responsible for a woman's death when her husband lost his job at a Bain-controlled company.* **But the Jeep ad was brazenly false.** *(Emphasis added.)*[6]

Note the verbiage there: the Obama campaign lied, though PolitiFact won't use that word, in order to make Romney's views "seem more extreme than they actually were." PolitiFact was declaring that Mitt Romney, who by any measure was a moderate center-right candidate, was an extremist.

The "more extreme" part was bad enough, but ending it with

"than they actually were" is unambiguous. That's not reporting; that's editorializing.

Couple that with calling the ad "brazenly false" when it was absolutely true, and you reach a level of hackery you'd expect to find on the celebrity blog pages of the Huffington Post.

As an example of the hive mind in the media, the "Jeep lie" wasn't flagged only by PolitiFact. The *Washington Post's* "fact-checker" took a crack at it, awarding it its top rating: four Pinocchios.

Post fact-checker Glenn Kessler, in giving the ad the most critical score possible, wrote, "The ad's reference to Jeep production in China is technically correct but misleading, particularly in light of Romney's comments on the campaign trail."[7]

Romney's ad, which was declared the most egregious of lies by the *Post*, was "technically correct" but somehow still "misleading" because of something Romney had said at a campaign stop a few days before. The *Post* wrote:

> *The unspoken message is that American jobs are being sent to China, even though the ad carefully tiptoes around that claim. (The ad, in fact, includes brief text quoting Bloomberg as saying Jeep production was returning to China.)*[8]

The *Post*, in admitting that the ad was unambiguous in its word choice, rated the whole thing the biggest lie on its scale because of what is "unspoken" in it. Moreover, Kessler noted that the ad contained text making clear what was ultimately confirmed by Reuters after the election: that Fiat-Chrysler was, in fact, returning Jeep manufacturing to China.

The words "technically correct" are used again by the *Post* in its conclusion. After ascribing the ad a motive, declaring its creation an indication "that we have entered the final, desperate week of the campaign," Kessler once again undercut his own argument:

> *The series of statements in the ad individually may be technically correct, but the overall message of the ad is clearly misleading—*

especially since it appears to have been designed to piggyback off of Romney's gross misstatement that Chrysler was moving Ohio factory jobs to China.[9]

How can a series of statements be correct when taken individually but when put together be "clearly misleading"? That's like finding all the characters on *The Big Bang Theory* individually hilarious but complaining that the series is unfunny. According to the *Post* fact-checker, they can if you happened to have noticed a campaign speech a week earlier, remembered one line from it, and imposed that line on an ad that contains clarifying text on the screen.[10]

Again, even if someone not paid to nitpick Republicans for a living had noticed all of this and found the harmonic convergence hidden in its obsessive-compulsive disorder, how does something "clearly misleading" receive the ultimate mark on a lie scale? Answering "yes" when you know the answer is "no" should rate four Pinocchios. Saying the equivalent of "maybe" should not.

When the Reuters story reaffirmed the accuracy of the ad, technically or otherwise, the *Post* surprisingly revisited the story and declared its original "four Pinocchio" rating still true.

In his January 25, 2013, follow-up, initiated by an email from Romney campaign strategist Stuart Stevens, Kessler concluded, "To some extent, this may be a matter of semantics. Stevens says Chrysler is 'moving production' to China. We think it is more accurate to say that Chrysler is expanding—in fact, returning—production to China."[11]

So believing that there is a "more accurate" way to convey information is now the basis for calling something a complete lie? Declaring that a child "ate the last cookie" is inaccurate because there are still cookies in the world; would saying only that he "ate the last cookie in the house" rate as true? That's a hell of a lawyerly answer.

In an attempt to validate his obstinacy, Kessler revisits what neither he nor PolitiFact "fact-checked" in the first place. "Romney first said 'all production' of Jeeps would be moved to China. Not true," he wrote.

Yes, Romney did say that one time in a campaign speech. But PolitiFact wasn't fact-checking that campaign speech, it was critiquing a campaign ad that said nothing of the sort.

"With all due respect to Stevens, the claim that Romney turned out to be right is simply not accurate," Kessler concluded. With all due respect to Kessler, this is the Beltway way of saying, "I know you are, but what am I?"

The speed with which the media fact-checked (and ultimately butchered) Romney's claim leaves light in the dust. And it was awarded the "Lie of the Year" less than two months after the ad hit the air. When President Barack Obama was finally passed the mantle of the year's top lie, it was years after he told it and long after it could affect his political fortunes.

Clearly, the media aren't checking facts. So what are they checking?

The 2013 "Lie of the Year" was something Obama had been saying for five years: "If you like your plan, you can keep your plan. If you like your doctor, you can keep your doctor."

Conveniently, PolitiFact didn't even call this a full "lie," let alone the biggest of the year, until after Obama had faced voters for the last time and he was insulated from any blowback.

In 2009 and again in 2012, PolitiFact did check the oft-repeated declaration, rating it "half true" both times. During the 2008 campaign, it declared it to be "true."

The first time PolitiFact checked it, it entitled the piece "Obama's Plan Expands Existing System."[12] That piece says of the lie, "Obama is accurately describing his health care plan here. He advocates a program that seeks to build on the current system, rather than dismantling it and starting over."

In its conclusion, PolitiFact doubled down on the regurgitating of Democratic campaign talking points:

It remains to be seen whether Obama's plan will actually be able to achieve the cost savings it promises for the health care system.

But people who want to keep their current insurance should be able to do that under Obama's plan. His description of his plan is accurate, and we rate his statement True.[13]

How did the people at PolitiFact know what people "should" be able to do under a theoretical plan that didn't yet exist? They didn't, but that didn't matter—Obama said it, so it must be true. Conservative guesses about the future are made in bad faith, they seem to be saying, and liberal guesses are made in good faith.

The second time PolitiFact checked the statement, less than a year later, it downgraded what had once been "true" to "half true."

The piece was called "Barack Obama Promises You Can Keep Your Health Insurance, but There's No Guarantee."[14] But if it acknowledged that "there's no guarantee," how could an unequivocal statement that used to be true be even half true?

"On one level, Obama is correct," PolitiFact declared.

And what was that level? "Now, close to a year later, we finally have detailed bills to examine. They closely mirror what Obama promised during the campaign," it wrote. "But the plans also introduce new ways of regulating health insurance companies that will surely change the current health care system. That could prompt employers to change their health plans, and we find Obama's statement less clear-cut now than it once seemed."

Of course, it wasn't the employer-provided plans that were decimated but the individual medical insurance market, where millions lost both their coverage and their doctors. PolitiFact wasn't even looking in the right place.

Either undaunted or obtuse, it concluded:

Still, the legislative details that have emerged on health care reform indicate that if reform passes, we're headed for some significant changes in how health care operates. Obama certainly intends to leave the current system intact. But at this point, it seems too pat to say, "If you like your health care plan, you can keep your health care plan." It seems likely that at least some people will have employers who decide to change plans when different plans become available, most likely any small businesses that currently offer health insurance. They will be allowed into the exchange right away, and it seems likely some might find a better deal there and change plans.

Until the legislation gets closer to a final stage, it's difficult to say how many employers will likely opt to change coverage. But clearly some change is coming. It's not realistic for Obama to make blanket statements that "you" will be able to "keep your health care plan." It seems like rhetoric intended to soothe people that health care reform will not be overly disruptive. But one of the points of reform is to change the way health care works right now. So we rate Obama's statement Half True.[15]

Again, it was "fact-checking" something that didn't yet exist and siding with its liberal advocates. Don't worry; it was a half lie "intended to soothe people," so it was all good. It's not as though it were a "technically accurate" campaign ad that is still somehow a lie because it was said to help a Republican.

After the Supreme Court ruled Obamacare constitutional in June 2012, the president made the following statement:

If you're one of the more than 250 million Americans who already have health insurance, you will keep your health insurance. This law will only make it more secure and more affordable.

PolitiFact decided to take another crack at it. This time it found that the statement had grown in inaccuracy: "The claim Obama made after the Supreme Court decision on June 28, 2012, was a broader statement, and as a result, it's less accurate."[16]

Magically, although the claim had become "less accurate," it was rated exactly the same way: half true.[17] It's good to be a Democrat.

PolitiFact claimed that many of those changing insurance would do so "voluntarily" because people routinely seek "better health care options outside of their employer's plan." That was true, as most people will seek better options for themselves and their families. However, PolitiFact acknowledged, "Other switches will be involuntary."

Why? Not because of what became the case—their former plans were declared insufficient by the federal government under the new law—but because "Your employer may change insurance carriers, for instance, or your insurance carrier may unilaterally modify the terms of your plan."

See, it wouldn't be the law's fault, it would be the fault of your greedy damn employer and those evil insurance companies.

PolitiFact concluded, "Obama has a reasonable point: His health care law does take pains to allow Americans to keep their health plan if they want to remain on it. But Obama suggests that keeping the insurance you like is guaranteed."

So a law that essentially federalized one-sixth of the US economy, imposing new standards of minimum coverage on every American, took "pains" to ensure that it didn't disrupt people's plans?

And "Obama suggests" that you can keep your plan? The man made a firm "You can keep your plan" statement thirty-six times.[8] There's no hedging there, no wiggle room. Even if you grant wiggle room, the 5 million people in the individual market who received cancellation letters sure as hell were the ones feeling "pains."

Their final paragraph in the "fact check" is editorializing gold:

> In reality, Americans are not simply able to keep their insurance through thick and thin. Even before the law has taken effect, the rate of forced plan-switching among policyholders every year is substantial, and the CBO figures suggest that the law could increase that rate, at least modestly, even if Americans on balance benefit from the law's provisions. We rate Obama's claim Half True.

Again, your mean employers might switch your plan or an evil insurance company could, but that would all be natural and would have nothing to do with the law. Sure, the law might make things a little worse, but it would for your own good, you stupid American, because, "on balance" you'd "benefit from the law's provisions."

At the core of fact-checking is the assumption that if readers really understood the issues, they'd side with the Left.

By the next year, with reality looking it in the face and 5 million people receiving cancellation letters for their medical insurance plans, PolitiFact, after declaring it "true" once and "half true" twice, said that Obama's "promise was impossible to keep."[19] The poor dear, he tried.

"So this fall, as cancellation letters were going out," PolitiFact flippantly wrote, " . . . the public realized Obama's breezy assurances were wrong."

Not that they were a lie. Not that it was a political calculation designed to mislead people and not lose votes—the thirty-six separate occasions on which the president unequivocally pledged to the American people that they would not be adversely affected were just "breezy assurances." Oopsie!

Except it wasn't an oversight or an unfortunate "breezy assurance," it was a deliberate lie.

On October 28, 2013, a month and a half before PolitiFact awarded Obama the Lie of the Year, NBC News reported that the White House had known as far back as 2010 that the individual insurance market would see mass cancellations. It reported:

> Four sources deeply involved in the Affordable Care Act tell NBC NEWS that 50 to 75 percent of the 14 million consumers who buy their insurance individually can expect to receive a "cancellation" letter or the equivalent over the next year because their existing policies don't meet the standards mandated by the new health care law. One expert predicts that number could reach as high as 80 percent. And all say that many of those forced to buy pricier new policies will experience "sticker shock."[20]

Nowhere in PolitiFact's "Lie of the Year" write-up is this fact mentioned. Weird, right? Of course, PolitiFact won a Pulitzer Prize for its coverage of the 2008 election, the one in which it declared its future "Lie of the Year" to be true. From the moment it won that award, other news organizations immediately set out to get their own piece of that glory pie. But the path to Pulitzer was paved with bias.

Bias is bias, even when it's couched in fact-checking.

Of course there's nothing inherently wrong with fact-checking. Politicians should be held accountable for their words and how they match their actions. Keeping them honest is an important part of what journalism is supposed to be. But what it has become in the age of Trump is an opportunity for journalists and news organizations to call the president a liar by proxy.

During the second presidential debate in 2016, NBC News ran a live "fact check" on its Twitter page. The NBC News team of fact-checkers ran six real-time fact checks of Donald Trump—all were deemed to be lies—and none, zero, nada on anything Hillary Clinton said.[21]

What did NBC deem worthy of fact-checking?

In reference to Clinton's deletion of 33,000 emails from her secret, private server, Trump said:

But when you talk about apology, I think the one that you should really be apologizing for and the thing that you should be apologizing for are the 33,000 e-mails that you deleted, and that you acid washed, and then the two boxes of e-mails and other things last week that were taken from an office and are now missing.

And I'll tell you what. I didn't think I'd say this, but I'm going to say it, and I hate to say it. But if I win, I am going to instruct my attorney general to get a special prosecutor to look into your situation, because there has never been so many lies, so much deception. There has never been anything like it, and we're going to have a special prosecutor.

When I speak, I go out and speak, the people of this country are furious. In my opinion, the people that have been long-term workers at the FBI are furious. There has never been anything like this, where e-mails—and you get a subpoena, you get a subpoena, and after getting the subpoena, you delete 33,000 e-mails, and then you acid wash them or bleach them, as you would say, very expensive process.

NBC deemed that worthy of a fact check, declaring "Nope." But which part of that statement is false?

Hillary Clinton did delete 33,000 emails she declared to be personal, turning over 30,000 she said were work-related from her time as secretary of state. Her emails had been under subpoena by the House of Representatives at the time of their deletion, so that was true, too. Was it the statement that people at the FBI were "furious"? That can't be proved or disproved. It wasn't even Trump's claim that "there has never been so many lies, so much deception" in regard to Hillary's emails.

What's to check? The words "acid washed."

Yes, that's right, NBC thought that part of a factual answer was not only worth fact-checking but a lie.

"FACT CHECK: Trump says Clinton "acid washed" her email server. She did not," NBC News tweeted. The tweet contained a picture that included a "The Claim" section that read, "Trump says Clinton 'acid washed' her email server." Okay, a little redundant, but it repeated it.

But the picture also contained a "The Truth" section that read, "Clinton's team used an app called BleachBit; she did not use a corrosive chemical."

If you made this up, no one would believe you. Trump said "acid washed," so he lied. But later, in the same answer, he said, "you acid wash them or bleach them." There it is, right there. "Bleach," as in BleachBit. But since he didn't say the actual name of the program Clinton's team used, only half of it, NBC News took it to mean that Trump was saying Hillary had sprayed her private server with battery acid or dumped it into a pool of hydrochloric acid.

It doesn't exactly rise to the level of lie of the year, but it clearly is an abuse of the trust journalists are entrusted with by virtue of their job. What people remember is "Trump lied," not the lie itself or that the lie was not a lie at all but a semantic mistake at best. The fact-checkers have become the fact-inventors.

Just over a week later, the fact-checking team at NBC News was back at it, fact-checking a claim by Trump not against facts, but opinions. On October 19, 2016, it fact-checked the following statement by Donald Trump: "Let me just tell you before we go any further, in Chicago, which has the toughest gun control laws in the United States, probably you could say by far, they have more gun violence than any other city. So we have the toughest laws and you have tremendous gun violence."

Chicago has been experiencing an incredible number of murders and shooting in recent years, with 762 murders and a stunning 4,331 shootings in 2016.[22]

Chicago also is noted for having notoriously tough restrictions on gun ownership, which leaves law-abiding citizens vulnerable to criminals, who obviously don't obey those laws. That would seem self-evident in what Trump said.

Although what officially constitutes "the toughest gun control laws" in the country is open for debate, it's not up to NBC News to decide.

However, "Chicago officials dispute that their laws are the toughest, as Trump claimed," NBC's fact-check declared.[23] Not any organization, not any proof, just "Chicago officials" say. Nor was there any attempt to describe the restrictions on the Second Amendment the city has in place; just a pronouncement by unnamed officials taken as fact when compared to something NBC deemed not a fact.

NBC acknowledged this ambiguity, in a sense, when it glossed over the first part of its "check" and continued, "but either way, strict city laws are undercut by more lax laws elsewhere. To wit: A majority of Chicago's illegal guns were first bought out of state."[24]

There are zero gun stores in the city of Chicago. Its laws, which may or may not be the toughest in the country, have outlawed the opening of one. It only makes sense that a large percentage of guns used in shootings in the city would come from elsewhere. But from out of state? That's where things get a little murky.

The *Washington Post*, through a weird coincidence of hive-mind thinking, fact-checked the same seemingly innocuous statement by Trump on the same day. It wrote, "Data from the Bureau of Alcohol, Tobacco, Firearms and Explosives from between 2010 and 2014 found that a remarkable number of guns in Illinois came from Indiana, according to The Trace."[25]

What is "The Trace"? It's a liberal anti–Second Amendment group, of course.

What constitutes "a remarkable number," according to the *Post*? Well, The Trace (its source) states that "more than half" the guns recovered by police in Chicago "came from outside the state."[26]

This report, cited as proof of Trump's lie, states:

Data from the Bureau of Alcohol, Tobacco, Firearms and Explosives (ATF) backs up the president's point. The agency cannot trace every gun taken in by law enforcement. But between 2010 and 2014, it was able to source between 40 and 60 percent of the firearms recovered in Illinois, the vast majority of which were crime guns. Statewide, most of those weapons came from elsewhere in Illinois, a pattern seen in other states. But thousands found their way into Illinois—and often, Chicago—from parts of the country with weaker gun laws.[27]

The agency was able to source only 40 to 60 percent of the guns recovered in Chicago, and basic math would tell anyone that "the vast majority of" 40 percent, or even 100 percent of it, cannot constitute a majority. Conceivably, if 85 percent of the high end—60 percent—were from out of state, there would be a simple majority of the small percentage of the guns the agency was able to trace as being from out of state. With such a small amount of the data available, it's impossible to declare anything definitively. Yet the *Post* did, as did NBC News.

Still, weirdly, neither of those fact-checks seemed to notice that Trump didn't mention anything about the origin of guns used in the shootings and murders in Chicago. It's as irrelevant as where a drunk driver's car was manufactured or where the beer he drank was brewed—he got behind the wheel drunk; the guy who filled his tires didn't put him there.

Both the *Post* and NBC News claimed that Trump had been telling a falsehood because of cooked stats from a liberal activist group based on something he didn't say.

It was all they could do, because they couldn't address what he actually did say: that violence in Chicago is out of control, and all the gun control laws in the world haven't put a damper on it.

Of course, that reality had to be ignored because President Obama is from there and Democrats have controlled the city's government since the earth cooled. To tell the reality of what's happening in Chicago could lead some people to recognize the same deterioration and societal breakdown in Democrat-controlled cities across the country and the abject failure of gun laws. But that can't be allowed. So they argued against something not said and declared it to be a lie.

Those who choose the unit by which success is measured will always win.

When NBC News reporter Ali Vitali tweeted that Trump had told a Teamster he'd met at a Wawa that "Teamsters are all with me" and NBC News felt the need to fact-check it, you know you've hit bottom. Of course, the Teamsters leadership endorsed Clinton.[28] The Teamsters never poll their members when they endorse, they just find the candidates with the (D) after their names and open their checkbooks.

The Teamsters have given more in forced union dues to Democrats over the decades than the GDP of many small countries, but Trump making a crack about how blue-collar workers support him could not be allowed to stand.

The statement might not have been allowed to stand, thanks to NBC, but the membership, particularly in states such as Pennsylvania, Michigan, Ohio, and Wisconsin, stood against the collectors of their dues on November 8.

There are, of course, countless fact checks by every "mainstream" outlet screaming that Donald Trump is a liar, but the chorus of voices from the activists with press credentials went unheeded by voters. Actually, they probably hurt their cause.

If everything is a lie, nothing is true.

The hyperbolic hyperventilation over everything, significant or not, has led to a rightful drop in the credibility of the media. Their irresistible desire to bandwagon the idea that Trump was P. T. Barnum with worse hair rather than simply report what he was saying and allow people to make up their own minds triggered millions of Americans to turn a deaf ear in their direction. They "fact-checked" their way out of their audience's trust.

That lost credibility didn't turn audiences away from news—from a sales perspective, 2016 was a banner year for every outlet, particularly conservative sites—they just didn't believe much of it anymore.

––––––––––––

President Trump might have popularized the term "fake news," but he didn't invent the phenomenon any more than poets invented the sunrise simply because they wrote about it. Had journalists and journalistic outfits stuck to conveying facts, their credibility would still exist.

One thing about journalism in the age of Trump is how all the corrected and retracted news stories have been in "error" in only one direction. There hasn't been one mistake that made the president look better, only worse. Weird, right?

ABC News reported that former national security adviser Michael Flynn had been "ordered" by Trump to reach out to the Russian government during the election, implying that it was the smoking gun of collusion the media was desperately searching for. The only problem was that Flynn had been asked to reach out to the Russians *after* the election, when Trump was president-elect, which is a normal practice for an incoming government to start building relationships with its foreign counterparts.

The story was retracted hours later, after it had been splashed across headlines and reported on cable news all day. The reporter, Brian Ross, was suspended for spreading a story that perfectly fit the liberals' dream narrative—that Trump had worked with the Russian government to "steal" the US election; it was simply too good to fact-check.[29]

And that has been the major problem with the "arbiters of truth" reporting on the Trump administration—the narrative that he is a corrupt incompetent is unquestioned, so stories that reinforce it are not given the basic scrutiny they otherwise would receive.

The ABC News story was just one of many stories that fit the pattern of "Report first, check facts later," but it was by no means the only organization to "shit the bed" when it came to reporting fake stories.

Also in December, on the heels of the bogus ABC News report, CNN jumped into the deep end of the fake news pool without checking if there was any water in it first. It had itself a blockbuster, a real "stop the presses" moment. It had sources telling it that there was proof, in the form of an email from a man named Michael Erickson to members of the Trump campaign, that showed the Trump campaign had been given access to emails hacked from the Democratic National Committee before they were made public by the website WikiLeaks. Since WikiLeaks, it's generally assumed, served as a conduit for information stolen by the Russian government to influence the outcome of the presidential election, this was yet another "smoking gun" of collusion. But a funny thing happened on the way to impeachment. . . .

After hours of breathless reporting on CNN and "confirmation" of the story by CBS News and MSNBC (coupled with their own breathless reporting and "analysis"), the wheels came off.

"Candidate Donald Trump, his son Donald Trump Jr., and others in the Trump Organization received an email in September 2016 offering a decryption key and website address for hacked

WikiLeaks documents, according to an email provided to congressional investigators," CNN reported.[30] It was a scandal—until someone saw the actual email.

It turned out that the email from Erickson, who was just an average person with no connection to the Trump campaign or politics at all, was sent *after* WikiLeaks had publicly released the emails on the Internet.

The date of the email was reported as September 4, 2016, when it was actually September 14, a full ten days later and after the public release of the documents. CNN scrambled to save face, changing its story to say, "the individual may simply have been trying to flag the campaign to already public documents."[31]

CNN, CBS, and MSNBC didn't just have egg on their faces, they had a chicken farm on their heads.

Curiously, as they all hurried to retract or correct their stories, all of which they'd claimed they'd "independently confirmed," none would say where the original bogus information had come from. Either all of their sources independently could not read a date clearly visible in the heading of an email, or they had been played by someone who knew something like an impossible chronology wouldn't stand in the way of a good narrative.

Moreover, the outlets remained adamant in protecting their source. The liberal journalist Glenn Greenwald called it "one of the most embarrassing days for the U.S. media in quite a long time."[32]

To this day, the source of the bogus information remains protected by the reporters they burned. Greenwald wrote, "The humiliation orgy was kicked off by CNN, with MSNBC and CBS close behind, and countless pundits, commentators, and operatives joining the party throughout the day. By the end of the day, it was clear that several of the nation's largest and most influential news outlets had spread an explosive but completely false news story to millions of people, while refusing to provide any explanation of how it happened."[33]

That was the culmination of a year of faulty reporting, suspect claims, and anonymous sources recounting alleged events that only people closest to the president could have witnessed—all of which conveniently fit the liberal narrative of a bumbling chief executive one step away from either indictment or impeachment who never should have won the election in the first place.

When it comes to the credibility crisis in journalism, for all the complaints by reporters of criticism by the president damaging their profession, their own actions have done more to harm their credibility than any president ever could. If they really had an interest in honest fact-checking, they might want to start with that one.

Chapter 3

Blind to the Truth

Fact checkers assume that lying Democrats are the exception and lying Republicans are the rule. Those stereotypes also direct which politicians get covered and how.

When the trial of New Jersey senator Robert Menendez started, the *New York Times* ran a 1,288-word piece on it. Menendez, a Democrat, was charged with taking bribes in exchange for helping a wealthy businessman procure government favors. Never once did the original story mention that Menendez was a Democrat. It wasn't until hours later, in the online edition, that the story was changed to make mention of that fact, in the fourth paragraph.[1]

At least the *Times* mentioned the trial. Over the course of the sixty-two days of testimony, CNN spent only thirty-six minutes total on the story, with fourteen minutes and thirty-five seconds of that coming from one show: *The Lead with Jake Tapper*. Its prime-time lineup, *Erin Burnett OutFront*, *Anderson Cooper 360*, and *CNN Tonight* with Don Lemon, never once talked about the corruption trial of a sitting US senator.[2]

CNN was in familiar company. The three broadcast network nightly newscasts on NBC, ABC, and CBS made zero mention of the trial during its run as well.[3] It can't be that what happens in New Jersey isn't "national newsworthy" (as much as we might secretly like it to be); the networks had just spent a year reporting on two closed lanes of a bridge that had impacted a few thousand people as though they'd found multiple dead bodies and gold bullion in Republican governor Chris Christie's trunk. Something else had to be in play.

Bribery trials of sitting members of Congress don't come along all that often (probably not nearly as often as they should), so they are big news—or at least they are when they involve Republicans.

The Media Research Center (MRC) found that, in contrast to the way CNN covered the Menendez trial, when a Republican stood trial for roughly the same thing, the network recognized it as news and covered it as such.

In 2008, then–Republican senator Ted Stevens of Alaska was accused of failing to report about $250,000 in home improvements and other gifts from the CEO of VECO Corporation.[4] Stevens was convicted, but that conviction was thrown out a year later when it was discovered that the prosecutor had withheld evidence favorable to the senator.[5] The charges were ultimately dismissed.

But the damage to Stevens had already been done; he lost his bid for reelection in 2008 and died in a plane crash in Alaska in 2010.

At the time, Stevens's trial was of great interest to CNN. The MRC found that

When it came to reporting on Stevens, CNN rarely missed a day, and often updated viewers on the status of the trial multiple times in the same day. In the first three weeks of his trial (Sept. 20, 2008, to Oct. 11, 2008), CNN aired 36 stories about Stevens, compared to only 7 for Menendez in the exact same time period (Sept. 5, 2017, to Sept. 26, 2017)—a six-to-one disparity.[6]

Stevens had been charged with failure to report, Menendez had been charged with the more serious bribery. Yet CNN found one newsworthy, the other not so much.

But forget corruption; how does the media cover perversion?

In 2006, just before the midterm elections that year, Florida congressman Mark Foley was accused of sending obscene messages to teenage boys in the congressional page program. Foley, a Republican, quickly resigned from Congress after massive pressure from GOP leadership. It was absolutely a story worth covering, and cover it the media did—long after Foley resigned on September 29, 2006.

The MRC reported:

> On the ABC, CBS, and NBC morning and evening news programs, from the story's emergence on Thursday night, September 28, through Wednesday morning, October 11, the Big Three networks have aired 152 stories. On October 11's Good Morning America, news anchor Christopher Cuomo spoke insistently: "Less than a month before the elections and the Mark Foley scandal just keeps growing." Reporter Jake Tapper added, "This is the scandal that will not go away."[7]

It's hard for a scandal to go away when you won't stop reporting on it.

The Democrat who beat Foley's replacement on the ballot that year, Congressman Tim Mahoney, found himself in a sex scandal only two years later. Mahoney resigned after he agreed to pay his mistress, a former staffer, $121,000. The married Mahoney "promised the woman, Patricia Allen, a $50,000 a year job for two years at the agency that handles his campaign advertising."[8]

While the story was broken on the ABC News website, the network's nightly newscast never mentioned it. Neither did NBC or CBS.[9]

When New York Democratic congressman Anthony Weiner was exposed sending lewd texts and tweets to multiple women by Andrew Breitbart, the liberal media laughed off the story. Weiner's claim that his account had been hacked was accepted as gospel truth, and the man who'd married Huma Abedin, Hillary Clinton's closest aid, nearly skated free.

CNN's legal analyst, Jeffrey Toobin, whose job it is (still) to provide legal analysis of a story, not political spin, unquestioningly accepted Weiner's claim that he had been hacked.

When Andrew Breitbart told CNN that Weiner had sent lewd

images to "young followers," Toobin was outraged. "What Andrew Breitbart was insinuating about [Weiner] with young girls and stuff is outrageous. And frankly, it's too bad that he got to say that stuff on CNN," he said.[10]

Toobin continued, attempting to dismiss the whole story, including the allegation that the prominent Democrat had sent lewd images to young girls, by saying "Look, this is a light-hearted story. This is a silly little thing that happened, it's not a big deal."[11]

When it's a Republican, it is "the scandal that will not go away," long after the Republican in question resigned. When it's a Democrat, if it's reported on at all, "it's not a big deal."

Were it not for double standards, liberals would have no standards at all.

Weiner ended up resigning from Congress in disgrace, then running for mayor of New York City. While he was leading in the polls, more examples of him sending lewd and nude photos to women online emerged, and he lost badly in the primary. After counseling, Weiner was again discovered to have been sending and soliciting sexual photos online, this time with a fifteen-year-old girl. He was ultimately charged and pleaded guilty to a "charge of transferring obscene material to a minor."[12]

His wife, Huma, filed for divorce, and he was sentenced to twenty-one months in prison, a term he started serving in November 2017.

While he won't be able to meet anyone for lunch anytime soon, he is actively seeking pen pals.[13] No texts, please, as he won't have access to a cell phone for a while.

No matter the story, if it is about a politician, it is covered differently based upon the party affiliation of the person accused.

This is classic groupthink that can come about only when the media have alienated and expelled not just conservatives but anyone who isn't a down-the-line liberal. Stories about "them" are scandalous, newsworthy, and important, while stories about "us" are a chore that must be acknowledged, sometimes, but hold little news value. The bias may not even be conscious, but it is very real.

When reporters, producers, and editors think about what might be interesting or important today, they do it within an echo chamber of people who've spent two decades living by WWJSD, or the "What Would Jon Stewart Do?" standard.

———————

The double standards don't stop with scandals. Liberals lecture conservatives on the "tone" of their rhetoric while engaging in some of the vilest rhetoric ever to exit a human's mouth.

There is, or at least was, an unwritten rule in politics: you don't compare your opponent to Adolf Hitler. Unless someone is actually advocating for or committing genocide, he should not be compared to history's greatest monster. That rule was set on fire after the 2016 election.

From day one of the administration of President Donald Trump, left-wing journalists and pundits have been comparing him to one of history's greatest monsters who, along with his fellow Republicans, was going to kill thousands of Americans. MSNBC's Chris Matthews called his inauguration speech "Hitlerian."[14] Bernie Sanders tweeted, "As Republicans try to repeal the Affordable Care Act, they should be reminded every day that 36,000 people will die yearly as a result."[15] The *Washington Post* ran the headline "Repealing the Affordable Care Act Will Kill More than 43,000 People Annually."[16] Not wanting to go the "full Chris Matthews," Salon declared, "Trump's not Hitler, he's Mussolini," so maybe it was toning down the rhetoric a bit. . . .[17]

Those are just a few examples of what could be volumes of headlines and statement by leftist politicians, pundits, journalists, and the celebrities who parrot them, claiming the country was being run by the Nazi Party and it was only a matter of time before the killing factories opened to start slaughtering anyone who dared oppose them. That none of those people were rounded up for their treachery should have been a tip-off that maybe, just maybe, they were making it up for political purposes.

The hypocritical venom still runs strong and permeates every-thing, even policy. Are you aware that Republicans are trying to kill you and as many of your neighbors as possible? That's not a smart election strategy when every vote counts, but that's what liberals would have you believe.

Vox claimed that the Republican plan to repeal Obamacare would lead to "more than 24,000 extra deaths per year" and "kill more people each year than gun homicides."[18] Democratic senator Elizabeth Warren, not two weeks later, said, "I've read the Repub-lican 'health care' bill. This is blood money. They're paying for tax cuts with American lives."[19]

Not one to miss the boat, the New York Times chimed in with a piece by the columnist Charles Blow (yes, that's his real name) entitled "Trump Isn't Hitler. But the Lying . . ." Blow allows for the fact that "Trump is no Hitler," yet he continues, "but the way he has manipulated the American people with outrageous lies, stacked one on top of the other, has an eerie historical resonance."[20]

One part of Blow's piece sticks out, where he writes, "One way he does this is by using caveats—'I was told,' 'Lots of people are saying'—as shields."

You can decide for yourself the value of Blow's claim, but the concept here is one that is routinely found in journalism. News sto-ries regularly tout "critics" in stories, when in fact they were some-times the reason for the story being written in the first place.

When Supreme Court justice Neil Gorsuch gave a speech at the University of Louisville in Kentucky, he was introduced by Senate majority leader Mitch McConnell. McConnell had refused to allow the Senate to vote on any nominee in the last year of President Barack Obama's administration, preferring to have the voters de-cide who would pick the replacement for the late justice Antonin Scalia. This caused liberals to collectively clutch their pearls; they had seen Scalia's death as their opportunity to seize control of the high court for a generation by replacing the staunch conservative with a malleable progressive. McConnell, in the face of relentless pressure and criticism, held his ground.

The speech should have been no big deal; it was just a speech, after all, and Supreme Court justices deliver them all the time. And it was uncontroversial in both tone and content. But that fact didn't stop the *Washington Post* from reporting what "critics say."

"Gorsuch's Speeches Raise Questions of Independence, Critics Say," the headline blasted. In the story's body, the critics cited were left-wing judicial advocates. "Whether or not this breaks any explicit ethics rules, it is certainly not the behavior you'd expect from someone trying to ensure the appearance and reality of judicial independence and impartiality," said Elizabeth Wydra, the president of the liberal Constitutional Accountability Center, according to the *Post*.[21]

How is a liberal criticizing a conservative news? It's not. So why was this criticism, if it was worth reporting, attributed simply to "critics" in the headline? Critics criticize; that's what they do. But when a Republican is critical of a Democrat, the media are unambiguous about who is doing the criticism.

You're more likely to see a unicorn than see a liberal policy or action attacked in a headline or see conservative beefs referred to as "critics say" in a mainstream media outlet. It doesn't happen. Because liberal orthodoxy is the default setting for journalists, and that default is reflected in headlines.

Most people don't read past the headlines of stories; they're just too busy. That's why headlines are written to convey what the author or editor of the story thinks is the most important point of the story, so at least that can get into people's heads if they don't read the whole thing. It's not necessarily done for deceptive purposes— you can't have a 500-word headline for a 700-word story—but it often ends up exposing the biases of the people involved.

When Senate Republicans released a version of an Obamacare replacement bill in June 2017, the *Washington Examiner* compiled headlines of the release that illustrate just how this works.

It wrote:

The BBC lead described a bill that "slashes taxes on the wealthy and cuts Medicaid funding."

USA Today took the same approach, "Senate GOP unveils health care bill that slashes Medicaid and taxes."

NBC News jumped on the slasher bandwagon, clarifying that the bill would "slash Medicaid."

Slate teased its readers, "Here are six lines of text that could decimate America's biggest health care program."

Yahoo News stated, "Senate GOP health care bill looks a lot like 'mean' House one."

The Daily Beast took a slightly different angle on the same theme. Referencing protesters at the Capitol, the Beast blared, "The government wants to kill me protesters scream at GOP."

CNN was more nuanced, but clearly saw the bill's Medicaid reforms in a negative light. Its top headline warned, "Senate health care bill includes deep cuts to Medicaid."

Of course, this was nothing compared to the more avowedly leftist outlets. Salon's blazing title declared "GOP Evil: Not just Trump," adding that the Senate bill is "gruesome." The Huffington Post huffed two separate headlines, "Disabled Senate protesters removed by force" and "Heartless health care."[22]

These headlines presuppose a few things, namely that Republicans hate the poor and disabled and that every dollar spent on Medicaid is a vital dollar and the difference between life and death for everyone enrolled. Both assertions are lies. But busy glancers at headlines absorbed those lies, unfamiliar with the fact that the assertions came from an editorial viewpoint or Democratic Party talking point.

To illustrate this point further, after the Las Vegas massacre in which fifty-eight people were killed, The Hill ran a story that read, in part, "The former chairman of the conservative Republican Study Committee said Wednesday that the device used by the Las Vegas gunman to **modify a semi-automatic weapon to shoot more rapidly** should be banned."[23] (Emphasis added.)

When The Hill tweeted the story, which would likely be seen by more people than actually read the original piece, the tweet read, "Top conservative lawmaker calls for ban on device Vegas shooter **used to turn gun into automatic weapon**."[24] (Emphasis added.)

Notice the difference? It's subtle, but important. An automatic weapon is a very specific thing—it means pulling the trigger only once and firing nonstop until the trigger is released. Being able to fire "more rapidly" is not the same thing, not by a long shot. But the argument in the immediate aftermath of the slaughter was for more gun control, with Democrats leading that push. The "bump stock" used by the Vegas killer does not turn a weapon into an automatic weapon, and automatic weapons have been banned for decades.

But with the gun control debate raging, giving people the impression that there is a simple $40 piece of plastic a crazed person can buy to turn a normal rifle into a machine gun is an important piece of propaganda, even if it is directly contradicted in the story to which it links.

Also from The Hill, its Twitter account blared the headline "DeVos Uses Private Jet for Work-Related Travel," about Secretary of Education Betsy DeVos.[25] That was in the wake of the resignation of Health and Human Services secretary Tom Price being forced to resign for his use of private and government jets for his official travel. The media were itching for another scalp.

The only problem was, like the Vegas tweet, the article told a completely different, harmless version of the story. It turns out that DeVos, who is an incredibly wealthy individual, does fly on a private jet for government business—her own private jet, at her own expense. "DeVos Flies on Her Own Private Jet for Work-Related Travel," the story's headline read, which is very different from the implication in the tweet.[26]

But more people would have seen the tweet and, given the news at the time, would come away with the impression that DeVos was bilking taxpayers.

All this may seem innocuous, but it really isn't. The painter

Georges Seurat was known for painting by tiny dots, each one insignificant but together forming beautiful scenes. Each story with a deceptive headline or tweet providing a false impression, by itself unimportant, helps reinforce a narrative, a left-wing narrative, and misleads the audience. This isn't by accident.

Liberal memes and narratives in the media aren't an accident, they *are* the media. When not advancing them actively, the media are creating them. No conservative idea can ever be uttered unchallenged.

———————————

The most widely held liberal narrative is that most conservatives are dumb, and Republican presidents are just plain stupid. It's been around since at least President Ronald Reagan, who was portrayed as a doddering old man, senile, playing the role of president, and has only picked up steam: Republican presidents (Reagan, W. Bush, Trump) are dumb, Democratic presidents (Carter, Clinton, Obama) are smart. The only exception was George H. W. Bush, whose résumé made it impossible to call him dumb, so he was portrayed as a "wimp." If it's not one thing, it's another—but it's always something. It's easier to dismiss your opponents by making them out to be something negative rather than refuting their points individually, especially when you can't.

"President Reagan proposed a missile defense program? We'll just call it 'Star Wars' and laugh at him." Now, thanks to that program, the United States is safer from a missile attack than it has ever been, and Israel still exists, in part, because of it.

Making fun of presidential gaffes is fun, and it should be done. No president is perfect, and none should ever be above mockery. Media outlets had a field day with President George W. Bush's gaffes—"Is our children learning?"

But no mainstream media outlet bothered to have any fun at the expense of President Obama when, in February 2010, referred multiple times to "Navy Corpse-men," instead of "Corpsmen." One is a member of the US Navy; the other is, presumably, a patriotic zombie of some sort. Yet nothing about it—delivered in a speech at the National Prayer Breakfast, so it wasn't some obscure event—was mocked the way Bush's mispronunciation of "nuclear" was. It's almost as though the media couldn't think of anyone who might find that funny. Weird, right?

It's not that conservatives mind being held to standards, it's that liberals not only aren't held to the same standards, they aren't held to any standards at all.

Former vice president Dan Quayle misspells "potato" with an "e" at the end, and he's forever dogged as a moron. Former vice president Joe Biden, a literal gaffe factory, says during the 2008 campaign, "Look, John's last-minute economic plan does nothing to tackle the number one job facing the middle class, and it happens to be, as Barack says, a three-letter word: jobs. J-O-B-S," and it's barely mentioned.

On the rare occasion that Biden's verbal screwups were mentioned, it was done so in a playful, "that's just part of his charm," kind of way. "Biden's Speech Likely to Spotlight Strengths, or Foibles," a *New York Times* story was headlined. It referred to Biden as "folksy and loose," not as a man who couldn't count.[27]

During the 2008 campaign, then-senator Barack Obama once claimed that there are sixty states—he said, "Over the last 15 months we've traveled to every corner of the United States. I've now been in fifty-seven states, I think one left to go. One left to go. Alaska and Hawaii, I was not allowed to go to even though I really wanted to visit but my staff would not justify it." That would mean "with one left to go" and his staff not letting him go to Alaska and Hawaii, that would be a total of sixty. But he's a genius.

Verbal gaffes happen to everyone and can be indicative of anything, but they're portrayed very differently depending on the party affiliation of the person making them.

Before Barack Obama even took office, the presidential historian Michael Beschloss called him the "smartest guy ever to become president" on *The Don Imus Show* in November 2008.[28] When asked how he knew it to be true, Beschloss had no answer. It was just a matter of faith presented and treated as a matter of fact, and it stuck.

Yet a verbal gaffe by a Republican in an otherwise well-delivered speech or press conference, and the person is forever labeled a fool. The only thing the Left loves more than someone they consider a smart person is being a smart-ass.

In fact, journalists—self-appointed, noble arbiters of truth— have now stumbled onto a way to cover politics in a manner that gets clicks, attacks conservatives, and defies the fact-checkers: covering celebrity comedians' political pronouncements. Forget double standards, they really don't have any standards at all.

Chapter 4

Bias by Proxy

On an average week, HBO's John Oliver has more stories written about his Sunday-night show than his show has viewers. Stephen Colbert can't make a joke about a Republican without the laughter from newsrooms in the DC/New York media nearly popping their insulated media bubble.

A search of just *Time* magazine's website from January 1 through April 1, 2017, returns thirteen stories about Oliver. That might make sense, given that it was thirteen weeks into the year, but Oliver's show, *Last Week Tonight*, didn't premiere its fourth season until February 12. That means he didn't have a show until the seventh week of the year, yet the following six weeks elicited more than two stories per week.

So what earth-shattering wisdom and Oliver utterances did *Time* deem newsworthy?

There was this gem: "John Oliver Compares Republicans' Health Care Coverage to Your Dad in a Thong."[1]

In this story, *Time* wrote, "The House and Senate have passed budget resolutions to start the process of repealing the Affordable Care Act, despite what their constituents may want."

Notice the "may" part? That's opinion, not reporting. It's more wishful thinking or projection than anything else. "People who elected politicians who'd run for seven years promising to repeal Obamacare might not really want it to be repealed . . . we just don't know."

Not stopping there, *Time* continued, "More than 20 million

Americans gained health coverage under the Affordable Care Act, but as Oliver pointed out, many people appreciated the coverage, but could never get over the fact that the act became known as Obamacare."

First off, it was always known as Obamacare. That was not some late addition to the political lexicon. Moreover, 13 million of those 20 million people, the Congressional Budget Office reported, were put on Medicaid, the joint state and federal program for the poor, or welfare. "[T]he total increase in Medicaid enrollment stemming from the ACA will average 13 million in any given month in 2016."[2] Hell of a deal, "You're now a ward of the state!"

But the hits keep coming.

Since Medicaid pays doctors such a low rate for their services, *Forbes* reported, "most physicians were also reluctant to take on many Medicaid patients in their practices because these patients often required much more time and attention than the average patient."[3] So congratulations to new Medicaid recipients—you have insurance, you just can't find a doctor without long wait times. How can you not love it?

As for the remaining millions, Obamacare caused 5 million to lose the plans they had before the law's passage because the federal government deemed them inadequate.[4] Whether they were happy with those plans was irrelevant; the plans were no longer legal.

Time and Oliver were citing "gains" that are like getting a new swimsuit while you're drowning. But don't worry, people have a negative reaction to it only because the new suit was called Obamacare.

That's just one paragraph from one of the "news stories" *Time* gushed about Oliver. Every Monday, after a new show, readers are treated to whatever the former *Daily Show* correspondent decided to "destroy" or "eviscerate."

Oliver was written up again just two weeks later, under the title "John Oliver Takes Out More Ads to Explain the Health Care Bill to Trump."[5]

Time wrote, "Oliver also pointed out that the bill's extensive tax cuts, which largely benefit the wealthiest citizens, are essentially 'taking from the poor and giving to the rich,' according to Oliver, who dubbed it 'a Reverse Bernie Sanders.'" Note the selective use of quotes and the editorializing in the first half of that sentence. "Oliver also pointed out that the bill's extensive tax cuts, which largely benefit the wealthiest citizens" are not Oliver's words, they're *Time* commenting.

Not mentioned by *Time* is the fact that Obamacare imposed billions of dollars in new taxes and hiked scores of others. If a law is repealed, the tax hikes in that law will necessarily go away, thus making it less a "tax cut" than a restoration of the way things were before the tax hike. Whose money is it, anyway? Liberals, don't answer.

The very next line reveals more textbook bias. "Oliver also noted the sad irony that those who have the most to lose in the repeal of the Affordable Care Act are the same people who largely voted for Trump," *Time* wrote. "The sad irony"? Why is it sad? Why is it ironic?

Lost to the staff of *Time* is the prospect that some Americans don't look to government to be the giver of things; they don't want to suckle the government teat. If there's one thing liberals can't wrap their mind around about middle Americans, it's that they have pride; they take pride in taking care of themselves, and, come what may, they'll do what they have to do to make that happen. Government assistance is not their first option; it's a last resort.

People in flyover country don't assume that if the government is spending money, things are going well. Isn't it possible that the people living in "Trump country" have seen Obamacare up close and know its frustrations and expense better than someone who lives in Brooklyn and saw three segments on *The Rachel Maddow Show* about how wonderful it is? Not everyone believed Hillary Clinton's promises to show up at their door with a gift basket of goodies as though they'd won the Publishers Clearing House sweepstakes. Democrats describe this as "voting against their interests," as described in the book *What's the Matter with Kansas?*

Well, there's nothing the matter with Kansas, or anywhere else where people live life not wanting "government largesse" to be how they support themselves and their families. If that means a second job or a smaller house, they do it.

The real question is, what's the matter with New York and Washington, DC? Why do the people there so desperately want to "take care of" people who don't want to be taken care of? Why can't they believe people when they say, "We've seen what government does, and we're not interested"? Why do they want to involve themselves in the lives of people who want to be left alone? Go to a dinner party in either city, and you'll see just how miserable those people are to be around, so it makes sense that they'd want to ruin other people's lives from afar—misery loves puppetry.

Either those elites think they know better what the uncouth ants need in their lives more than those people themselves do, or they simply don't give a damn.

No one takes more glee in dumping their shit on middle America than John Oliver. Jon Stewart was the old king, condescending with orgasmic glee to the great unwashed, but he's retired. Stephen Colbert does it on *The Late Show*, but he no longer does a show designed to mimic news for the uninformed.

Oliver's show is just him at a desk, pretending to convey news in a comedic way—a dorky, more pretentious Dan Rather whose lack of fundamental knowledge is shaded by a British accent. If he delivered the exact same words sounding as though he went to school with Miley Cyrus, no one would take him seriously.

But *Time* does take him seriously. Oliver has the freedom to say what it wants to say but can't because the last remaining veneer of journalism prevents it.

To drive home the point that everyone who disagrees with liberals is an idiot, one *Time* piece, dripping with contempt for the president and his supporters, focused on fake TV ads *Last Week Tonight* produced to "educate" Trump on the basics of the presidency. *Time* summarized them this way:

> *For the good of the nation, Oliver wants to help Trump succeed, though. To that end, Oliver and his team created a series of*

*educational commercials that will run on channels that Trump is
known to watch, including Fox News, CNN, and MSNBC. The
informative ads, which will air in the D.C. area, are filled with
helpful facts that Trump might need, like the name of one of his
daughters, the finer points of the Geneva Convention, and the
three parts of the nuclear triad.*[6]

"For the good of the nation," you see, he "wants to help Trump
succeed." The underlying tone is that Trump is a moron who doesn't
even know his younger daughter's name.

The studio audience ate it up, as did newsrooms across the country. It was something journalists couldn't write on their own, so
Oliver provided the perfect vehicle to say it without their saying it.
It's the equivalent of telling your significant other that someone
else said he or she was fat—there's no reason to say that other than
you want to say something yourself but don't want to sleep on the
couch for a month. Problem solved: use a proxy!

That's the real reason celebrities and comedy shows are treated
as if they were news—so journalists can "report" the things that
they wish they could say about politicians but the constraints of
their profession don't allow them to. You can't constantly call Republicans and conservatives idiots; you want some of them to watch
your shows and read your stories. So you build up otherwise insignificant people who will do it for you.

There's no "fact-checking" of John Oliver, Beyoncé, or Kim Kardashian. They're entertainers, not politicians or journalists. What
they say is put out there under the guise of entertainment, unchecked, unfettered, and imbued with a semblance of credibility
because it appeared in *Time* or some other "news" outlet.

It's the audience's fault that something offered as news, in a
news format, is taken as news, isn't it? Once, maybe. But a continual drumbeat of something presented as news will eventually
blur, then obliterate, the line. It becomes a distinction without a
difference.

Oliver becomes someone daring enough to "speak truth to

power." Kardashian becomes someone worth listening to because the outlets that are supposed to tell us who is worth listening to say so.

The most pernicious power the media has is the power to ignore. But the second arrow in its quiver is to elevate to a level of influence and importance that which should be ignored, at least as far as news value goes. None of it is done by accident.

———————

There was a time when the name Kardashian elicited thoughts of OJ's legal team and Paris Hilton was a destination. All it took for that innocent reality, and journalism, to change was two homemade porno tapes.

Paris Hilton came first, when her night-vision tryst with an exboyfriend hit the market. But then a funny thing happened: what just a few years earlier would have embarrassed someone into hiding led to celebrity status. Paris was inundated with offers and attention; television shows, endorsement deals, and millions of dollars on top of the millions she was born into soon followed.

Hot on her tail was Kim Kardashian's homemade porno. At the time, her partner in the video was the famous one—a rapper named Ray J, who is now the answer to a trivia question that will stump your friends. Three marriages later, Kim's every move is fawned over by the media and Ray J is on a milk carton . . . in a trash can . . . somewhere . . . probably.

Eventually Paris stepped back from the limelight, maybe even grew up a little, but the second child of O. J. Simpson's late lawyer sucked in every bit of it. From that one tape, which is the most viewed adult video in history, and with no discernible talents (outside of what is seen on the tape), the Kim Kardashian name rakes in tens of millions of dollars per year by simply existing in a way that gets people to pay attention.

The rise of the ultimate supermarket tabloid stars was the death of supermarket tabloids, as the mainstream media followed the trail of attention and usurped their creations. With the release and celebration of those private moments made public, the marriage between news and celebrity was consummated. The embrace of Hilton and Kardashian marked the obliteration of the line between famous and infamous, between honoring accomplishment and celebrating existence by "the beautiful people."

So much of what journalism is today consists of celebrity garbage. Not the kind of celebrity garbage the *National Enquirer* peddled before cracking the JFK assassination by outing Senator Ted Cruz's dad as a conspirator, but the gossip and bullshit that had moved from the newsprint pages of "rags" to the glossy pages of *US Weekly*, *People*, and *Entertainment Weekly*.

Entertainment journalism is still journalism, the way a wart is technically a tumor. Reporters interview celebrities with a team of publicists in the room on topics agreed to ahead of time—usually whatever movie, album, or book they're promoting at the time.

In exchange for essentially reprinting a press release with airbrushed, posed "candids" or airing well-lit video "interviews," entertainment journalists are rewarded with trips to exotic locales, as many of those "press junkets" are staged in places where the movie was filmed.

In other words, it's awful. Imagine a thirteen-year-old interviewing the Beatles in February 1964. Only there was an off-chance she would have accidentally asked something interesting; there's no such worry in modern entertainment media.

But entertainment media are no longer consigned to the grocery store checkout lanes. They've crept into the world of once great news outlets.

Nary a day goes by when *Time* magazine isn't tweeting about the latest action, inaction, or solid bowel movement of a Kardashian sister or calling some model "brave" for daring to eat carbs.

In between stories on America's obesity epidemic, the House That Luce Built can be found filling its website with stories of how some universally attractive actress "overcame her body issues."

Journalism at *Time* is dead, and it died of diabetes.

Time isn't alone, though it does have an unhealthy fascination with Chrissy Teigen, the model about whom it has tweeted more than Nancy Pelosi has called someone a misogynist; all outlets know there is money to be made off the celebrity set. And they are all fighting for their piece of the pie.

Clicks are money, and journalism is a business. Somebody has to pay the bills. But at what cost?

Print outlets are dedicating an ever-growing percentage of their websites to celebrity clickbait, and networks are following suit.

Unlike the days of physical print copies of periodicals, where what could be covered was limited by space, the Internet has no such constraints. That *Time* burns so many calories on celebrity pap does not mean it's at the expense of something else, per se. (Though when was the last time you remember *Time* breaking a major story?)

The nightly network news, on the other hand, has only twenty-two minutes per day to cover the events of the world. Yet, unfortunately, this trend has crept into those newscasts as well.

With the approach of the 2016 election, ABC News dedicated more than twice as many minutes to talking about the breakup of a Hollywood power couple than it did the US economy, according to analysis by Newsbusters, a conservative organization that monitors liberal media bias. [7]

The fact that Angelina Jolie filed for divorce from Brad Pitt undoubtedly upset some of their fans is unquestioned, and maybe it was worth the almost three minutes (173 seconds, to be exact) ABC News spent on the story in late September 2016. But when compared to the economy, the subject that even ABC's own poll found to be the top issue among voters, was it really deserving of twice the coverage?

In the month of September, ABC News spent 77 seconds on the US economy.

The following month, October 2016, ABC News found another shiny object by which to be distracted—a 101-year-old cheerleader.

You don't usually think of 101-year-olds being cheerleaders, and it was a lighthearted, feel-good story, so that it got mentioned isn't the issue. It's only when it's compared to the top issue of concern in the month-away election that you begin to see a pattern.

ABC spent 85 seconds on the story of Burnece Brunson, the elderly Tennessee State alumna who was a cheerleader at the college in 1934. And although there certainly is no harm in celebrating her as ABC's "Person of the Week," the problem comes in when you compare a one-time human interest story to what humans were really interested in one month before they were to pick their next president.

In October, ABC News spent barely half a minute—39 seconds—talking about the sagging US economy.[8] Anemic growth didn't serve Hillary Clinton's campaign, so shiny object distraction it was.

Chrissy Teigen is a favorite bit of clickbait and distraction for the media, particularly for *Time*. There was a time when short of being kidnapped, there wasn't much a model could do to warrant attention from one of the nation's top newsmagazines. Every issue had some fluff, but this was first and foremost a news organization, after all, and an attractive person whose job is to be attractive and not, say, cure cancer, isn't news. Anymore, not so much.

Between January 1 and April 1, *Time* ran twelve stories with Teigen's name in the title and ten more that mentioned her in the body of the story. What accomplishment warranted so much coverage of Ms. Teigen? Literally nothing. In one piece sure to be a finalist for the Pulitzer Prize, Teigen declared that she has "the utmost respect for mothers and single mothers who go to work and come home and make dinner. I do all these things because I have help."[9] That wasn't a random line from the piece; it was its crux. Entitled "Chrissy Teigen Has the 'Utmost Respect' for Working and Single Mothers," it was a rehash of an interview she gave to Yahoo Style, so it might have to share that Pulitzer. Still, *Time* deemed it worthy of a story of its own.

On February 13, 2017, *Time* added Beyoncé Knowles to the Teigen mix. Entitled "Chrissy Teigen Had the Perfect Reaction to Beyoncé's Grammy Performance," the piece offered a series of tweets from Teigen detailing how Beyoncé's performance had her crying.

"I am crying. My bey. I cannot breathe," she tweeted. This, according to *Time*, was "the perfect reaction."[10]

Beyoncé is one of the few celebrities to garner more attention from *Time* than Teigen. A search of *Time* for the same period returned no fewer than sixty-four stories with Beyoncé as the subject and hundreds more that mention her.

On February 24, 2017, *Time* stopped all the presses for the earth-shattering story "Beyoncé Posted a Snapchat Photo and the Internet Can't Handle It."[11] What, pray tell, was the Internet unable to handle, according to the once-storied news outlet?

> *While Beyoncé cancelling her Coachella appearance might have bummed out some Bey Hive members on Thursday, they had no time to lament because Queen Bey graciously provided an engrossing diversion: a photo suggesting she has a secret Snapchat.*[12]

Fear not, the Internet survived.

Beyond Beyoncé's secret Snapchat and Teigen's ability to raise her children with "help," *Time* doesn't restrict itself to simple celebrity lifestyle developments. When celebrities act as political pundits, all presses are stopped yet again and their declarations, usually in the form of tweets, are treated as though they were carved into stone tablets by a burning bush.

When, on February 3, 2017, Teigen called President Donald Trump evil, *Time* could not contain its excitement. President Trump, in regard to his temporary travel ban, tweeted, "We must keep 'evil' out of our country!" In response, the model wrote, "What time should we call your Uber?"

Amusing, sure. But "epic"? That's how *Time* described it. "Chrissy Teigen's Latest Tweet to President Trump Is Epic" was the headline.[13] News, in this case, stems from what is the equivalent of a "Your momma" fight.

When Trump rolled back late-term orders by President Obama that mandated genderless bathrooms in all government-funded buildings, Beyoncé took to her Facebook page to express her support for LGBTQ youth. "Beyoncé Supports LGBTQ Youth After Trump Rolls Back Guidelines Protecting Transgender Students," *Time* headlined the story.[14] Beyoncé's Facebook post was 19 words, which included a hyperlink. *Time*'s story about that post was 130 words.

Beyoncé, of course, is free to support whatever cause she wants, and she routinely does. The question is whether an innocuous social media post is "news" if it requires nearly seven times the words to explain it.

If freaking out over Beyoncé news were an Olympic event, *Time* would win the media gold. But the podium would be crowded and the competition stiff.

When the singer announced that she was having twins with her husband, rapper Jay-Z, not only did *Time* overblow the announcement, it ran a story on how other celebrities had lost their minds at the news that a married couple was reproducing.

"10 Celebrities Who Lost It When Beyoncé Announced She Was Pregnant with Twins" blared the headline on February 2.[15] Some of what *Time* declared about people "who lost it" did, indeed, seem a little too excited about news that wouldn't affect their lives in the least. Yet others were not all that outside the realm of a normal reaction. But *Time*'s narrative is that "Everyone loses their damn minds when Beyoncé does anything," so the tweets were lumped together to continue that narrative.

The Oscar-winning actress Brie Larson, in all caps, declared, "NO—YOU ARE CRYING BECAUSE BEYONCÉ IS HAVING TWINS." Okay, that does seem a little like someone who lost it. Point for *Time*.

Also in that "lost it" category would be Hailey Baldwin. At this point you may be asking yourself, "Who is Hailey Baldwin?" You wouldn't be alone.

Baldwin is a model, a daughter of the actor Stephen Baldwin, of the lesser Baldwins. On what planet is she a "celebrity"? On Planet *Time*, where people's status is elevated to fit the narrative of a particular story's needs.

Baldwin's reaction was a bit unhinged; she tweeted, "I feel like I'm more excited for Beyoncé to be pregnant than I will be for my own child." But *Time*'s line about her tweet gave her a run for her money. "Hailey Baldwin embodied the thoughts of many Beyoncé fans with her tweet," *Time* wrote.

Another unhinged response was from the author and transgender celebrity (because that's a thing now) Janet Mock, who tweeted, "Queen came through to give us new life in these dismal ass times"—the "dismal ass times" being the Trump presidency.

Still, lacking in major celebrities losing consciousness over the pregnancy of a singer, *Time* had to project reactions onto some.

The little-known actress Issa Rae simply suggested names for the babies. "Should she name them Yellow and Lemonade? No? Okay. *Nods and escorts self out*" *Lemonade* was the name of Beyoncé's latest album and "Yellow" is a song by Coldplay she and Jay-Z sang together in an HBO documentary. That's not "losing it," it's making a joke.

Time also blew up the singer Zendaya's reaction, which was simply tweeting "Absolutely radiant" in reaction to the picture of the pregnant Beyoncé. *Time* described that as "Zendaya couldn't contain her excitement for Bey."

That "excitement" seemed pretty well contained in just two words: "absolutely" and "radiant."

Celebrities can make news, and celebrity news is a valid form of journalism. But not every move, every utterance of a celebrity is newsworthy.

In the digital age, clickbait equals money, and there's no larger worm to put on a hook than a big-name star. Yet what once was a domain of supermarket tabloids is now haunting the pages of once-great newsmagazines.

But the printed page, dead tree or digital, is not the only hunting ground for mindless content. Cable news now dwells in the bowels of celebrity obsession, too.

Whereas the Internet is endless, time is not. Cable news shows have a finite number of minutes per hour and only twenty-four hours in a day, yet that time, too, finds itself being devoured by breakups and gossip. How else to explain MSNBC spending almost nine minutes on a Saturday with a panel discussion on a Twitter feud between Taylor Swift and Nicki Minaj, wondering what it "says about bias in the industry, feminism in the music world, and the success of women of color in popular culture."[16]

When Kanye West stopped by Trump Tower to meet with then president-elect Donald Trump, you would've thought the pope had declared abortion a good thing based on the amount of coverage given the event by MSNBC and CNN. Analysts rushed to describe what it could mean for fans of both. In the end it meant nothing, because, well, West is a musician and Trump is president. Presidents meet musicians, and those meetings never amount to anything.

But it was the merging of two worlds—the political and the entertainment—that now dominates so much of what is called journalism. When they temporarily converge, as they always have, the gravity of it is like that of a black hole; it sucks all the life from everything else. It must have deeper meaning because so much meaning is projected onto both professions by the profession covering them. That Bill O'Reilly and two guests spent almost six minutes of a one-hour show on the subject of Kanye's Trump Tower visit is a testament to that—and a condemnation.[17]

Perhaps it's a sign of the times that everything is political now, or maybe it always was and people simply like to think that the time in which they live is the worst. Whatever the case, some of what celebrities do is newsworthy, but most of the media attention they receive is not journalism.

Chapter 5

As Seen on TV

Liberals lost their collective mind when Trump beat Hillary Clinton. As a way to keep angry liberals angry and motivated, several marches were organized in the hope of mobilizing demoralized activists. The Women's March, the March for Science, A Day Without an Immigrant, and so on, all liberal causes centered around left-wing identity groups and causes created to keep liberal talking points in the media and indoctrinated masses scared. They are perfect events for television.

"Science believers" becoming an identity group might be the most consequential and frightening thing that's happened on the left in the past decade or two. It has moved science from an area of life in which the truth is sought to one in which "truth" is what people with that identity say it is.

Onstage as an honorary cochair of the March for Science, Bill Nye, "The Science Guy," could not have written himself better press. *Esquire* wrote:

> *Who knew, when watching Saturday morning reruns of* Bill Nye the Science Guy, *that the enthusiastic, bowtied man teaching us about electricity would become the spokesman for saving our planet from certain doom? The outspoken environmentalist gave an emotional speech at the Washington, DC, March for Science on Saturday.*[1]

Stalin could only dream of such loving coverage from state-run media with the threat of a one-way trip to a gulag behind it. Yet liberal causes and liberal-approved champions bathe in such coverage like a mermaid in a hot spring. If you're on the side of the Left, you're on the side of the media, and that media will shower you with love that makes Spanish fly look like saltpeter. This sort of fan letter is what happens when liberal activists are granted press credentials.

The coverage of the March for Science was indicative of the coverage of every left-wing cause. "Marches also took place in hundreds of other cities around the world, according to organizers," declared *Variety*.[2] CNN said, "Besides the Washington march, organizers said more than 600 'satellite' marches were taking place globally in a protest timed to coincide with Earth Day."[3] "Why Scientists Are Marching on Washington and More than 600 Other Cities" was the headline in the *Washington Post*.[4] Vox reported, "In all, organizers say people marched for science on Earth Day in more than 600 cities and towns across six continents."[5]

Those were just a few of dozens of examples of "journalists" parroting the "these protests are happening in more than 600 cities" claim without providing one scintilla of proof. They were effectively publishing a press release, unquestioned, as fact.

This isn't new, though it is unique to the Left. The annual March for Life, a pro-life march in DC on the anniversary of the *Roe v. Wade* decision, draws hundreds of thousands of people every year and barely rates a mention in the media. But the "fight for $15," the push by liberal activists to raise the minimum wage for fast-food workers (sorry, if you can be replaced by a touch screen kiosk and credit card swipe, you aren't worth $15 per hour) gets stories that declare protests nationwide.

"Workers in more than 200 cities walked out on jobs or joined protests bankrolled by organized labor on Wednesday in latest bid to raise minimum wage," said the UK *Guardian*.[6] Reuters said, "Thousands of U.S. fast-food workers and supporters marched in nearly 200 cities around the United States on Thursday including Chicago and Boston to advocate for a $15 minimum wage and other labor rights."[7] "A Tax Day strike by fast-food workers in more than

200 American cities is expected to be the largest of its kind," reported the Daily Beast.[8] The *New York Times* reported, "in the wave of actions on April 15, organizers say more than 60,000 people will join strikes and protests in 200 cities nationwide. They also predict there will be strikes and support actions in 35 other countries."[9]

Protest marches happening in two hundred cities would mean an average of four per state. Did you see one? Most people live near a major city and consume some sort of news; did you read about one or see a report on your local news about one in your state? If you don't live in New York, Washington, DC, Detroit, Chicago, St. Louis, Dallas, Houston, Seattle, Portland, or Los Angeles, probably not. Or at least not one about a local march, as television packages consisted mainly of footage from one of the cities listed.

Yet that two hundred cities number was reported as fact, many times before the day of the protest itself, without question. Reporting without proof is not reporting, it's publishing a press release; it's activism.

There is no list of cities where the protests occurred, just a declaration that they would. There is no list of cities that held Marches for Science, just reports that they would or did happen based on the word of the organizers. Organizers have every incentive to lie, to inflate their effectiveness and reach, because it means fund-raising dollars. It's a scam actively aided by "objective journalists" because they support the causes and do not verify such claims; waiting until an event actually occurs to see if it lives up to the hype would be too much like work and could damage the cause if it didn't clear the bar organizers set for themselves.

In the activism game, being a liberal is akin to having a twelfth man on the football field.

An event is wildly popular because, according to the people writing the story, it's wildly popular among the people they know. It's a bit like the spirit of the quote falsely attributed to the late *New Yorker* film critic Pauline Kael that she didn't understand how Richard Nixon had been elected president because "I don't know anyone who voted for him."[10] But, just as someone doesn't have to know a supporter for a candidate to win an election, someone doesn't have to be wildly popular to be portrayed as wildly popular. And he or she doesn't have to be knowledgeable on a topic such as, say, climate change, to be portrayed as an expert on the topic.

Bill Nye was a celebrity, if not a scientist, who could parrot talking points with the best of them, making him perfect for television activism for liberal causes.

In what reads like a rock star taking the stage, the *Washington Post*'s lede in a story on the March for Science portrayed Nye like a conquering hero:

> *The moment he emerged onstage in a black jacket and red bow tie, the crowd noise hit near-deafening decibels. A sea of iPhones appeared, everyone stretching and jostling for the best possible photo angle. They cupped their hands to their mouths, screaming his name.*[11]

Who would have thought pretending to be a scientist would earn a guy groupies? "Near the foot of the stage, a young woman with a bright green pixie cut shouted, 'I love you!'"[12]

The finger on the scale in favor of Nye (and people like him) in the media extends to anything he does or says—when you create a demigod, you must protect that demigod from exposure at all costs. When Nye suggested that NASCAR switch to electric cars, a suggestion not only contrary to the sport but stupid and logistically impossible, Huffington Post declared, "Bill Nye Has a Brilliant Idea to Transform NASCAR," continuing, "In an emotional new blog post, America's beloved 'Science Guy' urges the popular stock car racing series to replace the 'ancient tech' internal combustion engines that power the series' race cars for clean-running electric motors."[13]

Nye wrote:

> *Just think what an electric race would be like. It would be faster, and quiet. You could talk to the person next to you. The drivers could probably hear the roar of the crowd rather than having to*

imagine it as they do now. And most significant from my point of view, everyone in the crowd, every race fan, would want an electric car! The market for electric cars would go crazy. Manufacturers could not produce them fast enough. We could convert our transportation system to all-electric in less time than it took to go from horse-drawn to horseless carriage, 20 years maybe.[14]

Aside from the dangers of high-speed crashes with hundreds of pounds of batteries in the car and the environmental problems the batteries themselves pose,[15] electric cars are not all that environmentally friendly. The electricity to charge those batteries has to come from somewhere, and coal-fired power plants are the most common source.

Scientific American reports shifting to electric cars may sound like an environmentally sound idea, but "those [power plants'] smokestacks, many attached to coal-fired power plants, are the single-largest source of greenhouse gas pollution in the U.S., at two billion metric tons of CO_2 per year."[16]

So the "cure" could be worse than the solution, if you believe there is a problem in the first place. Still, Nye comes through unscathed, even praised.

The protective shield the Left builds around those they deem useful is nearly impenetrable. The only time it goes away is when the person has outlived his or her usefulness.

———————

You wouldn't accept as gospel medical advice from a plumber, nor would you take the word of a pediatrician on car maintenance. Yet every single day millions of people take the advice of people who have zero experience of or firsthand knowledge about the subjects they're so assertively speaking of, simply because they're on television.

You wouldn't know it by watching cable news, but there is no such job as "Republican strategist" or "Democratic strategist." When you see those words following someone's name on cable news chyron, it's shorthand for "This person was available and willing to talk about the subject at hand."

Most "strategists" are simply people who are known to producers, able to string together a coherent sentence, and willing to speak passionately on subjects they may or may not know anything about.

They do make for good TV, even if they don't necessarily make for informative TV. But good TV is what matters now, even in the news business.

Ever wonder why you see the same people on CNN, for example, all the time? There are several reasons for this.

First, they're easy to get. A cable news contributorship is one of the most sought-after gigs in politics—it's easy money and brings a measure of fame to the people who land one. Nobody had ever heard of Ana Navarro before she started making a clown of herself on television. She's now CNN's "Republican," which would normally be akin to being a vegan group's butcher. But she's on the network more frequently than the voice of James Earl Jones because she's a "cable news Republican"—shorthand for someone with any type of Republican pedigree who now expends more energy complaining about the party than calories burnt by a participant in an ultramarathon does in a top-five finish.

It's the medium more than the message, or even the messenger, that has the impact. No medium is or has ever been as powerful as television. Print came close in its heyday, but too few people read books and newspapers to truly saturate the nation the way television does. Print still has its place; in news nothing can influence what is discussed on television like a print story. But nowadays newspapers' "scoops" have an impact only insofar as they get attention on cable news programs.

Even with the cost, the saturation of cable television is nearly complete in all income brackets, minus the Amish and general Luddites. The mere act of appearing on television imbues a participant with a level of credibility no other medium can.

Viewers assume that the person speaking is knowledgeable about the subject at hand because there are entire staffs whose job it is to make sure that what goes out on the air is true and accurate. TV wouldn't lie, would it?

The fact is, the majority of people now debating important issues on cable news have no firsthand knowledge of the stories they discuss, nor any information beyond having read a story or two before airtime.

The five words that are killing cable news are "For reaction we turn to . . ." which translates directly to "The people you are about to hear from know nothing more about this story than you do."

The power of TV, coupled with confirmation bias in the audience, turns a conversation that most people would move away from were it happening at the table next to them at a bar into successful "news." Without television this would not be possible. The medium encourages misinformation. On any given day, there simply isn't twenty-four hours' worth of news to fill a cable news station's schedule, nor is there twenty-four hours' worth of information about the news of the day to warrant that much time spent on it. Opinion, which started out as the filler, is now the main course. It's the peanut butter and jelly sandwich of knowledge—cheap and easy to make but of little value beyond simply keeping you alive.

The power of television to create "media stars" and therefore elevate the importance of stories while formulating and advancing a narrative is unparalleled. No credentials are needed; all you have to do is be on the "right side of history" on an issue, and you could be the media's chosen star.

Two prime examples of this are the aforementioned Bill Nye, "The Science Guy," and Neil deGrasse Tyson.

Would you take home-remodeling advice from an astrophysicist? Probably not. Nor would you take investment advice from an actor with an engineering degree. Or at least you shouldn't.

When it comes to important decisions, from your personal life to government policy, expertise is important. The experts giving advice have to be honest, of course, willing to put their personal preferences aside and go where the facts and data take them, but study and experience are what make them experts.

Then there are people who simply excel at . . . being good on TV.

Neil deGrasse Tyson is, undoubtedly, a smart man in the field of astrophysics. If you want to know about deep space and distant planets, he's your guy. Yet his input is not limited to his area of expertise. In fact, it's nearly unlimited.

The media themselves so love Neil deGrasse Tyson that *People* magazine named him "Sexiest Astrophysicist" in 2000.[17] Quick, name a second astrophysicist. You can't. The world, it seems, needs only one.

But why does it have one so well known that the media seeks his input on everything from climate change to politics in the first place? Because Tyson is engaging on TV.

Space has always fascinated human beings since the first virgin was sacrificed during an eclipse. We've evolved some since then, but we're still incredibly curious about the unknown beyond the stars.

That curiosity led to shows such as *Star Trek*, countless successful movies, and documentaries about actual scientific discoveries. It's there that Tyson entered the public consciousness.

In 2000, Tyson appeared on the PBS series *Closer to Truth*. He was interviewed for the three episodes related to the cosmos, his area of study.[18] After that, for the next few years, he was involved in other documentaries on space. But in 2007, things started to change; he began making the transition from scientist to celebrity.

On March 15, 2007, Tyson was a guest on *Late Night with Conan O'Brien*, then more documentaries, *The Tonight Show with Jay Leno*, and *Who Wants to Be a Millionaire?*, the host of science TV shows, and a guest on scores of other shows. In all, Tyson has over a hundred appearances as himself on his IMDb page.[19]

The credibility instilled in him by appearing in documentaries, going on *The Daily Show*, and the like, and simply appearing on TV as an expert led him to being a listened-to expert on nearly any issue.

When Tyson speaks on climate change, for example, his opinion is reported as if it were the result of years of intense, personal study during which he arrived, finally, at a provable, irrefutable truth. In reality, an astrophysicist knows as much about climate as an accountant does. Yes, both might have read studies, but reading someone else's work and being able to recount it is not understanding it. Anyone can read a paper on performing an appendectomy, but allowing someone with that as his extent of knowledge on the subject to take yours out would be like letting a random person off the street do your taxes because he stayed in a Holiday Inn Express last night.

When it comes to climate change, Tyson is essentially a fortune cookie. "Odd. No one is in denial of America's Aug 21 total solar eclipse. Like Climate Change, methods & tools of science predict it," Tyson tweeted before the eclipse.[20] For an astrophysicist, he seems blissfully unaware of how the orbit of the moon around the earth relative to the sun compares with the climate of the planet. One is easily determined by the laws of physics; the other is a best-guess computer model system with a history littered with failure.

No one was "in denial" over the eclipse because there was no question it was going to happen. No climate model can say what will happen in the future, which leads to predictions of doom and gloom all accompanied by words such as "should," "might," and "possible." No one thought there "might" be an eclipse on August 21, 2017; people didn't plan vacations in the path of the eclipse on the off chance that the moon would block the sun.

When it comes to weather, Tyson is equally as deep. "Hmm. Don't see much denial of @NOAA climate scientists who have predicted Hurricane Harvey's devastating path into Texas," he tweeted.[21] He was right, there wasn't. What he didn't elaborate on, either because he couldn't or he didn't want his audience to think about it, is the fact that the National Oceanic and Atmospheric Administration (NOAA) admits that its modeling of hurricane tracks is an ever-widening cone, meaning that the farther out in time they go, the wider the possible path of the hurricane is.[22] And those predictions cover days, not years, as do climate change computer models. Also, they don't allow for hurricane "wobble," a slight, last-minute shift in tracking that, for example, spared the east coast of Florida from a hit by Hurricane Matthew in 2016.[23] Florida was prepared, the warnings had gone out, the water and canned goods had been purchased . . . the only thing missing was the hurricane, which shifted slightly east and missed the state completely. Was Hurricane Matthew a climate change denier?

No one event or cluster of events means much of anything in the long term, and climate data has been available for only about 150 years, as far as basic information goes, and 50 or so years from a satellite gathering perspective. To put it another way: there is almost nothing we can surmise about patterns in the past based on the data we have from then, nor is there much we can accurately predict about the future based on the tiny amount of reliable data available. Yet to Tyson, if you don't feel comfortable ceding more power, control, and money to the government over an eclipse and one storm, well, you're in as much denial as someone saying that the Holocaust didn't happen. See the logic there?

Of course there's no logic there. Any rational person would reject the idea of never flying because planes have crashed, and he'd completely reject uprooting his way of life because people with a political agenda swear that not surrendering to their desires will bring about the end of the world.

Ironically, Tyson himself undercut his own argument on climate change when he said, "The press will sometimes find a single paper, and say, 'Oh here's a new truth, if this study holds it.' But an emergent scientific truth, for it to become an objective truth, a truth that is true whether or not you believe in it, it requires more than one scientific paper. It requires a whole system of people's research all leaning in the same direction, all pointing to the same consequences. That's what we have with climate change, as induced by human conduct."[24]

With respect to the age of the planet, the fifty years' worth of reliable data that technology has enabled us to gather from all levels of the atmosphere equals about as much time as it took you to read this sentence. And this doesn't include the fact that in those fifty years there have been dramatic disagreements over what the future of the climate will be and what any possible cause is.

Using the "do it my way and do it now" tactic of the Left, Tyson warns that it may already be too late. "I worry that we might not be able to recover from this because all our greatest cities are on the oceans and water's edges, historically for commerce and transportation. And as storms kick in, as water levels rise, they are the first to go," he said.[25]

This might be good news for anyone looking to find an inexpensive apartment in New York City. But one thing celebrities such as Tyson and his fellow travelers in the climate change doomsday cult don't do is move away from the places they say are going to be decimated by climate change. Tyson lives in New York, as do many of the celebrities who preach about the flooding of coastal cities. And Los Angeles, the last time anyone checked, was not only the center of the movie industry but on the Pacific Ocean. Shouldn't all the climate change promoters move to bunkers in the Rocky Mountains?

Of course, a scientist is a scientist, but what that scientist studied matters. What an entomologist knows is significantly different from what a chemist knows; you would likely take medicine cooked up by only one of them. So why should people take climate advice from an astrophysicist?

Yet the Daily Beast labeled Tyson "this generation's preeminent scientific voice" with no concern about the field of discussion because it agrees with what he says, no actual expertise required.[26] The Beast has asked him about Scientology, religion in government, homophobia, and whether or not President George W. Bush was antiscience because he "believed in 'intelligent design' and is widely known to have suppressed scientific discussion of global warming during his administration."

So believing in God makes one "antiscience" and something was "widely known" yet somehow suppressed.

Tyson defended Bush because "the budget for the National Science Foundation went up" and "he appointed me" to government commissions.[27] All politics, it seems, really is local—and as close as in one's wallet.

But why ask Tyson about those topics in the first place? Because he's a liberal, and liberals automatically give credit on any subject to anyone who agrees with them.

There's no doubt Tyson is smart—he's an astrophysicist, for crying out loud—but outside his field of study his intelligence begins to wobble. As does, it seems, his integrity.

Tyson is a sought-after public speaker because of his television presence. And, like any good public speaker, he strays from the topic at hand to include more entertaining and interesting tidbits and anecdotes. While Tyson knows astrophysics, facts on topics beyond that evade his grasp.

———————————

In 2014, while giving a speech in Seattle, Tyson used two quotes to illustrate how dumb headline writers and politicians are (and there's no doubt many are). The only problem is that both the quotes were made up.

"Half of the schools in the district are below average," the first quote read, attributed to a "newspaper headline." You should always be skeptical of anything cited with the specificity of a can of generic beer.

The problem with this is twofold. One, Tyson wanted to mock the concept of half of some group being below average, but half of something can be below average. The median is different from the average. He didn't seem to understand the concept he was going to mock someone else for not understanding.

The second problem is that the headline was never actually written. "To start with, that's a terrible headline. Below average at what? Half the schools in which district? It's such a terrible headline," wrote The Federalist.[28] Moreover, it found zero results for the headline or any headline close to it, in a Nexis search of the archives of all newspapers. In other words, either Tyson made it up or he heard it somewhere and thought it was too good to check.

In the same speech, Tyson quoted an anonymous member of Congress as saying "I've changed my views 360 degrees on that issue." Again, no citation, just a PowerPoint slide with the attribution of a "member of Congress." Generic "cheese," anyone?

The problem, again, is that there is zero record of any member of Congress saying such an absurd thing anywhere.[29]

In a vacuum, these false statements by the smartest man on the planet might be forgivable, if he at least acknowledged he had been wrong to use them. But that's not how Neil deGrasse Tyson rolls.

Though Tyson chose not to avail himself of the opportunity to attack President George W. Bush in an interview with the Daily Beast, that wasn't always the case. After he'd already been appointed to one White House Commission on science, his loyalty hadn't, apparently, taken hold yet when he said:

> Here's what happens. George Bush, within a week of [the 9/11 terrorist attacks] gave us a speech attempting to distinguish we from they. And who are they? These were sort of the Muslim fundamentalists. And he wants to distinguish we from they. And how does he do it?
>
> He says, "Our God"—of course it's actually the same God, but that's a detail, let's hold that minor fact aside for the moment. Allah of the Muslims is the same God as the God of the Old Testament. So, but let's hold that aside. He says, "Our God is the God"—he's loosely quoting Genesis, biblical Genesis—"Our God is the God who named the stars."[30]

What a buffoon, right? That's the image Tyson was trying to convey to his audience, anyway. But, again, none of it is true.

What President Bush actually said, in a speech addressing the space shuttle *Columbia* disaster, was:

> The same creator who names the stars also knows the names of the seven souls we mourn today. The crew of the shuttle Columbia did not return safely to Earth; yet we can pray that all are safely home.

May God bless the grieving families, and may God continue to bless America.[31]

That speech was delivered on February 1, 2002, after the *Columbia* tragedy, which was decidedly not "within a week" of September 11, 2001, unless Tyson has discovered a rip in the space-time continuum and kept it to himself.

According to Tyson, Bush's unfortunate God quote came long before Tyson was in Bush's Rolodex—long before he was selected to serve on commissions to advise the president—otherwise the all-knowing Dr. Tyson would've set him straight and prevented him from ever saying such a stupid thing. Seriously, Tyson claimed that.

Except that's also false.

When Bush allegedly uttered Tyson's fake quote—within a week of 9/11, according to Tyson—Tyson had already been selected by President George W. Bush to serve on a White House Commission. On August 22, 2001, the White House press office announced that the president would appoint one Neil deGrasse Tyson of New York to serve on the Commission on the Future of the United States Aerospace Industry. Again, I'm no physics PhD, but I am fairly certain that August 22, 2001, came weeks *before* September 11, 2001.

Literally not a single thing about Tyson's Bush story is true. Not a single thing![32]

You would think that fabricating stories and quotations would damage a person's credibility to the point that journalists might think twice before citing or interviewing that person on any topic, but you'd be wrong. Tyson's career and celebrity have been unencumbered by his failures. Nice work if you can get it.

Not limited to attacks on Republican presidents, nearly every thought of Tyson is treated as worthy of note.

When Tyson unleased a series of tweets on the movie *Star Wars: The Force Awakens*, of all things, it was written up in everything from *Time* magazine[33] to NBC News.[34] Why? Why not? The only problem with Tyson's "debunking" was that he got it wrong. "In @StarWars

#TheForceAwakens, BB-8, a smooth rolling metal spherical ball, would have skidded uncontrollably on sand," he tweeted. BB-8 is a ball-shaped droid with a floating head that stays on top of the ball, no matter how much it rolls. Tyson's claim that an autonomous ball would skid on the sand is exactly what someone would assume about a ball on sand if that person believed the improbable-looking machine were a computer-generated special effect.

But BB-8 was not CGI, it was a remote-controlled physical robot created for the movie. And there was behind-the-scenes footage released of it easily rolling over sand dunes.

Tyson simply assumed that he knew how robotics and physics worked, beyond question, and so did the media reporting on him. But knowing deep space does not mean knowing science fiction movies set in deep space.

Tyson has a history of getting things outside his field of expertise horribly wrong, but that hasn't deterred the media from citing him as an expert on climate change, something decidedly outside his field of expertise.

It's not as though this penchant for wandering into areas about which he knows little more than anyone else has somehow sailed under the radar; each instance is written up somewhere.

These aren't world-changing errors, but the sheer number of them would damage the credibility of anyone who did not subscribe to liberal orthodoxy on climate change.

"The Leap Day is misnamed. We're not leaping anywhere. The calendar is simply, and abruptly, catching up with Earth's orbit," Tyson tweeted on February 29, 2016. As CNN pointed out, "Matt Breunig was among those heaping sarcasm or scorn on Tyson's thoughts: 'if only there was a name for a sudden and abrupt lurch forward.'"[35]

Again, not earth-shattering, but a continual string of fortune cookie–level aphorism and errors would ruin the man if he were a conservative. Since he's not, it's all good.

Neil deGrasse Tyson is not the only expert on everything the media worships on the altar of "science." Nor is he the most egregious example.

There's a good chance that you or your children grew up watching Bill Nye, "The Science Guy," on television, and you probably learned a lot of basic science knowledge from his show. But Bill Nye is not a scientist; he's an engineer turned actor who spent a good part of his early adulthood attempting to be a comedian. In 1993, he developed his "science" show for a PBS station in Seattle and from that pulled the biggest joke of his career on all of us.

His show was successful because, (a) he is a charming man, and (b) the government subsidies that funded his show did not require him to attract an audience. After 100 episodes, *Bill Nye the Science Guy* ended without much controversy or fanfare in 1998.

Though his show went away, Nye did not.

After several attempts at new shows failed, Nye was a constant presence on news programs advocating for radical climate change legislation. With no background or expertise in climate science, he was still labeled "The Science Guy," and his assertions went unchallenged.

Nye's belief in human-caused climate change makes him a hero to the political Left, which has showered him with the attention he's craved since his failed stand-up days. When asked about how "denial" can be overcome, his answer was not "by proving" anything; it was to wait till people who weren't indoctrinated into the Holy Church of Global Warming as children die off. "Climate change deniers, by way of example, are older. It's generational. So we're just going to have to wait for those people to 'age out,' as they say. 'Age out' is a euphemism for 'die.' But it'll happen, I guarantee you—that'll happen," he said.[36]

Yes, people will die, but is that what constitutes science?

The administration of President Barack Obama recognized the power and importance of television and celebrity (hell, it owed its existence to it). As such, President Obama embraced Nye, elevating him further in the growing area of implied expertise by proxy.

Nye campaigned for Obama in 2012:

Nye, an engineer, comedian, author, and inventor, is best known
for playing the part of an energetic science teacher on the televi-
sion series "Bill Nye the Science Guy," which aired in the mid- to
late-1990s.

Nye handled lobsters, signed autographs and promoted the
president's re-election bid during his stop on the New Hampshire
Seacoast.[37]

From there, Nye's bona fides as a liberal icon were sealed. More
late-night television appearances followed, and he was named to
the cast of *Dancing with the Stars* for the 2013 season. His celebrity was assured, though his popularity lagged. He was voted off
DWTS in the third episode.

It's not just people who seek the spotlight who get endowed with
credibility from television by the liberal media; sometimes people
have it thrust upon them because they serve a particular cause.

Khizr Khan was a simple man who never sought the spotlight
but ended up in it anyway. Khan, an immigrant lawyer, had a son,
Captain Humayun Khan, who was killed in Iraq in 2004. A veritable unknown before late July 2016, Khan became a media sensation when, never having wanted the spotlight, he gave a prime-time
address at the Democratic National Convention, blasting Republican nominee Donald Trump as a racist who didn't understand the
Constitution.

"Donald Trump consistently smears the character of Muslims.
He disrespects other minorities—women, judges, even his own
party leadership. He vows to build walls and ban us from this country," Khan said on national television, in a shot at Trump's stance
against illegal immigration, even though he was a citizen who'd
immigrated to the country legally decades earlier.

"Have you ever been to Arlington Cemetery? Go look at the
graves of the brave patriots who died defending America—you will
see all faiths, genders, and ethnicities. You have sacrificed nothing
and no one," he concluded.

Liberals wet themselves with glee as the shy Khan appeared on every major news program over the coming weeks. Never once was it pointed out to him that sacrifice was not a requirement to run for president, nor that Hillary Clinton had also "sacrificed nothing and no one," unless you count the humiliation of staying married to Bill after his countless affairs.

When Trump responded via Twitter, refuting things Khan had said, liberals screamed about how the candidate was "attacking a Gold Star father!" Though the horror of being a Gold Star parent is something only a Gold Star parent knows, it does not immunize such a person from being wrong or criticized, as evidenced by Democrats' subsequent attack on Trump's chief of staff, General John Kelly, who'd lost a son in Afghanistan. Every word spoken by the Khans was off limits; saying that General Kelly is a "disgrace to the uniform," as Democratic congressman Luis Gutiérrez did, is fair.[38]

Khan, who had never sought attention, hit the campaign trail for Clinton, signed fund-raising emails for Democrats, wrote a book, toured the country selling that book, and resurfaced in the media from time to time when liberals needed him to attack President Trump. Imagine how much attention he would have gotten had he *wanted* attention.

Khan became a television star by virtue of his son's sacrifice; an untold number of "think pieces" were written about his sacrifice, heroism, and courage for . . . telling Democrats what every Democrat already believes, then repeating it to Democrats in the media.

The loss the Khan family suffered is unimaginable, but the sacrifice of the son does not immunize the father from criticism.

Khizr Khan is useful to liberals now, but today's "unimpeachable hero" is tomorrow's "Didn't you used to be someone?" Liberals have a penchant for elevating people in their time of need or grief to advance their agenda.

Does the name Cindy Sheehan ring a bell? During the administration of President George W. Bush, Sheehan was a liberal celebrity. Casey Sheehan, Cindy's son, was killed in Iraq in 2004.

Soon after, in her grief, Sheehan became a vocal Bush critic and therefore a media celebrity.

Sheehan demanded a meeting with President Bush to get answers to why the United States was in Iraq in the first place. Liberals ran with the story, accusing Bush of ducking Sheehan, who had set up "Camp Casey," a tent city of left-wing activists, near Bush's home in Crawford, Texas. NBC News even ran a story entitled "Anti-war Mom Glad She Didn't Meet Bush."[39] The *Washington Post* added, "Refusal to See Sheehan Is Second-Guessed," writing, "When Cindy Sheehan showed up outside President Bush's ranch on the fourth full day of his five-week working vacation to talk about a son who had been killed in Iraq, he declined to meet with her—a decision that has been widely second-guessed, even by some Republicans."[40]

The problem was that President Bush had already met with Sheehan after her son's death, in April 2004 at Fort Lewis in Washington State. That fact was rarely mentioned by liberals, usually relegated to the later paragraphs of stories about Sheehan's latest protest, if mentioned at all.[41]

There wasn't a Sunday show or evening liberal broadcast that didn't have Sheehan on every time the Iraq War was in the news—until 2009. Then, curiously, she disappeared from television screens and the liberal consciousness. Around that time the antiwar movement disappeared as well, as did the cries of "No war for oil" and daily media coverage of the war.

The date of those disappearances roughly coincided with the election of Barack Obama to be the forty-fourth president of the United States. Weird how that worked.

Cindy Sheehan had outlived her usefulness and was tossed aside, memory-holed by the media and Democrats. The fate of Khizr Khan will be similar once every ounce of usefulness is milked from him.

Television giveth, and television taketh away.

The power of television to create celebrities and endow them with credibility is unparalleled in human history. It can make the host of a kids' show and a specialist on deep space into experts on climate change, and it can take the mother of a slain soldier to the pinnacle of moral authority against a president, only to discard her when a new president liberals support assumes office.

This power is nefarious, it's dangerous, it's manipulative, and it makes a mockery of what it purports to be. And none of it is accidental. They don't call television the "idiot box" for no reason.

Chapter 6

The Doomsday Cult

Nothing exemplifies the rise of "science believer" as a progressive identity like global warming doomsayers.

There is so much more at stake for them than the exact measurements of how much hotter the earth has grown over the past hundred years. They are a persecuted minority that sees how close we are to disaster: cities destroyed, animals extinct, plagues rampant, and humankind barely hanging on. They know the end is coming, because they can feel it in their hearts. Everyone asking for more proof before being required to drive Flintstones-style foot-powered cars is oppressing them and should be silenced.

The most amazing part of the idea behind climate change is the fact that the climate has always changed and always will. It's also the least reported part. That big ball of fire in the sky that gives us our light also gives us a lot of our heat, and that heat fluctuates over time. That's the dirty little secret about "climate science"—that activist scientists know very little, that they make it up as they go along.

When a major storm hits, it is blamed on climate change. When a predicted major storm fizzles or the weather is quite nice and normal for a particular season in a certain area, we are told that weather isn't climate, so something happening as expected cannot lead to any sort of conclusion.

Climate science and the politics of global warming are the ultimate three-card monte—you'll never find the red queen because the con artist on the other side of the table constantly redefines what a red queen is.

In the 1970s, the idea of global cooling was a commonly written about scientific probability. "There are ominous signs that the earth's weather patterns have begun to change dramatically and that these changes may portend a drastic decline in food production—with serious political implications for just about every nation on earth," a 1975 *Newsweek* article entitled "The Cooling World" stated. It predicted famine, doom, and gloom and everything we hear now associated with global warming, only from the exact opposite cause. "The evidence in support of these predictions has now begun to accumulate so massively that meteorologists are hard-pressed to keep up with it," it continued. "In England, farmers have seen their growing seasons decline by about two weeks since 1950, with a resultant over-all loss of grain production estimated at up to 100,000 tons annually." We were all going to die. "Climatologists are pessimistic that political leaders will take any positive action to compensate for the climatic change, or even allay its effects," the article concluded.[1] Sound familiar?

It wasn't the first time. Some time ago, scientists found "evidence" that "an Ice Age will result from a slow warming and rising of the ocean that is now taking place." That was in 1958, written by none other than the liberal icon Betty Friedan for *Harper's* magazine. The scientists, she reported, were certain that "the glacial thermostat, the present interglacial stage is well advanced; the earth is now heading into another Ice Age."[2] Though they didn't know why.

As in 1958, in 1975 scientists were not reluctant to admit when they didn't know something about an issue. As the *Newsweek* article pointed out, "Just what causes the onset of major and minor ice ages remains a mystery. 'Our knowledge of the mechanisms of climate change is at least as fragmentary as our data,' concedes the National Academy of Sciences report. 'Not only are the basic scientific questions largely unanswered, but in many cases we do not yet know enough to pose the key questions.'"[3]

Today, climate activists, both with and without degrees in the field, speak with absolute certainty—with a lot of qualifiers—about the future.

There was no solution offered in the 1950s, but the solution in the 1970s was different from today's. In its infancy, climate science hadn't yet been blamed on civilization, so treating everyone who drives a car as though he's a Bond villain with a personal weather control machine wasn't at the forefront of the activists' mind. They were too busy trying to save the whales from capitalism to recognize the opportunity that saving the planet by destroying capitalism presented.

Newsweek wrote about "solutions" such as "melting the arctic ice cap by covering it with black soot or diverting arctic rivers," though it conceded that doing so "might create problems far greater than those they solve."[4]

Still, the article did latch on to what would become the mantra of the Left on this issue—that we must act now, before it's too late! "The longer the planners delay, the more difficult will they find it to cope with climate change once the results become grim reality," it ended.[5]

That has been the calling card of left-wing activists on the subject since before it became known as climate change, back when it was still global warming. It's no longer the search for truth, it's "settled science." But history is littered with scientists who were certain that they'd discovered a truth, only to find out later, through questioning and skepticism, that they were wrong.

As climate has evolved into a religion, former vice president Al Gore has emerged as its pope. Pope Goreus I, as he should be known, has made hundreds of millions of dollars during his crusade against greed in the name of the planet.[5] Who knew that fighting for the poor and saving the planet could be the key to getting rich?

Pope Goreus I has been the Jim Jones of climate alarmism since his 2000 presidential election defeat. He and his apostles have been predicting doom and gloom since he realized he'd need a job in the private sector for the first time in his adult life after losing to George W. Bush.

In 2006, Gore described the climate as "a true planetary emergency," with the Associated Press reporting "politicians and corporations have been ignoring the issue for decades, to the point that unless drastic measures to reduce greenhouse gases are taken within the next 10 years, the world will reach a point of no return, Gore said."[7]

It's now more than ten years since 2006, and we're still here. Moreover, we haven't seen the death and destruction we were warned of.

Gore isn't the only snake-oil salesman who has had his arrogant "We have only this long to do something or it'll be too late" bluffs called by time. Activists had been predicting the end of life if we didn't turn away from capitalism and embrace government control of our lives for decades before he found himself in need of income.

All those dire predictions have one thing in common: they didn't happen.

Even Sting eventually stopped singing about the rain forests when we didn't all run out of breathable air, but the Holy Church of Global Warming simply repackaged itself and devotees kept singing right along.

A subtle change in tactics occurred, however, because con artists do learn from their mistakes. A movement once known for its near-term predictions started to lengthen the time span a bit.

As with Gore's "ten years or it's too late" talk, people who predict the end of the world in their lifetimes have some explaining to do when their followers wake up the day after and realize they maxed out their credit cards for nothing and now have to find a way to make it up to a boss they told to kiss their ass to get their old job back.

The predicted end time came and went, yet life continued, hardly noticing. Coastal cities weren't under feet of water. People had heard that something would happen in their lifetimes and it didn't. That's bad for business.

Rather than engage in self-reflection or question why what they had said would happen hadn't, believers simply moved the goalposts back. Suddenly ten-year predictions of doom and gloom became hundred-year predictions of doom and gloom.

If you say that something awful will happen this weekend, come Monday the people who believed you will have some questions for you and probably won't believe you the next time. But if you say that something awful will happen in a hundred years, well, no one will be around to call you out for being wrong, if they even remember the prediction in the first place.

That's been the latest trend in climate alarmism—undisprovable dire predictions.

One prediction is that global warming might increase lightning strikes by 50 percent by the year 2100. Notice the qualifiers?

Scientific American reported the "study" by citing the fact that there are 8 million lightning strikes per day on the planet but that "Now, a new study finds that lightning strikes could flash through the sky even more often than that as the planet warms, at least over the continental U.S."[8]

Again, note the use of the word "could." The study found that lightning could increase, it might happen . . . in eighty-two years. But this possible problem is something that must be addressed now, not tomorrow, NOW!

It's an impossible claim to prove, but, more importantly, it is impossible to disprove, and when it is merged with the urgency of the very survival of the human race, well, it becomes a moral imperative. To question it, to ask for proof and not just theories and predictions, isn't just immoral, it's heresy.

And poof, just like that, the party that spent decades lecturing conservatives about how, on social issues, "You can't legislate morality," created a moral imperative that must be legislated.

Scientific American rolled all this into one:

It is fair to say that citizens and politicians intend for Miami, and indeed the whole State of Florida, to exist well beyond 2100. Same for New York City, Boston, Washington D.C., London, Shanghai, Amsterdam, Mumbai and so on. Yet the same people discount staggering losses these places face beyond 2100. That's wrong, and immoral too.

That's because a crucial fraction of airborne carbon from the industrial revolution, plus that coming this century and next, will persist for tens to hundreds of thousands of years. The CO_2 stemming from just 150 years ago to a mere two centuries ahead may commit the world by inertia to tens of thousands of years of impacts.[9]

You see, we have to be controlled now, because if we're not, that will mean devastation not only in a hundred years but in tens of thousands of years. That's like saying we must change our policies now so all the people who have been cryogenically frozen have a pleasant world to come back to. Of course, that is believable only if you buy into the idea that the world will be unpleasant otherwise, which, again, no one can prove or disprove. Like religion, it's simply a matter of faith.

So the message remained, but the timeline changed.

The activists who'd been advocating for decades for more and more government control over the economy and the population found the perfect vessel in the weather—who can argue with the weather? Then they went bigger, to climate. The climate has always changed, so if that could be made into something to fear and ceding control made into the avenue along which safety lies, well, it doesn't get any better than that.

The issues may change, but the solutions of the Left always remain constant: more government control and regulation and higher taxes for people who just want to be left alone. Every new crisis seems to require capitulating to the will of the people on the coasts and destroying the livelihoods of everyone else.

"Weather is not climate" is a regular refrain of devotees. They use it when it's not oppressively hot in the summer or it's particularly cold in the winter. "Weather is not climate," they say when trying to explain where the planetary warming went over the course of two decades.

Yet weather events, when they are bad, are used by the faithful even in the middle of those events.

Hurricane Katrina devastated the Gulf coast, particularly New Orleans. But it was just a strong hurricane hitting a city that lies below sea level and sits on the sea. Much of the city would be under water naturally, were it not for a series of levees holding back the Gulf of Mexico. So the fact that the city was flooded was not a huge surprise. The devastation came from the failure of city and state officials to evacuate residents and to take the storm seriously until it was upon them. However, the lack of timely evacuation was not a focus of the alarmists or the media. Activists, with or without media credentials, never miss an opportunity to move the ball.

After Katrina, that weather event was used as a harbinger of what was to come—meaning that weather was bastardized into climate. Newsbusters, a project of the Media Research Center, compiled media "reports" on Katrina that made it clear that news organizations were on board with a weather event being climate. They were all wrong.

The day after Katrina's landfall, Robert Bazell, the chief science correspondent for NBC News, said, "Even with its slight weakening, Katrina was one of the biggest ever, and many scientists say we can expect such storms more often as global warming increases sea temperatures around the world." CBS correspondent Russ Mitchell said, "Hurricane Katrina was the most destructive storm this country has ever seen. But a growing number of scientists believe it is just the beginning of what could be a long stretch of wild and devastating weather." Mitchell again, a month later, said, "since 1990, the number of big hurricanes in the Gulf is up again, and there's no end in sight."[10]

In spite of all the scaremongering declarations to the contrary, another major hurricane, meaning one above a category 3, did not hit the United States from Hurricane Wilma in October 2005 until Hurricane Harvey in August 2017, more than a decade later. It was a forty-five-year low for major storms.

Those miserably failed predictions did not deter activists from making more of them in the wake of the devastation from Harvey, because, hey, why not?

Michael E. Mann, the director of the Earth System Science Center at Penn State and a noted activist in the climate change fight, took to his Facebook page during Harvey to ask, "What can we say about the role of climate change in the unprecedented disaster that is unfolding in Houston with Hurricane Harvey?"[11]

In his post, Mann did what climate activists always do—carefully qualified every declaration to leave wiggle room. "There are certain climate change–related factors that we can, with great confidence, say worsened the flooding," he wrote. Note the "with great confidence" part. "So Harvey was almost certainly more intense than it would have been in the absence of human-caused warming, which means stronger winds, more wind damage, and a larger storm surge," he wrote later. Again, note the "almost certainly" part. His conclusion read, "while we cannot say climate change 'caused' Hurricane Harvey (that is an ill-posed question), we can say that it exacerbate [sic] several characteristics of the storm in a way that greatly increased the risk of damage and loss of life."

That's so much couching, it's basically a furniture store.

Yet that is what we are expected to cede liberty to government based on: qualified predictions of what might happen a century from now.

In 2014, the *New York Times* asked if we've seen the "end of snow" thanks to climate change:

> The planet has warmed 1.4 degrees Fahrenheit since the 1800s, and as a result, snow is melting. In the last 47 years, a million square miles of spring snow cover has disappeared from the Northern Hemisphere. Europe has lost half of its Alpine glacial ice since the 1850s, and if climate change is not reined in, two-thirds of European ski resorts will be likely to close by 2100.[12]

There's that 2100 again, and the qualifier "will be likely to."

The winter after the *Times* lamented that "a million square miles

of spring snow cover has disappeared from the Northern Hemisphere," there was record snowfall across the United States. Boston received 110.6 inches, breaking its old record by 3 inches.[13] The
storm dubbed "Snowzilla" dumped between 22 and 35 inches on
the Baltimore/Washington area, including an all-time record for
a single storm in Baltimore.[14] People who sold their shovels after
reading the *Times* story a year earlier hopefully canceled their sub-
scriptions to the newspaper.

Of course, one storm doesn't indicate any sort of pattern, but
there was little more upon which the declaration of a pattern was
made in the previous year. Still, devotees wasted no time in pro-
claiming that "Snowzilla" was the result of, you guessed it, climate
change.

A reported piece entitled "The Surprising Way That Climate
Change Could Worsen East Coast Blizzards" ran in the *Washington
Post* the day after the storm, because why waste time?

The news story, not just the headline, was replete with qualifiers
(emphasis added):

> *As the East Coast digs out from the enormous snowfalls of Winter
> Storm Jonas, a prominent climate scientist* **has drawn a provoc-
> ative connection** *between the storm, warm ocean temperatures
> off the U.S. and a slowdown of ocean circulation in the North
> Atlantic that* **may also be behind** *a much discussed cold "blob"
> to the southeast of Greenland. . . .*
>
> *We certainly can't say that his argument is,* **at this point, a
> matter of scientific consensus or anything close to it.** *As Rahm-
> storf himself admits,* **it's pretty novel.** *. . .*
>
> *Take, for instance, a study just out in the* Journal of Geophys-
> ical Research: Oceans, *by eleven researchers with the National
> Oceanic and Atmospheric Administration. They used a high res-
> olution climate model to examine* **what will happen** *in the North
> Atlantic region as global warming proceeds, and found that for a
> doubling of atmospheric carbon dioxide above pre-industrial lev-
> els, the upper ocean waters in the northwest Atlantic continental*

shelf region **would warm** *"nearly three times faster than the global average."*[15]

Now is an important time to point out that the predictions for future calamities are just that: predictions. They're based on computer models, best guesses of what might happen in the future.

More than that, they are simply made up. Computer models for climate are notoriously unreliable. Given that data exist for only the last 150 years or so, and in the nineteenth century they didn't have the reliable and accurate instruments we have today, that leaves us less than a hundred years, realistically, of data from which to work. And in terms of the planet's life, that isn't even a pimple on a radar screen.

When climate scientists put together models to predict the future, they are basing them on an incredibly tiny amount of information from which they claim they can predict the future. But if those models are correct about what will happen, shouldn't they be accurate in showing what has actually happened?

Should they not be able to take their models and plug in the relevant data from, say, 1950 or 1960 and accurately map the following years up to the present day? They can't. Their models fail because so very little is actually known, not believed, about how climate works.

Dr. Roy Spencer, principal research scientist at the University of Alabama in Huntsville, has been studying climate since the 1980s. He has pointed out something about the climate models that devotees do not want to admit: that they are horrible at predicting the future. "These are all interesting exercises, but they miss the most important point: the climate models that governments base policy decisions on have failed miserably," he wrote.[16]

He explained:

I've updated our comparison of 90 climate models versus observations for global average surface temperatures through 2013, and we still see that >95% of the models have over-forecast the warming trend since 1979, whether we use their own surface temperature dataset (HadCRUT4), or our satellite dataset of lower tropospheric temperatures (UAH).

Whether humans are the cause of 100% of the observed warming or not, the conclusion is that global warming isn't as bad as was predicted. That should have major policy implications . . . assuming policy is still informed by facts more than emotions and political aspirations.

And if humans are the cause of only, say, 50% of the warming (e.g., our published paper), then there is even less reason to force expensive and prosperity-destroying energy policies down our throats.

I am growing weary of the variety of emotional, misleading, and policy-useless statements like "most warming since the 1950s is human caused" or "97% of climate scientists agree humans are contributing to warming", neither of which leads to the conclusion we need to substantially increase energy prices and freeze and starve more poor people to death for the greater good.

Yet that is the direction we are heading.[17]

What Dr. Spencer is pointing out is not just the failure of climate models to predict the future, though he does that beautifully, but how their failure is irrelevant to the push forward with their left-wing agenda by members of the Holy Church of Global Warming in spite of that reality. It's like surviving members of the Heaven's Gate cult still insisting on the divinity of Marshall Applewhite, their crazed cult leader who led members to commit suicide in order to hitch a ride on the spaceship hidden behind the Hale-Bopp comet. "Sure, there was no ship there to take our souls to another plane of existence, but that doesn't mean the guy who had us castrate ourselves to show our devotion wasn't onto something."

We're looking at an economic version of that self-castration, funded largely by government grants.

The joke in Washington is that if you want a grant to study the mating habits of, say, squirrels, aside from needing a hobby, you aren't going to get it. But if you apply for a grant saying you want to study the impact of climate change or global warming (it's a distinction without a difference at this point) on the mating habits of squirrels, that's a different story.

Climate change is a major funder of all manner of research nowadays, or at least the guise under which that funding is allocated. And much of that funding is spent on predicting the future, which by its very nature cannot be researched or studied because it hasn't happened yet.

And, as Dr. Spencer discovered, more than 95 percent of predictions have been wrong. But in academia there are no consequences for being wrong.

You miss sales projections time and again in the private sector, and you're going to be fired. You wildly underestimate costs, and you'll have a lot of explaining to do to shareholders. You regularly misproject projected temperatures or get caught conspiring with other climate scientists to "hide the decline" in global temperatures, and you're back in the lab the next day, hammering government grant checks.[18]

One area the followers of Pope Goreus I don't like to talk about is the inconvenient truth called the "Medieval Warm Period." The Medieval Warm Period was a roughly four-hundred-year stretch from 900 till 1300, when the planet's temperatures inexplicably rose, making the planet warmer.

Unlike today, there was no one around to profit from wild "end of life as we know it" predictions, nor were there any government grants to fund jobs based on the unexplained phenomenon. But it happened.

And it happened before the first SUV or coal-fired power plant. Also, it made life better for people.

A warmer planet in the Middle Ages meant a longer growing season, which meant more crops could be harvested, which meant more food. It wasn't all shits and giggles, life was still a struggle, but it was made slightly less awful by there being more food available.

Scientists have no idea what caused it, as record keeping and equipment to accurately measure relevant data didn't exist, but it did happen and it ended long before mankind had what is now declared to be the ability to change the planet's climate.

As inexplicably as it started, it ended. The world eventually moved into the "Little Ice Age," which, coincidentally, lasted until near the time global warming caused by humans started to be "measured." Weird how, after a period of unusually cool temperatures, temperatures would begin to rise, isn't it?

Of course, the original Ice Age ended, too, which led to unprecedented global warming, all long before the internal combustion engine or even human beings. It's almost as though the planet has cycles, based largely on that big ball of fire in the sky. . . .

Believers label skeptics "deniers" in an attempt to associate them with evil Holocaust deniers. But they've also recently sought to criminalize not accepting climate castration.

New York state attorney general Eric Schneiderman declared, "'Climate change is real.' He went on to say that if companies are committing fraud by 'lying' about the dangers of climate change, they will 'pursue them to the fullest extent of the law.'"[19]

Schneiderman was part of a group of more than a dozen liberal states' attorneys general who are seeking to criminalize skepticism of man-caused climate change.

Asked during congressional testimony whether she would consider investigating companies that deny man-caused climate change under RICO laws as the government did with the tobacco industry, then–US attorney general Loretta Lynch said, "This matter has been discussed. We have received information about it and have referred it to the FBI to consider whether or not it meets the criteria for which we could take action on."[20] Though she was talking about civil action, not criminal, the federal government suing corporations into oblivion is the threat of death.

California, often the tip of the insanity spear, nearly passed legislation in 2016 to criminalize skepticism as well. The California Climate Science Truth and Accountability Act of 2016 would have made George Orwell blush.

> *"This bill explicitly authorizes district attorneys and the Attorney General to pursue UCL claims alleging that a business or organization has directly or indirectly engaged in unfair competition with respect to scientific evidence regarding the existence, extent, or current or future impacts of anthropogenic induced climate change," said the state Senate Rules Committee's floor analysis of the bill.* [21]

As with every dumb liberal idea, it never really dies, it simply waits. . . .

The media's favorite "Science Guy," Bill Nye, who isn't a scientist at all but an engineer hired as an actor for a kid's TV show decades ago, took it a step further. Nye is now one of the go-to people for the media to preach climate change gospel because he's very personable and a bit goofy and has a soft spot in the hearts of many adults who grew up watching him do innocuous experiments on his television show. In a 2016 interview with Marc Morano of ClimateDepot.com, a leading skeptic website, he made it clear that the idea of imprisoning "deniers" isn't beyond the realm of possibility.

MORANO: We interviewed Robert F. Kennedy Jr. RFK Jr., the environmentalists. He said climate "deniers," his words, Energy CEOs belong at the Hague with three square meals and a cot with all of the other war criminals. What is your thought on that and do you think some of the rhetoric on your side—as I am sure both sides—gets too carried away? What is your thought on jailing skeptics as war criminals?

NYE: Well, we'll see what happens. Was it appropriate to jail the guys from ENRON?

MORANO: Interesting.

NYE: So, we will see what happens. Was it appropriate to jail people from the cigarette industry who insisted that this addictive product was not addictive and so on? And you think about in these cases—for me as a taxpayer and voter—the introduction of this extreme doubt about climate change is affecting my quality of life as a public citizen. So I can see where people are very concerned about this and are pursuing criminal investigations as well as engaging in discussion like this.[22]

Though the fever dreams of an actor turned activist who believes his own press aren't exactly the law of the land, Nye's thoughts represent the thinking of a significant swath of the Democratic Party's members on climate change. So although efforts might be stalled right now, nothing in the progressive agenda stays stalled forever. It took more than sixty years for the federal government to take effective control of the medical insurance industry with Obamacare; criminalizing climate skepticism has only not had its day because it hasn't yet had its day.

That's the thing about science: if something is proven, it's proven. No one denies that water is made up of two parts hydrogen and one part oxygen because it has been proven. Not even the most expensive bottle of water claims, "We put extra hydrogen into our water to make it superhealthy." It is what it is and has been proven to be such. The same cannot be said for human-caused climate change.

The climate always changes and is always changing. No one disputes that. Giant glaciers once covered most of the Northern Hemisphere, tropical fossils are found in cold areas of the globe—things have changed rather dramatically, several times over, long before human beings were around to have anything to do with it.

That's why science is so important and the politicizing of science is so dangerous. Science is based on proof, the pursuit of truth, not a show of hands or a majority vote.

Perhaps the favorite statistic of members of the Holy Church of Global Warming is that "98 percent of scientists agree" that climate change is caused by humans. They repeat it more often than a devout Catholic repeats "God bless you" at a kissing conference during a cold epidemic. But it's meaningless and false.

So where does it come from?

It originated from an endlessly reported 2009 American Geophysical Union (AGU) survey consisting of an intentionally brief, anything-but-scientific, two-minute, two-question online survey sent to 10,257 earth scientists by two researchers at the University of Illinois. Of the approximately 3,000 who responded, 82 percent answered "yes" to the second question, "Do you think human activity is a significant contributing factor in changing mean global temperatures?," which, like the first, "When compared with pre-1800s levels, do you think that mean global temperatures have generally risen, fallen, or remained relatively constant?," most people would also have agreed with.

Of those, only a small subset, just 77 who had been successful in getting more than half of their papers recently accepted by peer-reviewed climate science journals, were considered in the survey statistic. That "98 percent of all scientists" referred to a laughably puny number of 75 of those 77 who answered yes to the second question.

The first question was "When compared with pre-1800s levels, do you think that mean global temperatures have generally risen, fallen, or remained relatively constant?" Few would be expected to dispute this; the planet began thawing out of the "Little Ice Age" in the mid–nineteenth century, predating the Industrial Revolution. (That was the coldest period since the last real Ice Age had ended roughly 10,000 years before.)

The second question asked, "Do you think human activity is a significant contributing factor in changing mean global temperatures?" What constitutes "significant"? Does "changing" include both cooling and warming . . . and for both "better" and "worse"?

And which contributing factors? Do they include land use changes, such as agriculture and deforestation?[23]

There you have it: that 98 percent number comes from a small sample of a small sample, chosen deliberately and asked a couple of leading questions. When you choose the unit of measure, you will always win.

If the question is "Are humans having an effect on the climate?" it makes you wonder who the 2 percent are who don't think so. Everything has an impact on the planet. The questions should be "Is it the main cause?" and "Is the impact negative?" But it's often held up as if the question had been "Will burning fossil fuels make the planet unlivable in our lifetimes?" which moves it from a survey to a matter of faith or cult. It's a testament to the laziness of journalism that this number is not only widely used but accepted as if it were carved into stone tablets by a burning bush.

Then again, the theory is really just tax-exempt status away from being a religion, so . . .

Rather than a Bible and apostles fanning out across the country, the Holy Church of Global Warming has Hollywood to spread its word.

Movies such as the disastrous *Waterworld* and the insane *The Day After Tomorrow* presented futures where warnings were not heeded and the consequences were dire. They're fun enough, which is really all you should ask for from a movie, but they are as scientifically based as that "98 percent of scientists" number.

The scripted movies are not alone. There are countless documentaries on the subject on every platform for streaming entertainment, including *An Inconvenient Truth*, *The Age of Stupid*, and *Before the Flood*, which indoctrinate viewers who are expecting to see an unbiased examination of the subject at hand. These films make Leni Riefenstahl seem like a dispassionate observer.

As long as there is power to be gained and control to be derived from the idea of man-caused climate change, facts will not matter. Weather will remain different from climate and climate will remain different from weather unless and until either option becomes advantageous to the cause.

The science of climate is not the real issue; the real issue is power. The idea of human-caused climate change is the popcorn of politics: a socially acceptable delivery device for salt and butter, or in this case regulation and control. Butter and salt are delicious, but you can't sit down, dip a stick of butter into a bowl of salt, and eat it. The otherwise flavorless, kind of Styrofoam-y textured plain popcorn is a way to eat butter and salt together without coming off as a weirdo.

Simply trying to sell government control over nearly every aspect of our lives is going to be met with as much enthusiasm as a fart in an elevator; it has to be packaged in a way people will accept it, give in to it. The destruction of the planet is a bit dramatic, but it's also the perfect mechanism because it can't be disproved.

Most people aren't scientists, and they don't understand science. They do, however, understand, or at least believe, that scientists are truth seekers (little do they realize that they are, more often than anyone would like to admit, grant seekers), so when they say something, people assume that they've done the work to back up their claims.

But their claims are not, in fact, findings of truth; they are predictions about the future—wild speculations, really. The people who can't tell what the weather will be like this weekend are pinky-swearing that they know what will happen long after everyone currently living is dead. They don't.

But that doesn't matter, really, because if you question their methods, they remind you that weather is not climate and climate is not weather. Question anything beyond that, and, if liberals have their way, you may soon end up in jail.

As California governor Jerry Brown put it, "At the highest circles, people still don't get it. It's not just a light rinse. We need a total, I might say 'brainwashing.' We need to wash our brains out and see a very different kind of world."[24] Very different, indeed.

If there's one term that would define the Democratic Party on the issue of global warming, it's "settled science." This is the idea that whatever someone is discussing is a done deal and therefore questioning results or highlighting evidence that does not conform with the liberal agenda does not need to be countered with facts, it can simply be dismissed because the overall conclusion is "settled science."

This allows, say, people who are curious as to why, in spite of the doom-and-gloom predictions of an ever-warming planet, the planet hasn't warmed in more than a decade. You'd think that people who've invested not only the fate of the entire planet but also their professional reputations would be curious as to why what they'd sworn would happen hadn't. But you'd be wrong.

Showing a lack of curiosity that is decidedly antiscience, true believers dismiss the "pause" as an anomaly or, in a bit of irony lost on them, they simply deny that it happened.

"Depending on which particular set of data you looked at, and how you calculated trends, there was an argument that temperature rises had slowed over a period of about 15 years," the UK *Guardian* said.[25]

Saying that it depends on which set of data you look at and how it's calculated is a fairly qualified statement. It's like saying that a baby is taller than an adult if you look at it from the right perspective. But science isn't supposed to change based on perspective, and reality isn't malleable based on how you calculate it.

Moreover, the BBC reported, "Many researchers had accepted that the rate of global warming had slowed in the first 15 years of this century"; however, they miraculously discovered "that scientists have underestimated ocean temperatures over the past two decades."[26]

So they estimated ocean temperatures, then found a way to estimate them in a way they like better—possibly because it gave them the measurements they preferred?

The BBC article continued:

Researchers from NOAA [National Oceanic and Atmospheric Administration] suggested that the temperatures of the oceans were being consistently underestimated by the main global climate models.

The authors showed that the ocean buoys used to measure sea temperatures tend to report slightly cooler temperatures than the older ship-based systems.

Back in the 1990s, ship measurements made up the vast majority of the data, whereas now the more accurate and consistent buoys account for 85% of measurements.

When the researchers corrected the data to take this "cold bias" into account, they concluded that the oceans had warmed 0.12C per decade since 2000, nearly twice as fast as previous estimates of 0.07 degrees.

As a result, the authors said that the warming experienced in the first 15 years of the 21st Century was "virtually indistinguishable" from the rate of warming between 1950–99.[27]

If true believers ever wonder why people have a hard time believing them, they might want to consider that they "correct" data years after their first prediction, and those "corrections" conveniently negate what was recently accepted as fact.

Again, this is why science is not a show of hands, it's not a majority vote, it's proof.

And notice the line about temperatures "being consistently underestimated by the main global climate models." Thermometers exist, and they're fairly inexpensive. There is no need to estimate anything, nor is there a need to create computer models to calculate temperatures; just read the damn things.

But that's not how science works when the main focus of that science is to advance a political agenda. Rather than discovering or exposing universal truths, scientists now make predictions such as "the chance of 'catastrophic' climate change completely wiping out humanity by 2100 is now 1-in-20."[28]

"We would never get on that plane with a 1-in-20 chance of it coming down but we are willing to send our children and grand-children on that plane," one of the scientists behind the "study" declares.[29] Yet we're supposed to put our liberty on a plane piloted by someone with a track record of flying to the wrong airport, when not smashing it into a mountain?

The doomsday cultists know no bounds when it comes to at-tempting to frighten people into conformity. Take, for example, the concept of mass extinction. This is defined as "the extinction of a large number of species within a relatively short period of geologi-cal time, thought to be due to factors such as a catastrophic global event or widespread environmental change that occurs too rapidly for most species to adapt."[30]

There have been five mass extinctions in Earth's history, the most recent wiping out the dinosaurs. The longer climate change fails to register as a concern for the public, the more desperate the rhetoric of its advocates becomes. They've now embraced the subtle concept of "WE'RE ALL GONNA DIE!!!!" without the caps lock. Okay, they sometimes use the caps lock.

"Climate change will have sent Earth on the way to its sixth mass extinction in less than a lifetime, new research warns," proclaimed the UK *Daily Mail*. "By the year 2100, about 310 gigatons of carbon will have been added to the oceans—a potential 'tipping point' for ecological disaster, according to the study."[31]

But the "study" did not come from a climatologist or even a bi-ologist, it came from a mathematician. And it offered a prediction, not proof. That's what's missing from so much of the "science" worshipped and weaponized by the political Left: proof. And proof is kind of an important part of science, or at least it used to be.

But science isn't about science anymore, at least in the public sector.

Most of the climate change studies are conducted by people at government agencies or funded by them at universities. If they're wrong or later proven wrong or their estimates and computer mod-els don't pan out, as they regularly haven't, there are few to no con-sequences. Professors and government scientists don't get fired for being wrong, for wasting taxpayer money. In the private sector their jobs would be gone, and quite possibly the company, their employer, would go out of business.

But science isn't about science anymore. The "Party of Science" is influencing what science says, no longer the other way around.

Liberals deny basic science every time it butts up against what they want to be true, either ignoring it or changing it to suit their needs.

When Michael Brown was killed by a police officer in Ferguson, Missouri, the media embraced and ran with the idea that this sweet, innocent "teen," as he was repeatedly called in news stories, had been executed—"Hands up, don't shoot" became their mantra.

It was accepted as fact that officer Darren Wilson had murdered Brown in the middle of his peaceful attempt to surrender. The problem was that it was a lie. Though eyewitness testimony differed, the forensic, or scientific, evidence was unequivocal: Brown had attacked Wilson, had tried to grab his gun, and was charging the officer for round two when he was fatally shot.

However, science saying that the story of Brown as a victim wasn't true didn't stop liberals from repeating the lie. As the *Washington Post* put it, "Perhaps the reason for this disinterest in the ballistics report, autopsies and other similar information is that for at least some of Brown's supporters the facts are, apparently, largely irrelevant because Brown is a metaphorical 'symbol' of injustice regardless of what actually happened."[32]

In other words, never let the facts, or the "science," stand in the way of a good narrative. Though the *Post* speculated that maybe the people advancing the lie and those eating it up were too dumb to know any better. "A related reason may be that working through this information is time-consuming—and thus beyond the capacity of many commentators."[33]

The reason why matters significantly less than the fact of the matter, and the fact of the matter is that millions of people still believe Michael Brown was executed by a white police officer who decided he'd just blow away a black guy in the middle of the street for shits and giggles on a sunny afternoon.

Science be damned when there's an agenda to be advanced. That's how the self-proclaimed "Party of Science" works.

Liberals wrap themselves in the name of "science" while denying even the most basic parts of it. After Hurricane Katrina flooded New Orleans, a city on the sea that lies below sea level, existing the way it does only because of dirt mounds and flimsy dykes keeping out the water, we were told that hurricanes were going to be even stronger and more regular occurrences because of science, in this case climate change. When there wasn't another category 3 or above hurricane that hit the United States for twelve years, we heard nothing from the Mr. Wizards because there was nothing they could say that would do anything other than remind people of their false predictions.

When, after that twelve-year gap—the longest in recorded history[34]—Hurricane Harvey hit Texas as a category 4, the *Washington Post* simply declared that our "lucky streak" had come to an end.[35]

Once the "drought" was quenched, an excuse needed to be given. The *Post* offered up, "In 2015, Timothy Hall and Kelly Hereid used a model to estimate that a decade-long U.S. major hurricane landfall drought can be expected roughly every two centuries."[36]

Notice how it says "every two centuries"? There has only been any semblance of reliable weather records kept since about the middle of the nineteenth century, about 150 years. That makes this claim impossible to prove, but, more importantly it is also impossible to disprove. The Party of Science has created a miracle—a "science"-based explanation for why what it had said would happen didn't. When, in 2017, major hurricanes Harvey and Irma hit the United States, they were, predictably, blamed on climate change. The media, naturally, went right along with it all.

The media's favorite celebrity astrophysicist, Neil deGrasse Tyson, declared two hurricanes in one year proof of human-made climate change and said that the United States' citizens' refusal to cede more power and money to the federal government indicates that the change has gotten so bad, the world "might not be able to recover."[37]

If it's already too late, you really have to wonder why anyone would bother to worry about it, right? At a certain point the people who didn't make it into a lifeboat on the *Titanic* accepted their fates, drank some booze, and engaged in polite conversation. But there can be no polite conversation when someone is trying to slice off a huge piece of control of a $21 trillion economy.

After the devastating, but not unprecedented, flooding in Houston, Tyson said, "We don't have a civilization with the capacity to pick up a city and move it inland 20 miles. That's—this is happening faster than our ability to respond. That could have huge economic consequences."[38]

That's an astrophysicist talking about climate in "WE'RE ALL GONNA DIE!" terms and the media soaking it up like gravy with the last biscuit on Thanksgiving.

Dictionary.com defines "astrophysics" as "the branch of astronomy that deals with the physical properties of celestial bodies and with the interaction between matter and radiation in the interior of celestial bodies and in interstellar space." Notice how it has nothing to do with climate. Yet Tyson was on TV as if he had not only created the medium but also pioneered climatology.

Would you let a proctologist remove your brain tumor, or would you prefer a neurosurgeon to do it? They're both doctors. Depending on who you're talking about, it may be appropriate for a proctologist to be involved in brain surgery—some people's heads seem to spend an awful lot of time up there, so it's natural that some people would conflate the two.

Yet the media runs to Tyson or Bill Nye, "The Science Guy," any time there is an issue related to climate or really any area of science.

They go to them because they're good on TV, not because they know anything more than a summary of the latest Associated Press story or whatever they've overheard at cocktail parties.

That, by the way, is the secret to getting on TV—a willingness to do so and being good at it. Knowledge of the subject at hand is a bonus, at best. Ask anyone who knows or has spent time around anyone in the television news business, and you'll learn that Ron Burgundy in the movie *Anchorman* was closer to being fact than anyone currently drawing a check in the industry is willing to admit. (That goes for most guests, too.)

Though climate change has been a favorite issue of the Party of Science for decades, there is a new favorite coming on strong in the stretch, and it's an area that for the entirety of human history was actually "settled science."

Chapter 7

The Party of Science!

If you went back in time ten years and told people that in 2018 there would be a serious discussion about what constitutes gender, people would laugh at you. If you went back thirty years and told people that there were more than fifty genders, they would think you were high. If you went back sixty years, you'd be institutionalized.

But that's where we are in 2018.

Subscribing to the idea of there being only two genders is now a hate crime that will have you chased off any college campus in the country by an angry mob of unwashed progressive activists who spend more time with their drum circle group than studying, especially for biology class.

In 2014, Facebook launched a new feature—the ability to choose among more than two genders—a lot more. The social media site offered up fifty-eight options for people who, after the totality of existence, felt constrained by, and confused over, whether or not they had an "innie" or an "outie."

The choices offered are:[1]

> Agender
> Androgyne
> Androgynous
> Bigender
> Cis

> Cisgender
> Cis Female
> Cis Male
> Cis Man
> Cis Woman

- Cisgender Female
- Cisgender Male
- Cisgender Man
- Cisgender Woman
- Female to Male
- FTM
- Gender Fluid
- Gender Nonconforming
- Gender Questioning
- Gender Variant
- Genderqueer
- Intersex
- Male to Female
- MTF
- Neither
- Neutrois
- Non-binary
- Other
- Pangender
- Trans
- Trans*
- Trans Female
- Trans* Female
- Trans Male
- Trans* Male
- Trans Man
- Trans* Man
- Trans Person
- Trans* Person
- Trans Woman
- Trans* Woman
- Transfeminine
- Transgender
- Transgender Female
- Transgender Male
- Transgender Man
- Transgender Person
- Transgender Woman
- Transmasculine
- Transsexual
- Transsexual Female
- Transsexual Male
- Transsexual Man
- Transsexual Person
- Transsexual Woman
- Two-Spirit

To say this is insanity would be unfair to the man downtown arguing with a lamppost, but it sure ain't normal.

Fear not, Americans, in the never-ending liberal game of "make shit up as we go along," the fifty-eight gender choices Facebook offered you are nothing compared to the seventy-one options offered in the United Kingdom.[2]

So what did Americans miss out on? Options such as "asexual," "T*man," "T*woman," "two* person," "hermaphrodite," "polygender," and—for some weird reason—"man" and "woman."

So what do these terms mean? Aside from the fact that people who spend more than a nanosecond trying to figure out which one applies to them had better have really good insurance that covers therapy, they mean pretty much just a few things.

First, male and female are obvious because, well, you're a normal human being who grew up recognizing basic biology and understands the definition of gender. Why the United Kingdom felt the need to add "man" and "woman" is just an indication that everyone has decided to make everything difficult and stupid.

But what about the others?

Most of them are simply variations of one another. "Trans man," "trans* man," and "transgender man" simply denote how annoyingly demanding and insistent the person using them is. If someone wants to be called this or that online, fine. But this isn't about that person; it's about telling the rest of us what to do. It gives the person using a term an easy, regular opportunity to be offended when the rest of us have no idea what the hell he or she is talking about.

As for what "cis" as a prefix means, think "normal biology," since "cis female" means that the person not only identifies as a woman, she was born as a woman and is attracted to men. Why is there a need for the prefix "cis"? Because liberals who conform to millennia of human gender norms felt left out of the victimhood game, and liberals love labels.

"Pangender" is not someone who identifies as a panda (at least not yet), though it can't be long until there are gender options for those. It is "noting or relating to a person whose gender identity is not limited to one gender and who may feel like a member of all genders at the same time."[3] Think of it as multiple personality disorder for your crotch.

"Gender nonconforming" is "a state in which a person has physical and behavioral characteristics that do not correspond to those typically associated with the person's sex."[4] So really, as you can see, it means whatever the person wants it to mean at any given moment, which means it means nothing at all beyond an excuse to be offended.

To really dig into the narcissism and attention seeking of the victim culture, you need look no further than "nonbinary." Non-binary "is an umbrella term to describe any gender identity that does not fit into the gender binary of male and female. Nonbinary-gender (also sometimes referred to as genderqueer) people may, for example, identify as having no gender, fall on a gender spectrum somewhere between male and female, or identify as totally outside binary gender identities."[5] In other words: they are insane attention seekers.

But the question must be asked: Who is more insane, people with a distorted view of reality or people who distort their view of reality to conform with the distorted views of others?

When 1976 Olympic decathlon gold medalist Bruce Jenner declared himself to be a woman, it was as if a light switch had been flipped on in the liberal media. Jenner went from being a celebrity or an athlete to being a cause; all references were to Caitlyn Jenner, and anchors and news stories immediately used the pronouns "she" and "her" without missing a beat. That's weird.

Most people don't really care what name people want to call themselves; they're too busy with their own lives to worry about what some pampered bit player on a trashy reality show wants to be called or how he or she wants to live. But to pretend it wasn't weird is, well, weird.

Another weird thing was how the arrival of Caitlyn tossed Bruce down the memory hole. People who woke up the day after Jenner declared himself to be a woman found a world that bordered on pretending that the previous decades of Jenner's public life, and to some degree Bruce himself, had never existed.

Even technology was in on the fix. Siri, the iPhone's personal assistant, wiped Bruce from the history books. Users who asked for information on Bruce Jenner were met with a reply about Caitlyn Jenner.[6] When you ask Siri, "Who is Kylie Jenner's father?" Siri responds, "Caitlyn Jenner is Kylie Jenner's father."

Again, you shouldn't really care how some rich guy lives his life, but once Bruce came out as Caitlyn, you weren't allowed not to care.

Within months of the announcement of Caitlyn's existence,

ESPN gave Jenner its Arthur Ashe Courage Award. It's a sports award for courageous work that "transcends sports." But Jenner hadn't been involved in sports since before ESPN was founded in 1979.

To baby boomers he was the guy on the Wheaties box, but to the successive generations—generation X and millennials—Jenner was the guy with bad acting credits such as *CHiPs* and *The Love Boat* or the awkward, tall butt of jokes in the background of *Keeping Up with the Kardashians*. That he had ever been an athlete was a long-forgotten and unimportant piece of trivia. It'd be a safe bet that more people alive today know Jenner for killing a driver in a 2015 car accident and getting away with it than for being a gold medalist.[7]

Still, there he was onstage at the ESPY Awards being showered with praise for changing his name and tucking his "junk." And good for him, if that's how he wants to live, but did we really have to celebrate it?

But celebrate it they sure did. The lede in the *Washington Post* story about the few people uncomfortable with awarding Jenner something previously so prestigious read:

> *Radiant in a white dress at the ESPY Awards on Wednesday, Caitlyn Jenner seemed a woman on top of the world. She was receiving the Arthur Ashe Award for Courage—one of the most prestigious awards in sports—not just for her athletic achievements, but for her very public struggle to come out as transgender.*[8]

Again, may Jenner find happiness, but you shouldn't need to wear hip boots while reading a newspaper.

Jenner may be the highest-profile person to come out as transgender but was hardly the last. But hey, it's better to be a former Olympian than a traitor, right? Sort of. Because under the new rules of gender fluidity, even being a traitor to the country can be granted immunity from consequences under the new "tuck rule."

Bradley Manning pled guilty to ten charges and was found guilty of seventeen more related to espionage. For his treachery, he faced up to 136 years in prison.[9] He was ultimately sentenced to thirty-five years, so he got off lightly.

Then he became a "she," and she became a hero to liberals. (For the purposes of this book, Bradley Manning's gender identity will be shown as much respect as he showed the nation's secrets with which he was entrusted and will be referred to as "he.")

Bradley's lawyers even claimed that his "gender identity" issues had contributed to his treason. "During the trial, Manning's gender identity and sexual orientation were mentioned several times, and the defense team suggested that struggles with those issues were part of Manning's decision to leak the classified information," the *Washington Post* reported.[10]

The media conveniently forgot that Bradley had committed treason in an attempt to become a self-professed whistle-blower, but had never known of any real crimes to blow the whistle on. Coming out as trans made them ignore the fact that he had committed treason at all.

"Chadley" became a hero of the Left, honored at gay pride rallies across the country. San Francisco, ground zero of liberal activism, originally extended, then rescinded the title of "honorary grand marshal" of its pride parade in 2013, just after his conviction.[11] But it's telling that its instinct was to honor a traitor simply because he said he was a woman.

> SF Pride board president Lisa Williams said in a statement that an employee of the organization had prematurely notified imprisoned intelligence specialist Manning this week that he had been selected for the distinction, which recognizes about a dozen celebrities, politicians and community organizations each year for their contributions to the gay, lesbian, bisexual and transgender communities.

"That was an error, and that person has been disciplined. He does not now, nor did he at that time, speak for SF Pride," Williams said. A committee of former San Francisco Pride grand marshals did select the 25-year-old Manning, who is openly gay, for the honor, but the Pride board decided his nomination would be a mistake, Williams said.[12]

The idea that a traitor should not be honored simply because he happens to be gay lasted exactly one year.

The 2014 gay pride parade in San Francisco not only named Manning an honorary grand marshal but its organizers apologized for rescinding the offer the previous year. "I want to publicly apologize to Chelsea Manning and her supporters on behalf of SF Pride, and we look forward to a proper honor this year," the new SF Pride board president, Gary Virginia, said.[13]

The Advocate said that "Manning's role is controversial because while some consider Manning a whistleblower, others see her only as a convicted criminal."[14]

No, he's a traitor who just happens to be gay. A traitor who also used his being gay as an excuse for his treason, by the way. But that reality is easy for some on the Left to ignore when politics is in play.

The mainstream media now bend over backward to be as politically correct as possible about trans people, which seems to include pretending they did not exist before changing names and identities. Imagine how weird it would be if you came out as gay and expected everyone to pretend that your life before that didn't exist.

But the real scandal is not the fact that the liberal media are doing what they always do. There may well be some things about gender that are cultural, but some things, decidedly, are not, such as where babies come from.

CNN, for example, ran a story with the headline "Transgender Man Gives Birth to a Boy."

Here's a refresher for anyone who hasn't been in a biology class for a while: men cannot give birth; men don't have the equipment to carry a child, and the birth would be essentially like driving a semitruck through a garden hose. It wouldn't be pretty.

But believing that a man is what a man has always been is not allowed anymore. The science is denied, if you will.

The mother, or father, or whatever, named Trystan Reese, had been taking testosterone to lower his/her/their (who the hell knows?) voice, grow facial hair, and so on, but had stopped for the pregnancy. CNN reported that Trystan "was assigned the female gender at birth."[15]

The science of misgendering is far from "settled." A family in Arizona says they were all "assigned" the wrong gender at birth. "Daniel Harrott, 41, the biological parent of two trans children, was assigned female gender at birth and is a transgender man. His son and daughter also say they were assigned the wrong gender at birth, and he has met a transgender woman, Shirley Austin, 62, who was assigned male gender at birth. Harrott and Austin are now engaged. 'The whole family is in transition,'" according to Austin.[16] The children are ages eleven and thirteen.

That's one hell of a coincidence, don't you think? That they'd all find one another and realize their misgendering only after Austin entered their lives?

These stories may be lots of things, but they're not science. If anything, they are denying science. And being accused of "denying science" is the new leftist heresy.

The story of Patrick Mitchell is one such heresy, though his age, fourteen, largely insulated him from the label of heretic himself. At twelve, Mitchell decided he was a she and was promptly diagnosed with gender dysphoria, the idea that a person was born the wrong gender. He started to take hormones so he could "transition." But when he turned fourteen years old, a strange thing happened: he realized he had been wrong.

"You have an image of what being a boy and being a girl is like, but when you actually experience it, it's very different," he said.[17]

Putting aside the obvious child abuse of allowing a twelve-year-old to make not only life-changing but body-altering decisions, how could the mental health profession get it so wrong? It turns out that it's not all that uncommon, though there is enormous pressure to keep that fact secret.

In December 2017, the Canadian Broadcasting Corporation canceled plans to air a documentary produced by the British Broadcasting Corporation called "Transgender Kids: Who Knows Best?" It was about parents of children who are said to show signs of gender dysphoria. But that wasn't the problem; the show was canceled because it contained interviews with experts who questioned the wisdom of allowing children to make incredibly complex decisions before they enter puberty.

The *Canadian National Post* reported:

> First broadcast in the U.K. in January, much of the film focuses on parents deciding whether to pursue a "gender affirmative" approach in which they fully support their child's wish to change gender identities.
>
> "Increasingly, parents are encouraged to adopt a 'gender affirmative' approach . . . but is this approach right?" reads an official synopsis.
>
> Even before the documentary had aired, a Change.org petition signed by 11,000 people warned that it "could spark a trail of prejudice; belittling transgender children, leading to them not being socially accepted by society."[8]

So the complaints rolled in before anyone in Canada had seen the documentary, most of which had actually been filmed in Canada.

The reaction in the United Kingdom, where the film was actually shown, was just as unhinged as the pre-action by activists in Canada:

> After the broadcast, the British charity "U.K. Trans Info" called the documentary "violent and one-sided." The chairperson of the U.K. group Coventry Pride said in a post it was "vile venom" that was "biased towards the denial of trans+ children."

The broadcast even prompted a swath of British medical agencies, including the British Psychological Society and the Royal College of General Practitioners, to draft a statement denouncing clinical efforts "to suppress an individual's expression of sexual orientation or gender identity."[9]

The reaction to the existence of a documentary containing views that stray from the liberal orthodoxy was the same an ocean apart: it was condemned with equal passion by those who'd seen it and those who hadn't. That's not a coincidence, and it sure isn't science.

Putting aside the brain, once someone "transitions," he or she takes his or her body along. This presents a whole new series of issues.

Biologically, and this is hardly breaking news, men and women are physically different. Men are, on average, stronger than women and have greater muscle mass and bone density. Though there are some women who are physically stronger than some men—who doesn't believe that Hillary could kick the crap out of Bill if he were outed with another intern?—it's not a fluke that every world record for weight lifting by a man is significantly higher than the corresponding world record for a woman.

It's not just strength, it's speed, too. Usain Bolt is the current world record holder for the 100-meter dash, completing the run in just 9.58 seconds. The women's world record is held by the American Florence Griffith Joyner at almost a second slower, 10.49 seconds. Flo-Jo's record would easily crush the speed of 99.9 percent of the world's population, and not just because there are more people better qualified to be competitive eaters than competitive runners. But she would be an afterthought if she ran in the men's race in the Olympics, as her women's world record would have been a distant last-place finish in the men's finals at the 2016 Olympics in Rio de Janeiro. The last-place finisher in the 100-meter finals posted a time of 10:06 seconds.[20]

That more women than men have long hair is a cultural construction. That the fastest, strongest men are faster and stronger than women is an unavoidable biological fact. Now, as liberals move to blur the lines between genders even further, men who identify as women are entering the women's sports arena—and many, though not all, are, predictably, dominating.

Fallon Fox was born a man. At the age of thirty-one, Fox had gender reassignment surgery to live as a woman. Then Fox began a career as a mixed martial arts fighter against other women.

In one fight, Fox gave her opponent, Tamikka Brents, a concussion and fractured her orbital socket, which required seven staples in her head to repair. Of the beating, Brents said, "I've fought a lot of women and have never felt the strength that I felt in a fight as I did that night. I can't answer whether it's because she was born a man or not because I'm not a doctor. I can only say, I've never felt so overpowered ever in my life and I am an abnormally strong female in my own right."[21]

Was Fallon's having been born a man the deciding factor in the fight? There is no way of knowing. It's worth noting that Fallon did lose a professional fight, just one, to a biological woman and retired with a record of five wins and one loss.

The story of Mack Beggs is very similar while being almost the opposite. Mack was born a girl and was transitioning to be a boy while in high school. As a junior in high school, Beggs was a wrestler who wanted to compete against the boys. But Texas law required high school wrestlers to compete against people of their biological gender at birth, so Mack had to wrestle other girls. But there was an issue: Beggs was taking testosterone to aid with the gender transition. Testosterone is considered a performance-enhancing drug[22] in sports, but it was ruled "well below the allowed level" by the board that governs high school sports in Texas.[23]

Beggs won the girl's state championship for the 110-pound division with a perfect record of fifty-seven wins and zero losses.[24] Whether or not those wins and the championship were tainted by the use of testosterone is a matter for debate, but it can't simply be dismissed out of hand because of the genitalia in Mack's wresting singlet. If an athlete born male were caught taking testosterone, he would be disqualified.

These are but two examples, a sneak peek of what's to come if people are allowed to pick which gender they compete under. Imagine an aging NBA star with no prospects for another season signing on with a WNBA team or Tiger Woods joining the LPGA and dominating simply because he made a declaration that he now identifies as a woman. It seems absurd, but further down the yellow brick road of gender fluidity lies an Emerald City of second careers for aging athletes and overwhelming social pressure to not say anything about it or risk being ostracized from polite liberal society.

If you don't believe it, try telling people that "trans" itself is a useless social construct. Or try asking out loud what scientific proof we have that transgender people are biologically different, rather than suffering from a mental illness. Be ready to duck.

Normally you could just ignore this sort of insanity—some kid named Wilbur wants to be known as "Lazer-Lightning," and you could just laugh at him and call him Wilbur. But there is a push to punish, even criminalize, using the wrong pronoun for people if they declare themselves to be transgender.

The wrong pronoun, by the way, means that if you call a woman who identifies as a man "her" or "she," that's a problem. Even if she was a woman yesterday. Also, if someone decides they don't like the available "gender-specific" pronouns, they can choose a made-up one, such as "xe" or "zie," or even "ham sandwich," and you have to use it once you're told that that's what the person wants to be called when not called by their name.

In New York City:

Employers and landlords who intentionally and consistently ignore using pronouns such as "ze/hir" to refer to transgender workers *and tenants who request them—may be subject to fines as high as $250,000.*

The Commission on Human Rights' legal guidelines mandate that anyone providing jobs or housing must use individuals' preferred gender pronouns.[25]

The effort hasn't succeeded—yet—but liberals don't stop just because an effort fails. The takeover of the nation's health care system through Obamacare was the culmination of a sixty-year effort.

This concept of punishing "wrong pronoun use" has found a home in California on a small scale. Nursing home employees and people working in long-term care facilities, thanks to a law signed into being by Governor Jerry Brown, now face a $1,000 fine and up to a year in prison if they continue to use a pronoun to refer to a patient that is not the pronoun that person prefers.[26]

The state senator who authored the LGBT Senior Bill of Rights, Scott Wiener, said, "Everyone is entitled to their religious view. But when you enter the public space, when you are running an institution, you are in a workplace, you are in a civil setting, and you have to follow the law."[27] Individual liberty and the First Amendment, it seems, extend only to your front door, as does everything you've learned about biology.

The insanity of this denial of science has not been without mockery. Grant Strobl, a student at the University of Michigan, used the opportunity afforded all students by the school to "choose" the pronoun by which they want (demand) faculty and the school to address them. Since the possibilities were literally endless, Strobl chose "His Majesty" as a way to protest.[28] This meant that all of his teachers, when not calling him Grant, had to address him as "His Majesty," as did all official letters from the school.

Fun, yes, but that it has come to this is insane.

When it comes to climate change, liberals demand absolute acceptance of the idea that human beings are causing it, in spite of history and facts, and demand complete compliance with their will about it. They call people who question the science behind future computer projections of what could happen with the climate "deniers," equating them not so subtly with lunatics who deny that the Holocaust happened. When it comes to biology, it is a completely different story.

To the Left, gender is fluid and open to interpretation, a social construct. People are free to live their lives any way they choose and dress and act anyway they want. People also used to be left alone to not care if someone else decided to do things that are, by the strict definition of the word, abnormal. Not anymore.

Now you've got Yale University eliminating the terms "freshman" and "upperclassman" because they include the word "man," and you wouldn't want to offend anyone who identifies as "transfeminine" or "neither."[29] You will be hammered publicly for using the wrong pronoun based on a whim and could eventually face government-enforced penalties for offending someone by applying the concept of gender that has been with us since Adam first hit on Eve.

The Party of Science should have an asterisk right after its name to denote that the self-imposed label applies only to science that supports its ideology and that it reserves the right to reject any other science, even in that field, that it doesn't like the conclusions of. It also reserves the right to deny this privilege to anyone else at any given time on any issue.

This won't fit on a business card, but at least it'd be accurate.

When all is said and done, if someone decides he can fly simply because he wants it to be so, you should still try to talk him out of jumping off the roof. Or maybe you should still try to talk xie out of it. Whatever.

Chapter 8

Survey Says

Remember the old saying "Figures don't lie, but liars figure"? That may be true in business, but when it comes to polling, figures can lie like Bill Clinton caught with his pants around his ankles in the intern housing.

Progressives love journalists and pundits who know the science of polling inside and out; it helps them explain away the unpopularity of Democrats and their ideas when needed.

You can see this well in polling about gun rights.

Few areas arouse liberal ire like the Second Amendment. They routinely wrap themselves in the First Amendment while wiping themselves with the Second. This can happen when you set a different unit of measure for the things you like as opposed to those you don't. If one participant in a race gets to define what constitutes the "best" at something, for example, he or she can ensure that he or she is always the best.

The "right to keep and bear arms," liberals contend, applies only to members of a "well regulated militia," because the Second Amendment reads, "A well regulated Militia, being necessary to the security of a free State, the right of the people to keep and bear Arms, shall not be infringed." But the end of this simple sentence does not say "the right of members of that well regulated militia to keep and bear arms," it says "the people."

English comprehension aside, liberals try another tactic: the conservative idea of originalism.

The idea of originalism is that the Constitution means what it says and says what it means; judges and politicians shouldn't read into it concepts that aren't there. The Founding Fathers were very specific about what powers the federal government was granted by the document, and everything outside those enumerated powers is reserved for the states and the people—à la the Ninth and Tenth Amendments.

Liberals hate this idea because it prevents the government from metastasizing into whatever whimsical areas they'd like to put it in. They prefer a government they can smear into any nook and cranny of life, like smooth jelly on an English muffin.

But on guns, they have an attempted "come to Jesus" moment and try a bastardized version of originalism—and fail miserably.

Their argument goes, "The Second Amendment was written at a time when there were only single-shot muskets; therefore it only applies to single-shot muskets. After all, the Founding Fathers could never have imagined the guns we have now."

This argument fails on a couple of levels. First, even though the guns in 1787 were single-shot muskets, you still didn't want to have one pointed at you. A gun is a gun, and not having one while facing off against someone who does is not something most people would enjoy. Taking a few seconds to reload does give the target some opportunities, but the advantage is still with the holder of the gun.

Second, and much more damaging to the liberal cause, is that if you were to apply this logic to the First Amendment, or at least to the part of the First Amendment liberals care about (they're not superkeen on the freedom of religion part), free speech and freedom of the press would not apply to the Internet, television, radio, and so on. A gun that can fire multiple rounds before needing to be reloaded is certainly more imaginable than the ability to communicate instantly with millions of people across the country and around the world.

Putting that aside, when it comes to issues such as gun rights, liberal journalists use their ability to defy the imaginations of the Founding Fathers to spread every bit of polling favorable to their side. "Support for Stricter Gun Laws Hits All-Time High in Poll," screamed a headline from The Hill.[1]

"Sixty percent of respondents in the poll said they support tightening gun laws, while 36 percent said they are opposed to doing so. The support for stricter gun control tops the previous high of 54 percent in a June Quinnipiac poll," declared the story, as if enumerated rights were subject to the whims of a statistical sampling of people weighted by the pollster to fit the perceived ideological makeup of the country.[2]

Of course, that poll was taken days after the horrific mass shooting in Las Vegas that killed 58 people and injured more than 500, so you could expect some bump in numbers. And that's a little secret of polls that the liberals don't bother to mention: they are snapshots in time, a very narrow slice of information about the exact second the person is contacted. They aren't reflective of deeply held beliefs. They're tugs on emotions that fade or revert to historical places after the emotions calm and logic returns.

Ever notice that you don't hear much about Americans' feelings about guns when there isn't some horrific event involving a gun just preceding it? The killing fields of Chicago and Baltimore are veritable legal gun-free zones, where owning and/or carrying a pistol legally is nearly impossible. Murders there rarely warrant a mention in the news because they destroy the narrative that legally purchased and owned firearms are a scourge of society.

When the *Wall Street Journal* and NBC News conducted a poll in September 2017, they found that among the top issues of concern to the American people were the usual suspects—jobs, the economy, war—but right behind them was gun rights. Not gun control, gun rights. The American people, if not the media, take their rights seriously.

NBC News, which paid half the cost of the poll, didn't report on that bit of data in its broadcasts; it was as though it didn't exist.[3]

It didn't exist, or at least didn't need to be reported to their television audience, because it didn't fit the media's narrative that the

American people dislike the Second Amendment and want gun control.

Memory-holing inconvenient information is nothing new for the media, particularly NBC News. When President Obama's popularity waned significantly, another NBC News, *Wall Street Journal* poll found his approval rating at only 40 percent with 56 percent disapproving. *NBC Nightly News* didn't mention the poll at all, as though it didn't exist.[4]

NBC's *Today Show* did mention the poll the company had paid handsomely for, it even had NBC News' "political director," Chuck Todd, on the show to announce the poll's finding. Todd stressed people's disapproval of "Washington" four times in the short segment but never how unpopular the president himself was.[5] Or, more accurately, how unpopular he was outside newsrooms.

Liberals have a habit of citing numbers that are, ultimately, meaningless. But they weaponize those numbers.

———————

Not citing Barack Obama's unpopularity in the middle of 2014 would not have mattered one way or another to him, as he was never going to face the voters again. But the 2014 midterms were just around the corner, and 2016 was lurking in the distance; a Democratic president being unpopular could harm Democratic candidates by reminding people that they are of the same party. Magically, the president being unpopular became Washington, DC, being unpopular. Congress was, after all, controlled by Republicans.

It's subtle, it's stupid, but it happens. No wall is built with a single brick, and no narrative is built with a single story; they build on one another to reinforce the whole.

It may, however, work for attitudes over the long haul— Republicans do have a steep hill to climb in the perception war courtesy of the media's constant reinforcement and the insistence that every Republican answer for any Republican.

When Congressman Todd Akin was running for the Senate in

Missouri in 2012, he made the incredibly ignorant comment that a woman's body has a natural way to prevent pregnancy if she's the victim of "legitimate rape."[6] It exposed Akin as a moron but somehow tainted every Republican running for any office in 2012.

It helped for the media and the Democratic narrative that Republicans were waging some kind of "war on women," the idea being that the GOP, should it obtain control of government, was on the cusp of repressing women by denying them abortions, equal pay, and the right to wear shoes and leave the kitchen while not ovulating. On its face it's absurd, but that was the tactic chosen by the Left and it became a drum it would beat for the entire 2012 election cycle.

Putting aside the fact that, say, making abortion illegal would require a constitutional amendment since the Supreme Court discovered a nearly unfettered right to it in 1973, the prospect of turning the country into *A Handmaid's Tale* seems less likely than finding a Kennedy who honors his marriage vows. Yet that is what was pitched in campaign tone and rhetoric from then to today, to one degree or another.

Mitt Romney, the Republican presidential nominee in 2012, could not have been a more upstanding human being, yet even he had to answer for the comment by Akin, a man he'd likely never met. "As I said yesterday, Todd Akin's comments were offensive and wrong and he should very seriously consider what course would be in the best interest of our country. Today, his fellow Missourians urged him to step aside, and I think he should accept their counsel and exit the Senate race," Romney unambiguously said.[7]

Notice the "As I said yesterday" part? He'd been asked, and he had unambiguously answered already, but he was asked again and would be asked again about something he had had zero to do with and zero influence over. A presidential candidate cannot "fire" a candidate for any other office.

Yet a week later, the media was still tying Romney to Akin because, well, liberals had decided that Republicans hate women.

"Why Akin Hurts Romney" was the headline in Politico in a piece "reporting" this:

> It's bad enough for Republicans that Akin has put the Missouri Senate seat at risk. And threatened the Republican campaign to win a Senate majority. And introduced a highly divisive social issue into the GOP campaign. And shifted the debate away from jobs and the economy, where President Barack Obama is vulnerable. And highlighted the inconvenient fact that the Republican platform calls for a total ban on abortions with no exception for rape. And opened up a split in the party between mainstream conservatives and the religious right.
>
> Akin is also making Romney look weak and ineffectual. If Romney doesn't have clout with members of his own party, voters may ask, how can he be an effective president?[8]

Not only was this one guy who'd said something stupid responsible for what he had said, the candidate at the top of the ticket, and every single one on down the ballot, was also somehow responsible for what that one guy had said, and if they couldn't get him to resign, voters would see it as weakness, according to the website.

Realistically, voters would not associate one guy running for office in one state with the person running for president, but the media made damn sure they did.

All Republicans are routinely held to account for the things other Republicans have said; Democrats often aren't asked about the things they themselves say.

In 2012, when Vice President Joe Biden made a clearly race-baiting comment about Romney and his policies, the media largely balked. They reported it, but in the context of Republican outrage, not outrage in general at the comment as was the case with Akin.

Campaigning before a predominantly black audience in Virginia, the vice president told the crowd that Romney's policies regarding the financial sector of the economy would "put y'all back in chains." Clearly a reference to slavery, unless the banking industry has a secret market set up that has escaped regulatory oversight for centuries.

Some considered it a gaffe and dismissed it as "Joe being Joe." The man had, after all, plagiarized a biographical speech about himself in 1988 and had developed quite a reputation for verbal diarrhea over his long career, so MENSA wasn't exactly beating a path to his door. But Biden knew exactly what he was doing, and so did the complicit media that covered him.

Race-baiting has a long tradition in the Democratic Party, starting with slavery, segregation, Jim Crow, and the progressive movement's embrace of Planned Parenthood and the grotesque idea of eugenics; that they'd still embrace that tactic, though in a different form, is no surprise.

The *New York Times* "covered" the Biden comments with the headline "Biden Warns Romney. Policies Would Put Crowd 'Back in Chains.'"[9]

In its story, the *Times* acknowledged that Biden had "created a stir" with his comments by angering Republicans, while Akin's comments had been unabashedly denounced as asinine for their content.

"President Obama and his surrogates have been campaigning heavily in Virginia, and the campaign's strategy relies in part on energizing the black vote to take the traditionally Republican state, which moved to the Democratic column in the 2008 presidential election," the *Times* reported. The paper continued, "Mr. Biden said his remarks had merely alluded to a term used previously by Republicans, including Mr. Romney's running mate, Representative Paul D. Ryan. In his response to Mr. Obama's State of the Union address in 2011, Mr. Ryan said, 'We believe a renewed commitment to limited government will unshackle our economy and create millions of new jobs and opportunities for all people, of every background, to succeed and prosper.'"[10]

But Ryan used the word "unshackle," not "unchain," which makes Biden's defense suspect at best. Akin apologized for his remarks, but that changed nothing in the tone of the press coverage of his race through election day. Biden's comments were forgotten. One was running for the Senate, the other to be reelected to the second highest office in the land.

There were no "Why Biden Hurts Obama" pieces written, no calls for an apology, as had been the case for Akin. Just headlines such as "Biden Warns Romney Policies Would Put Crowd 'Back in Chains.'"

Instead of calls for resignation, the headlines were couched in terms of "Republicans criticize," as if it were not something truly to be offended by, just partisan squabbling. Politico's headline was "GOP Slams Biden 'Chains' Remark."[11] The Huffington Post went with "Joe Biden 'Chains' Remark Seized Upon by Mitt Romney's Campaign."[12]

When the shoe was on the other foot, and that foot was in a Republican's mouth, the headlines told a different tale. For Akin, the *Times* headline screamed, "Senate Candidate Provokes Ire with 'Legitimate Rape' Comment."[13] For Richard Mourdock, the 2012 Republican candidate for Senate in Indiana, who made his own ill-conceived comments on rape, the headline of the *Times* was "Indiana Senate Candidate Draws Fire for Rape Comments."[14]

When a Republican is involved, the criticism is universal; when a Democrat is, the criticism is partisan.

All the comments were deserving of criticism, yet the way the criticism was framed was different. In the case of the Mourdock story, the only "critic" who offered "fire" for his comments happened to be the chairwoman of the Democratic Party, Congresswoman Debbie Wasserman Schultz. No other person was quoted in the piece on the candidate's comments, yet somehow that constituted "draws fire."[15]

When the media have the power to decide what constitutes a scandal or how that scandal is framed, they can have immeasurable influence over the outcome. That power, while real, is not absolute. No matter how hard it tried, the entire liberal establishment—from the political world to Hollywood to the media—could not get Hillary Clinton elected president.

In a classic case of spiking the football on the five-yard line, every major media organization that made election predictions before the 2016 election had Clinton winning in a walk.

The day of the election, the *New York Times* declared, "Hillary Clinton has an 85% chance to win."[16] The Huffington Post was slightly more optimistic, putting Hillary's chances of victory at 98 percent, with Donald Trump having only a 1.7 percent shot at the White House.[17] The remaining .3 percent must've been reserved for an asteroid destroying the planet.

Liberals loved the vaunted FiveThirtyEight blog, which had become famous for accurately predicting races in the past, until it gave Clinton only a 71.4 percent shot at victory.[18] Any gambler would happily embrace any game anywhere in the world with those odds, but Nate Silver saw himself attacked for his math from every corner of the liberal pollosphere. Forget the fact that the polling said Trump had a reasonable path to victory; it *felt* as though Hillary had a 98 percent chance of winning.

Those were the bibles of the Left, with predictions reported widely in the media throughout the race.

MSNBC's Lawrence O'Donnell did a segment on his show on November 4, four days before the election, with a Princeton professor named Sam Wang declaring Hillary to have a "99.5% chance" of victory the following Tuesday.[19]

That was it; game over, according to experts who'd "done the math." Months (years, really) of hard work polishing the turd that is candidate Hillary Clinton was about to pay off.

But when experts and journalists had nothing left to do but wait for the champagne to chill, the voters finally had their say and a million prewritten "The glass ceiling has been shattered!" celebratory pieces had to be scrapped for their worst nightmare—Freddy Krueger, the man who haunts their dreams, had won: Donald J. Trump was president-elect of the United States.

Newsweek even had to recall 125,000 copies of a special commemorative edition of its magazine celebrating "Madam President" and her victory, which had already shipped because the number crunchers were so certain of victory.[20]

That's what making a religion out of your math calculations gets you.

On election day, the *New York Times* compiled the predictions of nine organizations that analyze voter and polling data and published them. Every one of them had Clinton winning easily. Moreover, there was unanimity on Hillary winning the three states that ultimately cost her the election—Michigan, Pennsylvania, and Wisconsin; most had predicted a landslide in her favor.[21]

In their humiliating electoral postmortem, the Huffington Post's senior polling editor, Natalie Jackson (the boss of the department that had made the 98 percent prediction), admitted that she had "put too much trust in polls."[22]

Confessing that she had "assumed [the polls] would be right," Jackson continued, "In retrospect, it's easy to second-guess that assumption. There's more error in polls than most people realize."[23]

Knowing not only that polls can be wrong but can be so wrong, yet so obviously certain, that every prognosticator in the business would bet the farm of their reputation on them, why on God's green Earth would anyone attempt to govern by them?

On the issue of guns and the Second Amendment, as stated earlier, liberals cite any and every poll that can be even vaguely interpreted as supporting more gun control. But even they admit that polling data are flawed, perhaps hopelessly so. On issues involving emotion, such as the Second Amendment after a tragedy, the swing can be even greater.

The Founding Fathers set up the federal government to resist hasty actions based on emotion. They wanted a federal government to do very little. They'd just fought a war to rid themselves of an all-powerful government; the last thing they wanted to replace it with was one of their own. They hadn't rebelled against the location of their oppressor, they had rebelled against the very concept of one.

The entire Constitution was conceived under the notion that individuals are born with "certain unalienable rights," not that rights were granted by an external entity, a government. Any "right" granted by government can be rescinded by government.

That's why the amendments in the Bill of Rights are written as they are. "Congress shall make no law," the First Amendment reads, "respecting an establishment of religion, or prohibiting the free exercise thereof; or abridging the freedom of speech, or of the press; or the right of the people peaceably to assemble, and to petition the Government for a redress of grievances."

What it doesn't say is "Since the freedoms of religion, of speech, the press, to assemble and petition government are important, the people, hereby, have the rights to them." No, it says, "Congress shall make no law" infringing on those rights the people were born with.

Same idea with the Second Amendment, which ends with "the right of the people to keep and bear arms shall not be infringed." That "shall not be infringed" part is key. The Constitution wasn't granting anything; it was stating that the federal government could not go after that with which people were born.

The Third Amendment is out of date, unless there's a current scourge of soldiers moving into homes of Americans that isn't being reported.

The Fourth Amendment reads, "The right of the people to be secure in their persons, houses, papers, and effects, against unreasonable searches and seizures, shall not be violated, and no Warrants shall issue, but upon probable cause, supported by Oath or affirmation, and particularly describing the place to be searched, and the persons or things to be seized." Again, ensuring government not violate rights people have from birth.

Every amendment in the Bill of Rights is written the same

way—to prevent the government from growing and infringing on the rights of individuals; nowhere in the entire Constitution does it grant rights.

That being said, the idea of putting rights up to a popularity contest with the public or the majority of 535 elected members of Congress and one president is the antithesis of the concept on which this country was founded.

But even if you've bought into the concept that rights can be subjected to mob rule and shifting whims, to base your argument on polling popularity in the wake of tragedy is folly. But, as President Barack Obama's first chief of staff, now Chicago mayor Rahm Emanuel said, "You never let a serious crisis go to waste." He clarified, "What I mean by that [is] it's an opportunity to do things you think you could not do before."[24]

There is no static appetite for gun control or limitations on any rights when there isn't a "good crisis" to precipitate it. When "opportunity" knocks, liberals are ready to exploit it. In the wake of the Las Vegas shooting, liberals were calling for gun control before there was an accurate body count, so excited at the prospect of advancing their agenda were they. In fact, no matter the circumstance, every mass shooting has been met with cries for new laws. The cries are made without regard to how the current laws were not followed or were irrelevant.

California Democratic senator Dianne Feinstein admitted that nothing the government could've done would have made a difference in the Vegas shooting. The *Washington Post* reported, "Asked by CBS's 'Face the Nation' host John Dickerson whether any law could have stopped him, Feinstein said, 'No. He passed background checks registering for handguns and other weapons on multiple occasions.'"[25]

Admitting that did not, however, stop Feinstein and her fellow Democrats in the Senate from introducing an "assault weapons ban" bill the next month.[26] A good "crisis" had presented itself, polling data had swung in their favor, so . . .

The truth is that liberals call for such measures because it's a

Tuesday, they call for them because there is a stiff breeze, they wake up from a dream and call for them.

The political Left believes, or would at least like the American people to believe, that rights emanate from government, not birth (or, God forbid, God). That's why there have been prominent liberals who have declared that "health care is a right"[27] or that college "is a right."[28] Those things are goods and services, commodities to be purchased, not rights.

But the ideas of "free" health care and "free" college poll well because the question is usually framed like "Would you support the idea of health care being free?" Who wouldn't? It's never asked, "Would you be willing to have your taxes and your wait times to see your doctor increased, along with having your out-of-pocket costs and premiums skyrocket so someone else, someone you've not only never met but will never meet, can have the same access to care you enjoy, which will admittedly be lower for you but higher for them, so it balances out for everyone?" It'd be the first poll in history to find negative numbers.

But that's not how the questions about or reports on the concept are framed; it's all roses and sunshine.

This insanity of the government declaring rights has gone so far that in 2015, some House Democrats introduced a Children's Bill of Rights.

Congresswoman Karen Bass, a Democrat from California and one of the bill's cosponsors, let the cat out of the bag when she said, "If you think about it for one minute, the United States of America is the richest country on the planet. There is no reason in the world that we should not provide health care, housing, education, food, clothing and every other item that every human being needs, especially children."[29]

Remember when that used to be the responsibility of parents? Those were some crazy times; how did humanity survive so long without the government chewing our food and spitting it into our mouths as if we were baby birds?

Yet this is where liberalism and governing by polls would lead the country, any country. Questions can be finessed in such a way as to all but guarantee an outcome, and if the Constitution is bastardized to such a point that the federal government becomes a rights-granting machine, we'll be in for a world of hurt.

Imagine a government that declares something to be a "right." Then the next administration believes the opposite and rescinds that right, replacing it with another. Every four to eight years there would be massive shifts in how people exist and we'd end up with the exact type of government the Founding Fathers put quill to parchment to oppose in 1776.

Polls serve a purpose—it's good to take your temperature every once in a while—but they are no way to govern. Just ask President Hillary Clinton.

—————

Chapter 9

The Hate Crime Hoax

If polling is so accurate and useful, why don't we ever just ask people if they're racist? Could it be that the number of people answering "yes" would amount to a rounding error, and maybe, since polling is so accurate, we'd be able to stop obsessing about it and address real issues? How would that win votes for Democrats?

Racism and bigotry are disgusting, but they're also exceedingly rare. However, if you've watched the news or gone to the movies in the past few years, you'd think the Ku Klux Klan was not only in every city across the country but thriving and growing.

There's money and power in division, which is why politicians use it as a tactic to motivate voters to go to the polls. But those divisions are lies.

Liberals' go-to on hate crime issues is the left-wing activist group the Southern Poverty Law Center. The center has raked in hundreds of millions of dollars by labeling conservatives "hate mongers" and dangers to society. It even inspired a terrorist attack when one of its devotees, a man named Floyd Corkins, walked into the Family Research Council with the intent of murdering as many people as he could because the council opposed gay marriage.[1]

The SPLC had branded the FRC a "hate group" for adhering to a religious belief that marriage is between one man and one woman. Corkins, armed with a gun and a map from the SPLC, entered FRC headquarters and shot the building manager, Leonardo Johnson, who then wrestled the gun away from him and held him until police came. The map was a "hate map" showing locations of places the SPLC had determined were hate groups. Corkins attempted to use it to kill; instead he was sentenced to twenty-five years in prison.

So revered by the political Left is the SPLC that when CNN wrote up the story of Corkins's prison sentencing, its role in inspiring the choice of the FRC as a target did not warrant a single, even passing mention.[2]

The reason it's important to mention the SPLC's role in the FRC attack is to show how protected it is by the media because it is the burning bush on issues of "hate." Celebrities cite it and raise money for it, and journalists use its studies and statistics unquestioningly. And even the Southern Poverty Law Center estimates that there are only between 5,000 and 8,000 KKK members in the entire country.

"Today, the Center estimates that there are between 5,000 and 8,000 Klan members, split among dozens of different—and often warring—organizations that use the Klan name," the SPLC wrote in its report on the Klan.[3]

If you split the difference between the 5,000 and 8,000 estimate, making it 6,500 KKK members in the entire United States, that is not even a blip on the radar in a country of 330 million people.

To put the number into perspective, the wildly unpopular WNBA celebrated its 2016 season because average attendance per game was up to 7,655.[4] So the average attendance at one WNBA game is more than 1,000 more than the average of the estimated membership of the KKK. But you'd never know it by the amount of media attention the KKK gets.

When a group of racist "alt-right" mutants, neo-Nazis, and KKK members marched in Charlottesville, Virginia, in August 2017, you would have thought they were taking over the state.

The marchers, both at the idiotic Tiki torch march the night before their rally, where they chanted "Jews will not replace us" and rid the town square of mosquitos, and the following day, at their "piss everyone off and get a lot of attention" rally, amounted to only a couple of hundred people.

Clashes with Antifa, self-proclaimed "antifascists" who use

Benito Mussolini's playbook with his name scribbled out, led to the tragic death of a woman named Heather Heyer as a car driven by a "white nationalist" barreled into a crowd.

The world stopped, celebrities stopped, the media stopped. Though it is a horrible event anytime an innocent life is lost, the world kept spinning on its axis. But you'd never have known it by the way the media went all-in on the coverage. For more than a month Charlottesville became a rallying cry for the Left and a constant presence in the news. Everything was viewed through the lens of what had happened there.

The attempted assassination of dozens of Republican members of Congress while practicing for a charity baseball game against Democrats, at which the majority whip, Congressman Steve Scalise, was seriously wounded and nearly died, faded from the newspapers and cable news programs within three days, but one group of idiots fighting with a second group of idiots that resulted in the tragic death of a woman was a story that fit perfectly into the left-wing narrative of the United States of America being a horribly racist country, so it was given legs.

Remember the name James Hodgkinson? Probably not. He was the progressive activist and Bernie Sanders supporter who tried to murder as many GOP congressmen as possible that day on the baseball field. His name was reported, his motivations were glossed over, and his former existence was dropped like a rock by the media.

Hodgkinson's crime was the natural progression of what the left-wing media had been accusing conservatives of attempting to inspire for years.

After the mass shooting in Tucson, Arizona, that left six dead and fifteen injured, including then-congresswoman Gabby Giffords, leftists couldn't even wait for an accurate body count before they blamed Republicans.

New York Times columnist Paul Krugman wrote the day of the shooting, "You know that Republicans will yell about the evils of partisanship whenever anyone tries to make a connection between the rhetoric of Beck, Limbaugh, etc., and the violence I fear we're going to see in the months and years ahead. But violent acts are what happen when you create a climate of hate. And it's long past time for the GOP's leaders to take a stand against the hate-mongers."[5]

That became the mantra of the Left that day and in the days following: that the shooting had been caused by rhetoric coming from the right in opposition to Obamacare. More specifically, it was former Alaska governor Sarah Palin's fault because she had put crosshairs on Giffords's district on a map on her website.

In reality, the killer, Jared Lee Loughner, was an insane man who was generally apolitical. Eventually, after the allegations and accusations against Republicans had become the accepted, reported narrative and the story started to fade from headlines, the *New York Times* did a little journalism and discovered that Loughner was a fan of *The Communist Manifesto* whose "anger would well up at the sight of President George W. Bush."[6] That reality didn't matter; the narrative had been set. And there are, to this day, many people who still believe that Loughner was a right-wing extremist.

Proving that the editorial board of the *New York Times* doesn't even read its own paper, the day of the Scalise shooting, the *Times* ran an editorial entitled "America's Lethal Politics." In it, the "paper of record" wrote (emphasis added):

In 2011, when Jared Lee Loughner opened fire in a supermarket parking lot, grievously wounding Representative Gabby Giffords and killing six people, including a 9-year-old girl, **the link to political incitement was clear. Before the shooting, Sarah Palin's political action committee circulated a map of targeted electoral districts that put Ms. Giffords and 19 other Democrats under stylized crosshairs.**[7]

Later in the piece, the editors continued (emphasis added):

Though there's no sign of **incitement as direct as in the Giffords attack**, *liberals should of course hold themselves to the same standard of decency that they ask of the right.*[8]

Hilariously, the same day the *Times* ran its editorial falsely blaming Palin for the attack in Arizona years earlier, it ran a new story pointing out that although she was accused of inciting Loughner by liberals, including its own Krugman, "no connection to the crime was established."[9]

Again, the editorial board clearly doesn't read its own paper.

All this led to a rather epic correction the next day in the *Times*:

> *An editorial on Thursday about the shooting of Representative Steve Scalise incorrectly stated that a link existed between political rhetoric and the 2011 shooting of Representative Gabby Giffords. In fact, no such link was established. The editorial also incorrectly described a map distributed by a political action committee before that shooting. It depicted electoral districts, not individual Democratic lawmakers, beneath stylized crosshairs.*[10]

That didn't happen by accident, nor was it out of malice. It's just how leftists view anyone who isn't a leftist—as a violent hatemonger. Their default position when it comes to political opponents and those who are indifferent to politics is that they are the enemy; they don't assume the worst about them, they assume they are simply the worst.

So when a story fits that narrative, they run with it.

Every race/gender/ethnicity-based activist group knows this and keeps statistics on "hate crimes" because it knows they'll get ink. Journalists are all too happy to print a story about how someone in the racist/sexist/homophobic States of America was victimized somehow by a wrong-thinking Neanderthal.

The problem is that, more often than people realize, the stories are fake.

———————

When Donald Trump won the 2016 election, the political Left was gut-punched, as were many on the right. No one had seen it coming. But come it did, and with it came a wave of hate crimes sweeping across the country behind the victory of a violent racist winning the presidency.

At least that's how liberals saw it, and how liberals see things is, curiously, how things end up being reported by the media.

National Public Radio, the taxpayer-funded wing of the Democratic Party, exemplified this fetish for hate crimes in the Trump era perfectly in one interview. A madman had stabbed three people on a train in Portland, Oregon, two of whom had died after they intervened as the man was yelling anti-Muslim slurs at two Muslim women. It was immediately taken as an attack by a Trump supporter because he was reportedly yelling anti-Muslim slurs and the narrative is that Trump is anti-Muslim. No more evidence was needed for every news outlet to run with that story.

The truth, however, is more clouded than the narrative.

A guest from the media's favorite grievance-manufacturing group, the Southern Poverty Law Center, told NPR, "we're not entirely clear at this point what all was up with him, but it's clear from his social media postings that he had gone on anti-Muslim rants."[11]

And yes, the man, Jeremy Christian, had posted anti-Muslim rants on social media. He was also known for anti-Christian rants and for his support for a unified presidential ticket between socialist Vermont senator Bernie Sanders, who'd lost the Democratic Party's nomination to Hillary Clinton, and Green Party candidate Jill Stein, something he'd also ranted about on social media.[12]

This fact is something SPLC's Intelligence Project director, Heidi Beirich, passively acknowledged to NPR when she said of Christian's social media postings, "there was a lot of other material there as well which kind of clouds the picture."[13] Cloudy, it was.

"Sanders/Stein 2017!!! Let's stop these pipelines and reign [sic] in the Prison/Military Industrial Complexes!!! We the People have the right (As enshrined in our Constitution) to change any government by any means necessary!!! If Not Today Then Tomorrow!!!,"[14] is just one example of Christian's Facebook rants, so you can see how that kind of "clouds the picture" of his being a rabid right-wing Trump supporter.

Jill Stein didn't miss an opportunity to attack Trump, using one of her supporters, denouncing Christian's attack as "Another heart-breaking tragedy in Trump's America, as a white nationalist shouting anti-Islam slurs murders 2 on Portland, OR subway."[15]

Ignoring what she had clearly acknowledged moments earlier, Beirich told NPR, "Well, we have seen since the latter parts of the Obama administration an incredible rise in the frequency of attacks like this, hate crime attacks and domestic terrorism attacks. And the targets of those hate crimes have tended to be those populations demonized by the Trump campaign and now Trump administration."[16]

The SPLC knew that Christian was a mentally unstable person; it also knew he was a vocal supporter of Sanders who'd ranted publicly against all religions; but that didn't matter, there was a narrative to advance. And the NPR host, unless living in a bubble, knew that, too. Yet neither mentioned any of it directly, deliberately leaving the audience with a false impression.

In the same interview, NPR asked the SPLC guest about a stabbing death in Maryland that had just happened. "Do you have any evidence to suggest that this attack and what happened last week in Maryland are part of a pattern or perhaps not, perhaps a—just a terrible coincidence?" the host asked leadingly, attempting to tie together two different events three thousand miles apart in an attempt to blame the Republican president.

The man arrested for murder in Maryland was a twenty-two-year-old named Sean Urbanski, accused of stabbing Richard Wilbur Collins III, twenty-three, to death. Urbanski is white, Collins was black.

Urbanski allegedly belonged to a Facebook group called "alt-Reich," and that was enough for the media to label it a hate crime and blame it on Trump. But prosecutors, after a thorough investigation, didn't charge him with a hate crime. "After we have reviewed all the devices in the case we will look at the statute to determine whether or not the facts as we find them meet the hate crime elements, and so far, based on what we have, we have to continue to investigate. We didn't have enough today," they said.[17]

The motive certainly wasn't love, but the media had nothing on which to base the allegation of a hate crime inspired by Donald Trump other than a deep desire for it to be so. Turned out that that was enough, and they ran with it.

As if to plop a cherry on top of the false allegations against the president, the liberal journalists pounced on Trump for not speaking out about the Portland attack soon enough.

Here are some examples:

Dan Rather, who had lost his job at CBS over a report he did based on forged documents against President George W. Bush, wrote on his Facebook page:

> This story may not neatly fit into a narrative you pushed on the campaign trail and that has followed you into the White House. They were not killed by an undocumented immigrant or a "radical Islamic terrorist." They were killed in an act of civic love, facing down a man allegedly spewing hate speech directed at two teenage girls, one of whom was wearing a hijab. . . .
>
> This "extremism" may be of a different type than gets most of your attention, or even the attention in the press. But that doesn't make it any less serious, or deadly. And this kind of "extremism" is on the rise, especially in the wake of your political ascendency. Most people who study these sorts of things do not think that is a coincidence.[18]

Kyle Griffin, the producer of *The Last Word with Lawrence O'Donnell* on MSNBC:

> Trump tweets today attacking the media: 4
> Trump tweets today honoring the murdered Portland men who stood up to anti-Muslim abuse: 0[19]

Olivia Nuzzi, the Washington correspondent for *New York* magazine:

Out of Trump's 10 tweets today, most have been about the "fake news" media. 0 about Memorial Day. 0 about Portland. 0 about Mississippi.[20]

Bradd Jaffy, senior news editor and writer for *NBC Nightly News*:

The President of the United States has tweeted 10 times today—5 times about "fake news"—and not one word about the Portland train heroes.[21]

An actual beehive doesn't function with that much uniformity.

But not all alleged hate crimes involve murders, and many don't even involve actual crimes. Instead they involve something called a "bias incident."

What is a bias incident? The SPLC, the keepers of all things grievance, defines bias incidents this way:

A bias incident is conduct, speech or expression motivated, in whole or in part, by bias or prejudice. It differs from a hate crime in that no criminal activity is involved.[22]

So no crime, just basically offense given. But that offense given matters only if, somehow, the offended can divine the motive of the offender and it is more than them just being a jerk or the offended person being too sensitive.

It's a completely made-up unit of measure that is 100 percent arbitrary. Yet the SPLC, and therefore liberals everywhere, use such "incidents" to promote the idea that the country is a hateful place.

Bias incidents and hate crimes are used both interchangeably and simultaneously to pad numbers and mislead the public through the media.

After Trump's victory, the SPLC partnered with the liberal Pro-

Publica and other left-wing "news" outlets such as the *New York Times*, the *Boston Globe*, Buzzfeed, Vox, NBC News, PBS, *The Root*, *The Advocate*, and dozens more to "document hate."

"The 2016 election left many in America afraid—of intolerance and the violence it can inspire. The need for trustworthy facts on the details and frequency of hate crimes and other incidents born of prejudice has never been more urgent," the groups declared.[23]

Why is it so urgent now? Was it not urgent before November 8, 2016? Would it have not been urgent if Hillary had won?

The groups solicit reports and eyewitness accounts of hate crimes and bias incidents, which can be damn near anything, then catalog them for the purposes of showing what an awful country the United States is and how it's all Republicans' fault.

The SPLC declared that the groups had "collected 1,372 reported bias incidents between the day after the election and February 7."[24]

The *New York Times* launched a "This Week in Hate" series to blurb stories from around the Web that fit its narrative.

Curiously, most of the states with reports of hate crimes and bias incidences were very liberal states. California led the nation with 154 reports, followed by New York with 127.[25] Washington reported 65, and neighboring Oregon, 50.

Were those deep blue states harboring right-wing hatemongers just waiting for a Republican to win the White House so they could be liberated from holding in all their hatred for everyone else? Or could it be that since the project requires no verification, it simply solicits stories from anyone, and many reported "hate crimes" turn out to be hoaxes, that many people are making them up? Or maybe blue states are full of liberal snowflakes anxiously awaiting their opportunity to be melted, so any slight is a possible report?

Well, there are a lot of fake hate crimes reported by the media that are accepted as gospel when they first occur.

Remember the bomb threats called into Jewish Community

Centers after the election? More than a hundred JCCs received threatening calls about a bomb being planted in them. Footage of evacuations was all over the news along with experts blaming the "rise in hate" on the new president.

Many pundits and celebrities declared that Trump was responsible, that he was anti-Semitic and inspiring the threats. Ignored in the hysteria was the fact that his older daughter and son-in-law, two of his closest advisers, are Orthodox Jews. So if he's anti-Semitic, he's really, really, exceedingly bad at it.

Still, the threats were blamed on "right-wing extremists" because everything is blamed on them—at least until arrests are made.

Two people were ultimately charged with making the threats: a Jewish teenager living in Israel[26] and a black former liberal journalist.[27]

Suddenly—*poof!*—the stories disappeared from the headlines. The threats were still counted in the "hate crimes" data, but the narrative was gone. They could still be categorized as hate crimes and bias incidents, so they helped pad the numbers, but people rarely ask for details when quoted numbers.

The reality of an incident has little to no bearing on its usefulness.

In its "This Week in Hate" report for the week of the presidential inauguration, January 25, 2017, the *New York Times* wrote, "On Saturday, a liquor store in Newtown, Conn., was set on fire and vandalized with swastikas and an anti-Semitic message in an apparent robbery."[28]

This crime was under the banner that accompanies each of the reports, which reads, "This Week in Hate highlights hate crimes and harassment around the country since the election of Donald Trump." So everything is his fault, or at least preceded with a line designed to leave the reader with that impression.

However, the story of the attempted arson and swastika vandalism has a little update after it. It read, "After investigating, police believe the store owner staged the robbery, setting the fire and painting the graffiti himself. He has been charged with providing a false statement, among other charges."[29] Oops.

The original story was too good not to be believed, so the newspaper ran with it.

Notice the "after investigating" part. The *Times* didn't investigate it, nor had the police at the time. It fit the narrative, and that was all that mattered. People who read that story before the update will never know that they were lied to.

Another example of a hoax that was widely reported made the *Times'* list on December 6, 2016. "Last Thursday, a Muslim woman was attacked on the 6 train in Manhattan by three men who called her a terrorist, mentioned Donald Trump and attempted to rip off her hijab. 'No one said a thing,' she said of her fellow subway riders. 'Everyone just looked away.'"[30]

Awful, if true. And would really make you wonder why residents of New York City, the bastion of liberalism that it is, would sit by and do nothing as such a thing happened. They didn't, because it didn't happen.

The update reads, "According to police, the woman has since recanted her story and was charged with filing a false report." Oopsie.

The *Times* eventually stopped listing incidents altogether and appears to have ended the "This Week in Hate" column in July 2017. Guess "This Week in Corrections" didn't have quite the ring to it the editors were looking for.

There were many other "too good to fact check or wait for the facts to come out" hate crime and bias incident stories that were widely reported and turned out to be hoaxes. Listing them all would be a book unto itself, so here are just a few:

> A woman in Ann Arbor, Michigan, said she was attacked and her face slashed with a safety pin by a Trump supporter just after the election. She later admitted she had made it up and pled guilty to filing a false police report, saying "I was suffering from depression at the time."[31]

> A gay man claimed to have discovered "Heil Trump" and "Fag Church" spray-painted on the Brown County, Indiana, church where he served as organist. Later, after the story had been widely reported as a hate crime, he admitted he was the one who had spray-painted the slurs. The perpetrator, George Stang, "admitted to committing the crime out of fear of the election results. Stang, identified as being homosexual in court documents, said his parents are not very supportive of him because he is gay. He said he wanted to 'mobilize a movement' but didn't want the media attention that had resulted."[32]

> A Muslim professor at Indiana State University named Azhar Hussain received threatening emails and claimed to have been physically attacked while entering his office. Police investigated and discovered that Hussain had been not the victim but the perp. "Based upon the investigation, it is our belief that Hussain was trying to gain sympathy by becoming a victim of anti-Muslim threats, which he had created himself," police said.[33]

> A note was found on the windshield of a student's car at St. Olaf College in Minnesota that read, "I am so glad that you are leaving soon. One less nigger that this school has to deal with. You have spoken up too much. You will change nothing. Shut up or I will shut you up." Horrible. Also a fraud. Samantha Wells, the student who "found" the note, admitted, after giving tearful public speeches recounting when she had found it, that it was fake. "So, it looks like something made its way back to me in the investigation. I will be saying it was a hoax. I don't care. There is nothing more that I can do," she wrote on social media.[34]

There are countless more stories like these. Liberals are indoctrinated into believing the United States is a fundamentally unfair and racist country, rife with injustices and privileges that must not only be confronted but destroyed. It's a nation founded on racism, and propped up by the same.

These little social justice warriors boil over at the notion that other people don't know how racist everything is, so they commit to fighting. They leave their dorms, unshowered and angry, to hunt for the injustices, both micro- and macroaggressions, to "take down." But they don't find them.

They search their drum circles, they talk to like-minded people with similarly pierced privates in the social justice warrior army who are just as perplexed over the difficulty of finding droves of white men beating minorities on the streets or forcing women to carry babies to term and can't stand it anymore. They *know* it is out there, they *know* that's how the country is, but they can't find it. So they make it up.

"Is it really a lie if what you're doing is happening somewhere else, to someone else, even if they don't report it or even know it?" they wonder.

Actually, they don't wonder that at all. They see "woke" celebrities wearing "Hands up, don't shoot" shirts and lecturing the public from award show stages about the dangers of income inequality and how the president is a Nazi, so what's one little lie in the name of justice?

A crime, it turns out. Something these unwashed mutants might have learned had they chosen a major slightly more marketable than bisexual polar bear studies.

On the plus side, they don't really have to worry about a criminal record for filing a false police report being a hindrance to future employment; their attitude and college major choice already had that covered.

The lack of rational thought and the complete contempt in which these liberals, both the journalists and activists, hold their fellow Americans is, perhaps, the most disturbing part of this phenomenon.

Who are the Trump supporters who'd call him a Nazi? Maybe

the 6,500 remaining members of the dwindling KKK are running around tagging churches and schools with graffiti, but they're likely busier getting their swastika neck tattoos touched up and not mowing their lawns.

If it isn't those 6,500 who are harassing people and vandalizing things, it would have to be the other 62 million–plus people who voted for him. But realistically, how many normal Americans would feel compelled to tell the world, even anonymously, that they had voted for someone they think is a Nazi for president? The answer is not too many, if any.

Yet that is what liberals would have people believe.

The data gathered by the SPLC, ProPublica, the *New York Times,* and the rest of the clown car packed with liberal activists with press credentials showed something they probably didn't anticipate—that the farther away from the election, the fewer "reports" there were.

If the country were marinated to the bone in hate, as these groups would like people to believe, it doesn't explain why there was a precipitous drop-off of reports of "bias incidents" to them, even with the lack of a standard for what constitutes one, as time moved away from the election.

By the beginning of December, the "reports" had dwindled to next to nothing. How is that possible for a country based on hate? Did everyone forget he hates everyone else as the election faded into memory? Of course not. But that reality won't sell newspapers or inspire donations, so what's the point of it?

You can hate the country all you want, but there's something particularly manipulative about lying to justify it.

—————

Chapter 10

Millionaire Victims

Professional sports is entertainment in mega-taxpayer-funded arenas. So when then–San Francisco 49ers quarterback Colin Kaepernick chose to sit for the national anthem on August 26, 2016, it got the notice reserved for an actor wearing a ribbon at an award show, which is to say not much. What it eventually grew into was a cultural rift between rich elitist liberals from all walks of life and the people who put billions of dollars per year into their pockets.

Kaepernick's glory days were long gone. The former Super Bowl quarterback had been relegated to a backup slot on the team. Still, the NFL, as the line from the movie *Concussion* put it, "owns a day of the week. The same day the Church used to own. Now it's theirs." Everything people do around the game, even a benchwarmer, gets reported.

This was before taking a knee; Kaepernick sat. Why?

At the time, he was unambiguous. "I am not going to stand up to show pride in a flag for a country that oppresses black people and people of color," he told NFL.com after the preseason game. "To me, this is bigger than football and it would be selfish on my part to look the other way. There are bodies in the street and people getting paid leave and getting away with murder."[1]

He was protesting a myth—that police were murdering innocent, unarmed black men at will. Statistics gathered by the *Washington Post*, which won a Pulitzer Prize for the project, show that that was not reality.

In 2017, twenty unarmed black men were killed by police, as

were thirty white men and thirteen Hispanic men, according to data compiled by the *Washington Post*.[2] The circumstances around each incident differ, and all were undoubtedly sad for their families. But they are not indicative of an epidemic.

But the disconnect between the data and the media coverage, and therefore the perception of those whose worldview was informed by the mainstream media, became a chasm.

Riots over the deaths of Michael Brown in Missouri, who'd attacked a police officer and tried to take his gun, and Freddie Gray in Maryland, a heroin dealer who died in police custody of a spinal injury, were in the news, as was the condemnation of police before any investigation had been carried out or evidence was known.

The media whipped up a frenzy, covering these deaths as though they were political assassinations. Cable news was an endless stream of activists with a vested interest in strife-spewing conspiracies and allegations while alleged journalists reported rumors.

An absence of new information used to mean a lapse in reporting until new information emerged. Now, in the age of social media, confirmation bias and narrative reinforcement fill the void.

On Saturday, December 13, 2014, on *CNN Newsroom*, the "straight news" program became a vehicle for activism. After showing footage of protests, "CNN commentator Sally Kohn said, 'We want you to know that our hearts are out there marching with them,' as she and cohosts Mel Robbins and Margaret Hoover raised their hands up in the air, in an obvious nod to the 'hands up, don't shoot' chant associated with protests against police violence."[3]

The "Hands up, don't shoot" mantra was a staple of the protests and riots following the Brown killing. It was also a bald-faced lie.

"'Hands up, don't shoot' links directly to Brown's death, and it went viral. After the shooting, St. Louis Rams players raised their hands as a symbolic gesture entering the field before a football game," the *Washington Post* reported.[4]

The article continued, "'Hands up, don't shoot' did not happen in Brown's killing, and it is a characterization that deserves Four

Pinocchios. Politicians should step carefully if they try to highlight this expression in the future."[5]

That did not stop the lie or even slow it down. The Rams' engaging in it only served to spread it, showing the influence of the NFL. And CNN's embrace of the lie nine months later demonstrated just how deeply into the liberal media culture it had metastasized.

As Kaepernick's protest evolved from sitting to kneeling, the lies grew bigger and deeper. "A Black person in America is killed by a police officer or a person protected by the state every 28 hours," declared the Huffington Post, spreading what had become a popular liberal meme.[6]

That, too, was a lie. "This fact check focused on the claim that 'every 28 hours, an unarmed black person is killed by police'—which is not true, based on the findings in the Malcolm X Grassroots Movement report. The victims studied in the report were not all unarmed, and they were not all killed by police," the Post found.[7]

Still, Kaepernick and the protests continued.

Normally a backup quarterback goes unnoticed, but fed by the narrative-advancing media, Kaepernick became a growing spectacle, even as he rode the bench. Increasingly, it wasn't that he had an important or even correct opinion; it was that any other opinion was unacceptable.

"Protesters, pro athletes, Broadway performers and congressional staffers have used the gesture in public in a show of solidarity," declared CNN in a story entitled "Why 'Hands Up, Don't Shoot' Resonates Regardless of Evidence."[8]

It is rare for a "news" organization to declare facts and forensic evidence unimportant compared to a narrative, but there it was for the world to see.

Those "protesters, pro athletes, Broadway performers and congressional staffers" didn't let the facts get in their way; the lie persisted.

Other NFL players joined in. Not many, but more.

Then Kaepernick became a free agent, and no team wanted him. In addition to being a distraction, his skills had diminished.

Billion-dollar sports organizations tend not to keep people around for shits and giggles; they have to produce or be cut loose. Kaepernick no longer produced.

The decision of all the NFL teams not to sign Kaepernick was not seen as a valid one; it was declared racist. "Anonymous NFL execs say they're not blackballing Colin Kaepernick. They're just racist," stated Slate.[9]

Ironically, Kaepernick was on the verge of receiving an offer from the Baltimore Ravens when his girlfriend, radio DJ Nessa Diab, tweeted a picture portraying the team's owner as a racist.[10] So racism was involved, but it came from his end.

Usually when a player is no longer in a league, interest in him fades away—what is there to cover when he's not playing? He's just a wealthy private citizen; if anything, the media's glowing coverage of the Occupy Wall Street movement taught us that wealthy private citizens are the root of all evil.

But Kaepernick was different. His "sabotage by girlfriend" didn't matter; the narrative that he had not been signed because of his kneeling trumped reality.

Other players had adopted the kneeling pose during the national anthem, but Kaepernick was the leader, so attention still flowed his way.

Then came Donald Trump.

President Trump was hardly the first person to be critical of kneeling during the national anthem, but none of the other critics were as hated by the liberal establishment. When Trump, at a political rally in Alabama, said, "Wouldn't you love to see one of these NFL owners, when somebody disrespects our flag, to say, 'Get that son of a bitch off the field right now, out, he's fired. He's fired,'" the story blew up bigger than it had ever been.

Trump was not the first person to tie kneeling during the national anthem with disrespecting the country and the flag. But the power of the office is such that anything its occupant mentions becomes a national discussion.

And frankly, when you choose to protest *during* something, no matter what your cause, people will see it as a protest *against* that thing.

The following week, every team protested during the national anthem—with most players taking a knee and three teams refusing to take the field for it. It wasn't clear, exactly, what the protest was against, but it was clear that only "terrible" people weren't in on it.

A public relations nightmare ensued for the NFL and its players.

As team owners scrambled to control the damage with fans, journalists scrambled to spin the protest to be about anything other than the anthem and the American flag. Mostly, the media wanted it to be about race.

"The #TakeAKnee protests have always been about race. Period," declared CNN.[11]

President Trump's comments and subsequent tweets on the subject caused outrage in the liberal media and the NFL. What the president was saying, one journalist said,

> *misses the point of the protests entirely. These demonstrations are not about disrespecting the flag or the nation. They are not about disrespecting the military, especially given that some military veterans have participated in and supported the protests ever since Colin Kaepernick jump-started them.*
>
> *This is about systemic racism in America—and particularly police brutality.*[12]

But when you protest at a funeral, your protest becomes about that funeral; when your protest blocks traffic, it becomes about preventing people from getting to where they are going. Just as with the lunatic members of the Westboro Baptist Church, who routinely protest their wacko causes at funerals that will get media attention, and Black Lives Matter, which regularly blocks traffic and has become hated for it, the method drowns out the message. Neither of those causes is based in reality, but most people don't care; they just see people being assholes, and that's their takeaway.

But the media, athletes, and their ideological brethren in Holly-wood were not going to let their myth go—especially since if they did, it would give the appearance that the president, a man they de-spise, had a point.

Can't have that.

The modern Democratic Party is the AFL-CIO of identity politics—the common umbrella under which groups pool their re-sources to make their whole a force their parts aren't big enough to be. Except that those divisions are stoked by liberals for their benefit.

They present a grim picture of America, one that is racist, sexist, homophobic, Islamophobic—if you can identify certain people as a voting bloc and the Left can tell them they're victims, the Demo-crats can add them to the list. Just slap an "ist" or "phobic" at the end, and you're off to the races.

That is the party's strategy. No matter how inept the Democrats prove to be or how popular a Republican politician or plan might be, the Democrats will always say, "At least we're not the racist party."

Detroit has been in the clutches of the Democratic Party since 1962, when the city was still an economic powerhouse. Democratic congressman John Conyers represented a large part of that city from 1965 till his resignation in disgrace in 2017. Both the city and Conyers's district collapsed to near-third-world levels of economic depression in those years, yet the city repeatedly elected Democrats as mayor, and Conyers, the sixth-longest-serving member of the House of Representatives in history, had only one opponent get 20 percent of the vote against him in his fifty-three-year tenure.[13] It took his using taxpayer funds that were supposed to go to run-ning his congressional office to settle a sexual harassment claim against him to finally remove his carcass from office. Then, in the tradition of every self-entitled pompous ass who lets his political invincibility go to his head, he refused to repay the $27,000 his office had paid.[14] But even after that revelation, Democratic House leader Nancy Pelosi defended Conyers as "an icon in our country."[15]

Makes you wonder what you have to do to be seen as a disgrace to Democrats; what do you have to be accused of, and how many zeros must a taxpayer-financed check have? We've yet to find out.

Divided we are, but are we also conquered? It sure seems like it sometimes.

It must work, or why else would Democrats keep doing it? Why else would former first lady Michelle Obama say, 'Any woman who voted against Hillary Clinton voted against their own voice."[16]

To Democrats you are your skin color, you are your genitalia. Your vote should be determined by which bathroom you use. And if it's not, well, ask Clarence Thomas or Sarah Palin how tolerant and into equality liberals are.

This reality, aided by a media obedient to it, helped paint the NFL into a corner.

The racial paradigm so completely embraced by the political Left is how you can have a white *Good Morning America* coanchor declare, "it's hard to ignore the racial component here. The President went on this jag on Friday night in front of a largely white audience" when talking about the president's comments about NFL players protesting during the national anthem.[17]

It's actually very easy to ignore the race aspect of the story, unless you want to stir the pot and advance an agenda. Most sane people don't immediately think about the race of people involved in any discussion, let alone one that has nothing to do with race.

Who scans an audience at a political rally and makes mental notes about the racial makeup of the crowd? You have to really want to notice to be able to. And the media really want to notice.

You have to want to manufacture strife to go on *Meet the Press* and say, "Some of the words of the national anthem are white supremacist."[18]

And don't kid yourself, there's a lot of money in division. It's empowered Al Sharpton and Jesse Jackson to avoid getting real jobs their entire adult lives while living like kings.

As the controversy over the protests grew, so did the attempted rationalizing by the media. The Huffington Post declared, "White

Athletes Still Standing for the Anthem Are Standing for White Supremacy." Subtle. The article said, "The protest at the heart of all of this isn't about the anthem or the flag, it is about calling on America to live up to its self-professed values."[19] Never mind the fact that Kaepernick himself made it about the flag by staging his "protest" during the honoring of the flag and said, on day one, "I am not going to stand up to show pride in a flag for a country that oppresses black people and people of color."

———————

Liberals like to have it both ways on matters of race. Every commercial on TV looks like a Benneton ad, but they tell us that everyone is being oppressed. Which is it? Because it can't be both.

How many times have you seen an ad like this: five people of different races driving in a convertible, all smiling and laughing (but weirdly, no one talking), stopping to grab some fast food that not one of those professional models would eat on a dare, then sharing their food while sitting around a campfire and still laughing. They're laughing so hard you'd think there was a gas leak.

Or how about this one: a group of female models of every conceivable race are laughing and sneaking peeks at a group of similarly mixed male models across a New York rooftop set up to accommodate a band or DJ, dancing until the one really hot woman ends up next to the hot guy she was staring at with her friends, somehow able to have a conversation with him while the music is so loud everyone else dances like they're on ecstasy at a rave while they drink cheap beer. So someone is going to drop thousands for the permits that keep the police away while paying New York rent, but they'll only buy the beer that's $2.99 for a six-pack?

But everyone is getting along, everyone is having fun—all races together.

Then you turn on the news, and it all gets blown to shit.

"Racial hatred has never been higher," the anchors and actors insist. Search "hate crimes are on the rise," and you'll get almost 4 million results. Add "NFL" and that total drops by only 800,000. This is insanity.

The majority of the most popular athletes in the country are black; you won't find a list of most admired actors without Denzel Washington on it, and the country just twice elected a black man president of the United States. Do people forget how racist they are when it comes time to answer polls or go to vote? Or is something else at work here?

The tribal mentality that liberals seek to instill in people works only, to the extent it does, through constant reinforcement. That's how a criticism of protest can be made to be about race when it wasn't.

Are there still racists in this country? Of course there are. There are 330 million people; in a pool that big there will always be idiots of all flavors. But when the liberal Southern Poverty Law Center estimates that there are only between 5,000 and 8,000 members of the Ku Klux Klan left in a nation of 330 million and its peak membership was 4 million in 1920,[20] with a population of only 106 million[21] . . . well, if that's not progress, there is no such thing as progress.

Yet every year we are inundated with stories about how things are getting worse, movies about oppression, songs about how bad people have it. Why?

It's effective to tell people they have it bad when you want them to think you have the key to making it better. Detroit, Chicago, Baltimore, and cities like them with generational single-party control by Democrats don't keep electing the same party over and over because they expect a different result, they do it because their citizens have been manipulated into believing the alternative is somehow worse. The problems, they are led to believe, aren't the result of bad mayors and city councils, they're the result of the fact that Republicans have worked from outside the political power structure of those cities to make them worse. "How?" is never asked because people are conditioned not to ask, which is good for liberals because there is no answer beyond "the Reagan budget screwed us" or some other nonresponsible boogeyman.

None of it explains why the schools graduate people who can't read, of the few people they graduate. It doesn't explain why businesses fled or people with them. And there is no explanation for why all of these problems started decades ago. It's easier to just say it's the fault of racism. That goes unquestioned.

The racism excuse by corrupt politicians works beautifully because it allows people who believe it to absolve themselves of any responsibility for problems in their lives. Didn't get that job? It was because of who you are. Didn't get a promotion? Sexism. Got pulled over for a burned-out taillight? Racism.

Though this helps tighten the grip on power for the people peddling it, it strips the ambition of the people who buy into it. It truly is evil to absolve people of their responsibility and assign it to an external, nebulous force beyond their control.

Everyone has failures and disappointments, but they should serve as learning experiences. Those experiences lead to improvement and better outcomes in the future.

But people who are told they're victims of society's biases, many times, will be discouraged by a few simple failures. Why try if every time you try, the "systemic" bigotries and biases slap you back down?

Soon people stop trying, and as a result they stop improving. Once they accept the idea that there is a force out there working against them, it is a short drive to the idea that they'll let others, especially those who swear they're protecting them, handle their business. From there you get generational poverty and generational politics. Soon people pay little attention to what and whom they're voting for and simply vote for a party because they always have, and their children vote for that party because their parents did. Lather, rinse, repeat.

It's diabolical, really. But it wouldn't work on its own.

That leads to an important point: we're out of problems.

People do have real problems and struggles, but they're not societywide problems, not a part of everyday life for all Americans.

It wasn't that long ago, and throughout all of human history until the Industrial Revolution, that the focus of people's everyday life was simply to survive the day.

With the exception of nobles, daily life consisted of waking up, tending a farm, hoping to have enough food to feed your family, hoping you weren't killed by a random stranger, fearing getting sick and dying, even from something as simple as an infected cut, and getting to bed early enough so you could sleep and do it all over again the next day. With the fight for survival removed, people filled the void with the latest modern luxury: imagined problems. Being a victim became fetishized, a desired status for liberals. That status is both a weapon and a shield for liberals, wielded against all enemies, foreign and domestic.

Donald Trump is a monster for criticizing millionaires who play a child's game for a living because some of them happen to be black. Republicans were racist because they opposed Barack Obama's policies, but they weren't racist when they opposed those same or similar policies when they were pushed by Bill Clinton. Maybe they were redneck-ist?

The shield and sword of victimhood are even wielded against their own when it suits their needs.

When Congresswoman Linda Sanchez, a Democrat from California, said it was time to pass the torch of Democratic Party leadership in the House of Representatives to a younger generation, she was called a sexist by her colleague.

"I think there comes a time when you need to pass that torch. And I think it's time," Sanchez said. "I do think we have this real breadth and depth of talent within our caucus and I do think it's time to pass a torch to a new generation of leaders, and I want to be a part of that transition."[22]

Note "leaders," plural, meaning more than one. House Democratic leader Nancy Pelosi is seventy-seven; the Democratic whip, the second in command, Steny Hoyer of Maryland, is seventy-eight;

James Clyburn, the assistant Democratic leader from South Carolina, is third in command and is seventy-seven. Not only are they not spring chickens, they're young only for mountain ranges. When the average age of the country's leadership is higher than the average life expectancy of American men (76.4 years), the party might want to rethink its ability to recruit younger voters and bring energy to a campaign.

For stating this obvious truth, Sanchez was accused of sexism. "I have heard that argument used so many times before. I think it really reflects the sexism that still exists in politics today," Congressman Joseph Crowley said on the issue. "I think Nancy Pelosi is held to a different standard than others are."[23]

For the record, Linda Sanchez not only is a woman, she identifies as one as well. But facts don't matter to liberals; only the narrative does. They're nearly Pavlovian in their response to criticism, even from their own: declare victim status, and don't address the substance.

This would be laughed at as the absurdity it is were it not for a complicit media culture engaged in the same thing. In many ways, the media were pioneers in the concept.

As far back as June 2004, progressive Democrats were holding something called a Take Back America Conference, a gathering of liberal activists committed to defeating Republicans.[24] The events featured prominent Democratic Party members as speakers and participants, including then-senators Hillary Clinton and Barack Obama and actor/director Robert Redford at the 2006 edition.[25] The Huffington Post even touted its founder's speaking at the event,[26] and MSNBC covered the conferences.[27] The conference was billed by the *Washington Post* as "a chance for Democrats to highlight progressive politics."[28]

Curiously, after Barack Obama won the election in 2008, giving Democrats the White House and Congress, liberals stopped holding Take Back America conferences. The phrase was then adopted by the party out of power, and when Republicans started to use it, "take back America" suddenly became racist.

Attorney general Eric Holder said, "There's a certain level of ve-hemence, it seems to me, that's directed at me [and] directed at the president. You know, people talking about **taking their country back**. . . . There's a certain racial component to this for some people. I don't think this is the thing that is a main driver, but for some, there's a racial animus."[29] (Emphasis added.)

President Obama agreed with that sentiment:

> *But Obama, in his most candid moments, acknowledged that race was still a problem. In May 2010, he told guests at a private White House dinner that race was probably a key component in the rising opposition to his presidency from conservatives, especially right-wing activists in the anti-incumbent "Tea Party" movement that was then surging across the country.* **Many middle-class and working-class whites felt aggrieved and resentful** *that the federal government was helping other groups, including bankers, auto-makers, irresponsible people who had defaulted on their mortgages, and the poor, but wasn't helping them nearly enough, he said.*
>
> *A guest suggested that when* **Tea Party activists said they wanted to "take back" their country, their real motivation was to stir up anger and anxiety at having a black president, and Obama didn't dispute the idea.** *He agreed that there was a "sub-terranean agenda" in the anti-Obama movement—a racially biased one—that was unfortunate. But he sadly conceded that there was little he could do about it.[30] (Emphasis added.)*

Barack Obama spoke at the 2006 and 2007 Take Back America conferences. Guess he and Holder forgot.

David Remnick, the editor of the *New Yorker* magazine, had a similar exchange with Charlie Rose on PBS:

REMNICK: What's the phrase—"We want our country back." What does that really mean, Charlie, really? Is it about tax rates? Is it about health care debates? It seems to me some-thing even—

ROSE: What do you think it is?

REMNICK: Well, I think for some people—for some people, I want to emphasize that—that there is a—that race is attached to it, that ethnicity is attached to it. This is a country that is, in the words of James Baldwin, white no longer and will not be white in its majority.[31]

MSNBC found racism in the phrase as well. *Hardball* host Chris Matthews and *Washington Post* columnist Eugene Robinson decried the use of the phrase by the Tea Party in 2010:

MATTHEWS: It seems to me that there's a cake they're baking on the right, and very effectively. And all the ingredients are socialist, the delegitimizing of people, the birthers who say he's not really an American, the attempt to talk takeovers. All these terms seem foreign and . . .

ROBINSON: "I want my country back."

MATTHEWS: "My country back." You know, it seems like they're baking a cake so that people get this idea he's not one of us.

ROBINSON: He's not one of us and he's not legitimate.[32]

Oddly enough, Matthews covered Hillary Clinton's speech at the 2007 Take Back America Conference.[33] There was no mention of race then. What changed?

There was a Democrat in the White House is what changed, and he happened to be a black man. The opportunity presented to claim victim status was much easier than disputing any opposition or policy differences, so the race card cometh.

———————

The Pavlovian aspect of the victim card being played is illustrated when the liberal firing squad transitions from linear to circular. The Left has so fetishized being a victim and so indoctrinated its own function in a world of tribalism that it is often caught in friendly fire as it turns its guns down its own trench.

"Think pieces" are not uncommon, such as "Polite White People Are Useless," stating

> Polite white people—specifically, polite white people who call for decorum instead of disruption when attempting to battle and defeat bias and hate—aren't as paradoxical as tits on a bull. But they're just as useless. They provide no value, they move no needles, they carry no weight (metaphysically and literally) and they ultimately just get in the way. They're humanity's tourists: the 54-mile-per-hour drivers in the left lane refusing to get the fuck out of the way so others can pass. And if you get enough of them in one place, they cause accidents.
>
> Unfortunately, they're every-fucking-where. They're on Facebook threads and sitting behind you at work. They're your neighbors and (sometimes) your family members.[34]

Nor uncommon, lately, are stories of liberal-on-liberal complaints of "cultural appropriation," the idea that the skin color of the first person to ever do something somehow magically locks the ability to do that thing forever in the realm of people with that skin color and anything else is racist.

Braid your hair in cornrows when you're not black, and it's racist. Hall of Fame basketball player Kareem Abdul-Jabbar, on the subject of white women wearing their hair in cornrows, wrote, "In general, when blacks create something that is later adopted by white culture, white people tend to make a lot more money from it. Certainly, one can see why that's both annoying and disheartening."[35]

Abdul-Jabbar's piece called it "racial identity theft" and stated the idea of non-Mexicans liking burritos to be a problem. "Having said all that, here's the harsh reality. Whether we call it cultural appropriation, assimilation, exploitation, homage, plundering or honoring, it will continue to happen unabated or affected by complaints and protests," he said.[36]

Speaking of food, serving ethnic food at Oberlin College was declared to be cultural appropriation and racist, too. The *New York Times* reported:

> The students at the college in Oberlin, Ohio, are accusing the campus dining department and Bon Appétit Management Company, the main dining vendor, of a litany of offenses that range from cultural appropriation to cultural insensitivity.
>
> Earlier this month, students with the school's black student union protested outside of the dining hall at the Afrikan Heritage House, after demands for more traditional meals, including more fried chicken, went unmet, according to the campus paper, The Oberlin Review. . . .
>
> Another article, published by The Review in November, detailed what students said were instances of cultural appropriation carried out by Bon Appétit. The culinary culprits included a soggy, pulled-pork-and-coleslaw sandwich that tried to pass itself off as a traditional Vietnamese banh mi sandwich; a Chinese General Tso's chicken dish made with steamed instead of fried poultry; and some poorly prepared Japanese sushi.
>
> "When you're cooking a country's dish for other people, including ones who have never tried the original dish before, you're also representing the meaning of the dish as well as its culture," Tomoyo Joshi, a student from Japan, told the paper. "So if people not from that heritage take food, modify it and serve it as 'authentic,' it is appropriative."[37]

So unless you're Italian, don't even think about opening a can of Chef Boyardee!

This level of insanity might be understandable from college students marinated in left-wing identity politics on college campuses (it still really wouldn't be), but it isn't confined to college campuses.

Hollywood, a willing fellow traveler in the identity politics world, has been hit by it, too.

No one batted an eye when Samuel L. Jackson was cast to play Nick Fury in the Marvel superhero movies. Fury was created as a white man, changed only decades later. But there was no outrage and little notice when Jackson showed up in postcredit scenes as the eye-patch-wearing director of *Agents of S.H.I E.L.D.* He's a great actor and does a great job. That should be enough for any role, but liberals won't allow it to be.

Though comic book movies actually have a long history of black actors being cast in roles of characters that were white in the books—Michael B. Jordan as Johnny Storm in *Fantastic Four*, Michael Clarke Duncan as Kingpin in *Daredevil*, Billy Dee Williams as Harvey Dent in *Batman*, Idris Elba as Heimdall in *Thor*, Will Smith as Agent J in *Men in Black*—when casting decisions go in the opposite direction, all hell breaks loose.

None other than the *Washington Post* cataloged "100 Times a White Actor Played Someone Who Wasn't White."[38]

Imagine how miserable a human being, or how committed/indoctrinated into the progressive cause, you have to be to not only notice these but then think, "The world needs to know this important information" and set about cataloging it.

In 2002, the Tom Clancy novel *The Sum of All Fears*, starring Ben Affleck and Morgan Freeman, is another example of this concept. Unlike in the book, however, the villains in the movie were neo-Nazis—basically a bunch of white guys—hoping to start a nuclear war between the United States and Russia for reasons that are never quite explained because an all-out nuclear war would wipe out everyone.

In the book the villains were radical Muslims, but the Council on American-Islamic Relations (CAIR) lobbied against staying true to the novel. It didn't really need to lobby that hard.

By the time The Sum of All Fears *movie was being developed, CAIR launched a pre-emptive campaign to rid the adaptation of the novel's Muslim terrorists. ("Before we had typed a word on paper," producer Mace Neufeld has said, "I was getting complaints.") Harrison Ford, then slated for the lead, reportedly felt much the same way. Early script treatments cast Timothy McVeigh-style "super-*

patriots" as the heavies behind the bomb plot, not Muslims—a
PC move par excellence.[39]

The movie bombed because, among other things, the villains made no sense. Muslim radicals don't mind dying, it's a ticket to Paradise; people who want to take over the world, however, need a viable plan of conquest that doesn't involve the destruction of the planet.

The PC BS of race-obsessed casting did make its way into comic book projects when a white man was chosen to play the kung fu master Iron Fist in the Netflix series of the same name.

Buzzfeed reported on the controversy and "had the chance to ask Jeph Loeb, Marvel's executive vice president of television, if they ever considered casting an actor of Asian descent for the role."[40]

The weird thing is, although the character is a kung fu master, which evokes images of Asia, his name is Danny Rand and he was white in the comic books. The social justice warriors were protesting about something that was staying true to its source material.

But who produces that source material matters under the new rules, too.

In 2016, at a book festival in Brisbane, Australia, the author Lionel Shriver lamented the new push for political correctness in the literary world that says authors should not write about characters of races not their own; to do so would be—drumroll, please—cultural appropriation.

Shriver rejected the idea, saying artists should be free to make whatever art they like—a novel and dying concept, saying, "Otherwise, all I could write about would be smart-alecky 59-year-old 5-foot-2-inch white women from North Carolina."[41]

This idea, which goes against the entirety of written fiction and the concept of free speech and artistic expression, has found a growing audience in the literary world.

In response to Shriver's comment, author Kaitlyn Greenidge wrote:

This debate, or rather, this level of the debate, is had over and over again, primarily because of an unwillingness on one side to consider history or even entertain a long line of arguments in response. Instead, what often happens is a writer or artist acts as though she is taking some brave stand by declaring to be against political correctness. As if our entire culture is not already centered on a very particular version of whiteness that many white people don't even inhabit anymore. And so, someone makes a comment or a statement without nuance or sense of history, only with an implicit insistence that writing and publishing magically exist outside the structures of power that dominate every other aspect of our daily lives.[42]

Is anyone's life overwhelmed by "structures of power" dominating his or her daily life? Of course not, but people do obsess about such things. If that is the case, perhaps a hobby is needed.

As another author put it, "While some white people scoff at the complaints of minorities, they seem implicitly to understand that being a minority has not always been a pleasant experience—hence their fear of becoming a minority. These white people demand their country back, a more prosperous America where they once owned the culture. They too fear cultural appropriation, except that in this case it means the loss of the privileges that were long a benefit of whiteness, privileges which people of color appear to be taking."[43]

Imagine thinking that way, being so involved in race that it, rather than who you are, defines your every thought. This is the modern progressive movement and the mentality that dominates the modern Democratic Party and the media.

It's this obsession that divides, which is the liberals' goal and leads to dark places and an "us against them" mentality. It leads to the compiling of "a list of charities and organizations working to keep immigrant, Black, Latinx and other populations safe after Hurricane Harvey," rather than just helping people in need.[44]

That list was created by Race Forward: The Center for Racial

Justice Innovation, which, according to its website, was "Founded in 2002" and "catalyzes community, government, and other institutions to dismantle structural racial inequity and create equitable outcomes for all."[45]

Notice the "equitable outcomes for all" bit, a concept it elaborates on with "We define racial justice as the systematic fair treatment of people of all races, resulting in equitable opportunities and outcomes for all and we work to advance racial justice through media, research, and leadership development."[46]

This and myriad other similar groups find a receptive audience in the media.

Its goal? "Race Forward envisions a vibrant world in which people of all races create, share and enjoy resources and relationships equitably, unleashing individual potential, embracing collective responsibility and generating global prosperity."[47]

Karl Marx would be proud.

That's what this is all about, where the Left hopes this all will lead—to a collective world in which the individual is unimportant, nonexistent. The absence of real, life-threatening problems has created a void liberals have sought to fill with division and identity politics—the classic "us against them."

Unable to sell collectivism on its merits—because too many people remember the destruction that came in its wake everywhere it's been implemented—they push it as "justice" and "tolerance," implying that anyone who opposes them opposes those concepts.

But justice is being treated equally, not having an equal outcome; it's being judged for who you are and what you've done, not what anyone throughout history with your same skin pigment level did years or even centuries before you were born.

Victories do not transfer from generation to generation—children of Super Bowl champions are not Super Bowl champions, too—neither does complicity in crimes.

This wouldn't be an issue had liberals not needed it to cover their failures; it wouldn't be an issue if journalists weren't so eager to help. If the objective of waking up in the morning was working relentlessly so you and your family could wake up and do it all again tomorrow, it wouldn't be an issue.

As it stands, technological advances have liberated people in the Western world from most of their problems. Some manufacture or magnify problems as a means of manipulation; it's much easier to be a victim than responsible.

But if you have time to worry about how the race of a character in a movie lines up with the source material rather than simply enjoying the film or have gone from poverty to being a multimillionaire by playing a game but still believe the United States is designed at its very core to keep people down, you're out of problems.

Chapter 11

They're Making a Movie About It

Hollywood loves money; the folks there love it almost as much as they love themselves and sexual harassment. They didn't churn out three *Harold & Kumar* and *The Hangover* movies because the world needed to know what was going to happen next, they did it because it made them richer than they were before they made them.

The thing about Hollywood is that the people there don't like people knowing they love money, so when they go on late-night talk shows to plug their $100 million blockbuster, they talk about it as a "passion project."

Yes, we all believe you made a movie about wearing spandex and beating up aliens who were trying to destroy the planet because it's been a cause near and dear to your heart since you were a child . . .

The only people who have a problem with Hollywood being a money-driven industry are the people making Brink's trucks full of money working in the industry. We know that Mark Ruffalo isn't playing the Hulk in Marvel movies because he was a huge Bill Bixby fan or loved the comic books; he enjoys signing the backs of checks with a lot of zeros made out to him.

The people who watch the films are fine with that. They like to see Ruffalo playing a giant green monster on screen, so they also accept him being a giant "green" monster in real life. And he is.

On his personal Twitter feed, Ruffalo preaches incessantly about climate change, even exploiting tragedy as it unfolded to push his political agenda.

While it was still raining in Texas during the devastation of Hurricane Harvey, he tweeted, "It's time to get real and call it like it is! This storm the likes of which we have not precedent is because we are living in Climate Change."

Setting aside his awful writing, people will still go see the next Avengers movie because they're fun. What they won't go see is the next "important" movie attempting to beat audiences about the head and neck with a left-wing political agenda.

Hollywood is liberal, very liberal. The people there went from denying the "Red scare" to committing it when red became the color of Republicans on the electoral map. More than journalism, science, or academia, Hollywood has systematically rooted out conservatives and then started shaming moderates.

The people the entertainment industry holds in the highest contempt—its audience—haven't stopped going to the movies or watching TV altogether. They accept the personal pontificating of actors, directors, and writers when they are not playing characters. When Captain America fights the forces of evil on the screen, the audience can forget for two hours that the actor playing Captain America thinks a huge percentage of them are evil for how they vote and what they believe.[1]

Though that disconnect works for the average person, it's not good enough for the actors on the screen. It's as if they're in a constant dance-off to please some invisible studio executive who will hire only the most rabidly progressive actors for his next project.

Everyone has a cause, and that cause must be pushed.

The latest trend in celebri-care is the foundation.

Riddled with guilt over having earned so much more money than others in a time of growing income inequality, celebrities donate large portions of their massive salaries, royalties, and residual checks to average Americans to make things more "fair."

Just kidding, they'd never do that; it's too close to putting their money where their mouth is.

What they do do—likely on the advice of high-priced accountants who crawl through the bowels of the tax code, checking every nook and cranny for deductions—is create foundations to afford them sizable tax shelters.

You'll often hear celebrities talk about their foundations as if they're out in the world tackling important issues in the name of all that is good and pure. What they mostly are is a scam.

Here's how they work:

Say you made $100 million off your "This evil corporation has a plan to make trillions selling a product that kills everyone and poisons the planet until you come along and save the day" movie, in both salary and your piece of the back end. What are you going to do with that money? Unless you have an Olympic-sized cocaine problem, you don't have an immediate need for $100 million.

Do you just pay the taxes—37 percent to the feds, another 10 percent to the state, and whatever city taxes, if any, exist where you live? Keep in mind, this is after your agent gets 10 percent and your money manager takes a slice, not to mention your publicist and whatever other ass kissers you have on staff. That money shrinks quickly. It's still huge but nowhere near the original $100 million, even before taxes.

So what you do is you set up a nonprofit, some kind of foundation to help kids like you, the "good-looking kids in high school who weren't particularly bright but could cry on cue so it didn't matter if they couldn't get into community college" foundation. A foundation normally contains just the name of the celebrity sponsoring it, but for the sake of anonymity we'll keep it simple.

You then give the charity that your accountant set up for you a massive donation from that $100 million. The donation won't help you with your agent's or money manager's fees, but it will take a huge chunk out of your tax bill to Uncle Sam.

Let's hypothetically say you give $75 million to the foundation; you're thinking that's a little generous and maybe you'd like to keep some more of it just in case you want to travel with friends or something. Don't worry, you're covered. You're not cutting checks for $75 million to people who qualify for whatever your charity is supposedly set up for; your money manager buys Apple stock with it, and you disburse only something like $100,000 to the "winners" of whatever you're told to pretend the foundation is about. You take a gigantic tax deduction for the donation, spread it out over years if you want, and essentially live off the charity's money.

Want to go to Paris for a week to get away with some friends? List them all as some kind of advisers or make them junior board members or something, set up a meeting in Paris, and the foundation will pay for the private plane, the hotels, all the meals, etc., etc.

Always wanted to see the Great Wall of China? Same thing— find some reason to need to be there for foundation "work," and bingo, you're gold.

Every once in a while, when tragedy strikes somewhere in the country or world, you peel off $50,000 and make a donation "from your foundation" for a good cause. By the time the next tragedy rolls around, your stock will have increased enough to more than cover whatever donation you made last time, your money is continuing to grow, and you look as if you care. It's win-win. Though both wins are for you.

That's how many foundations and charities work—they're tax dodges designed to shelter as much money from taxes as possible on behalf of people who lecture the American people on the need for higher taxes and more federal spending on social programs.

Did you think the Hollywood types cut checks to the IRS for 40 percent of their earnings? Hell, no, that's for other people to do. Private planes to events where a celebrity can lecture everyone else on their need to reduce their carbon footprint don't stock themselves with nineteen-year-old Victoria's Secret models for nothing. That shit costs money.

Take, for example, the charity set up by the singer Wyclef Jean. Called Yéle Haiti Foundation, Jean's charity saw a major influx of money after an earthquake devastated Haiti, where the singer was born. Millions in donations flooded the charity, but what became of that money?

Some did help Haitians, while some appears to have helped Jean and other celebrities.

The UK *Daily Mail* reported, "The group allegedly shelled out $30,763 to fly Hollywood starlet Lindsay Lohan from New Jersey to a charity event in Chicago that raised $66,000." Additionally, "Yele spent nearly $58,000 on private jets to fly actor Matt Damon and Jean's other celebrity friends to Haiti," because flying commercial is for suckers, apparently.[2]

A forensic audit of the charity "considered it appropriate, though, for the charity to pay Mr. Jean $100,000 to perform at a Yéle fundraiser in Monaco because that was his market rate. It also found it acceptable for Yéle to spend $125,114 on travel and other matters related to a '60 Minutes' report on 'Wyclef's mission to help the people of Haiti and his personal success story' because it appeared to have heightened awareness of Yéle.'"[3]

So he was paid $100,000 by his own charity to perform at a fund-raiser for it.

Leonardo DiCaprio's charity, the Leonardo DiCaprio Foundation (LDF), came under media scrutiny when the *Hollywood Reporter* reported its ties to a Malaysian billionaire accused of embezzling billions from a sovereign wealth fund.[4]

Though the LDF has both raised millions and given millions in grants, it is also known for events such as a birthday party fundraiser for DiCaprio thrown in Saint-Tropez that attracted the actor's friends and a lot of models.[5]

As far as what the LDF does with its money, it's difficult to know. "Due to its unorthodox structure, the LDF is not obligated to disclose any specifics about its donations and repeatedly has been critiqued in recent years by Inside Philanthropy for its opacity as a prominent celebrity charity," the *Hollywood Reporter* found.[6]

It may all be on the up-and-up, but its gatekeepers have made it difficult to know. The report concluded:

That one of the most powerful figures in Hollywood—whom United Nations Secretary-General Ban Ki-moon in 2014 des-

ignated as a U.N. Messenger of Peace, with a special focus on climate change—has been sainted by his professional and social circles for his globe-trotting do-gooding may have permitted him to operate with comparatively little scrutiny so far. Notes Daniel Borochoff, president of Chicago-based CharityWatch: "[LDF's] structure allows them to shirk accountability. They aren't obligated to tell you, as a donor, anything. [DiCaprio's] able to fundraise with one because he's such a huge international celebrity. If you were an unknown, it would be a lot harder because people would quickly start asking questions."[7]

Forbes reported that singer and actor Justin Timberlake's charity "spent $146,000 on operating costs in 2006, according to tax records. This included $10,000 on travel, and $40,000 on loosely defined 'other services.' At the same time, it distributed $32,500, with $30,000 of that going to the Jane Goodall Institute."[8]

Perhaps the granddaddy of them all is a foundation that is a mixing of Hollywood and politics: the Clinton Foundation. The 2013 tax returns filed by the foundation show that, in addition to salaries and benefits for employees, it spent "$8.7 million in rent and office expenses; $9.2 million on 'conferences, conventions and meetings'; $8 million on fund-raising; and nearly $8.5 million on travel. None of the Clintons are on the payroll, but they do enjoy first-class flights paid for by the foundation."[9]

Charity Navigator, a nonprofit that monitors and rates charities for their effectiveness and how they handle and disburse their money, put the Clinton Foundation on its "watch list" in 2015. In the wake of the watch list story and in the heat of the 2016 election, the foundation scrambled to make changes to get into the organization's good graces.[10]

After cold, hard cash, hypocrisy is the currency in liberal politics and Hollywood. Okay, maybe cocaine and heroin first, then hypocrisy, but the point still holds.

Alec Baldwin can call a photographer a "cock-sucking faggot," but he's still a liberal in good standing because he's a progressive.[11]

Yes, he did lose his late-night show on MSNBC, but no one had noticed it was on in the first place. But Mel Gibson calls one female cop "sugar tits," and his cameo in *The Hangover 2* gets canceled.[12]

Hollywood is a place where what you believe matters. You don't have to know anything about the issues; as long as you're on the left side of them, it's all good.

And those issues not only permeate which fund-raisers you have to be seen at but the business itself.

Hollywood is about making money, but the people there also love to think they're making a difference at the same time. While they'll drop $200 million to make *Guardians of the Galaxy Volume 2*,[13] they'll also toss $1.5 million on a movie such as *Moonlight*.[14]

Moonlight, "A chronicle of the childhood, adolescence and burgeoning adulthood of a young, African-American, gay man growing up in a rough neighborhood of Miami,"[15] was the perfect Oscar bait, and it won Best Picture in 2017.

Moonlight was a rare example of a message movie that not only made waves during award season, it actually made money. But making money is important only for movies that aren't "important."

In an industry known for its love of blockbusters and its love of self, when it comes to "message movies" it showers them with awards and ignores whether they made any money or not. The agenda trumps the business, for likely the only time.

Since 2010, sixty-two movies have been nominated for Best Picture. Of those, only five were among the top ten grossing pictures of the year, and only twenty-three had a total box office return greater than $100 million. Only two winners, *Argo* and *The King's Speech*, earned more than $100 million.

Success with the general population isn't just not the key to success to winning a Best Picture Oscar, it appears to be the kiss of death. More accurately, what Hollywood thinks of as good and what everyone else thinks of as good are light-years apart. Being an entertaining movie loved by audiences isn't nearly as important as having an agenda. Actually, having a left-wing agenda.

Moonlight dealt with racism, abuse, and gay issues; not exactly a popcorn movie.

The 2015 Best Picture winner was *Spotlight*, the story of how child-molesting Catholic priests were finally exposed after decades of protection by the Church. Not exactly a date movie.

In 2013, the winner was *12 Years a Slave*, the awful true story of how Solomon Northup, a free black man, was abducted and forced into slavery. Though he eventually regained his freedom, it's a depressing story.

Other winners weren't left-wing, but many of the nominees were. Because Hollywood is willing to set money on fire only for the liberal agenda. Well, the liberal agenda and cocaine and heroin. And probably hookers, too, but that's it. How else could you explain Sandra Bullock signing on to star in a movie about former Texas Democratic state senator Wendy Davis's filibuster of an abortion law?[16] Not about Davis's life but about an eleven-hour speech the media heralded because she was filibustering a bill that would've banned abortions after twenty weeks. She ran out the clock and successfully blocked the bill . . . until later that year, when the Senate reconvened and passed the bill, which was signed into law.

No one in his right mind would fund a movie about a state senator whose most memorable moment came courtesy of her footwear—pink sneakers, which were written about in every major news outlet in the country—who ultimately lost by a humiliating 59.3 percent to 38.9 percent the next year in her attempt to be elected governor. Yet they landed an Oscar winner to play the flash-in-the-liberal-pan lawmaker in a story of a rambling filibuster because of, well, the agenda.

Hollywood loves agenda movies. The public, on the other hand, does not. But Hollywood keeps making them anyway.

It is bizarre how an industry that routinely focus groups and test markets movies, and forces changes to or abandons projects based on feedback from the general public, freely spends a lot of cash on movies seemingly for the express purpose of advancing a liberal agenda item.

Was the world really waiting for a movie about the disaster on an oil rig and therefore the dangers of oil drilling itself? If the box office numbers are any indication, it was not.

The movie *Deepwater Horizon* had a production budget of $110 million, which does not include the cost of marketing the movie. The worldwide take for it was only $122 million.[17]

You'd think every movie was produced for the sole purpose of making a profit, but you'd be wrong. Profit is clearly a motivation; you can't churn out movie after movie if they don't make any money because you'll eventually run out of money. But the message, in some cases, is just as important.

The company that produced *Deepwater Horizon* is a company called Participant Media, and it has an agenda.

Founded in 2004 by Jeffrey Skoll, the former president of eBay, Participant's business model was more of an activist model. When launched, Participant planned "to focus on projects that are both commercially viable and socially relevant." At the time, Skoll told *Variety* that his management team "will lead Participant in finding socially relevant projects with broad commercial appeal—stories like 'Erin Brockovich,' 'Gandhi' or 'Schindler's List,' which highlight these battles against injustices and bridge the gulf between 'haves' and 'have-nots.'"[18]

Skoll has a net worth of $4.2 billion, so if his movies didn't return a fortune on his investment, well, he already had a fortune to fall back on.

Participant, which describes itself on its website as "the leading media company dedicated to entertainment that inspires and compels social change," has produced dozens of films that appear to have the express purpose of changing people's minds on various political subjects. It has produced many documentaries pushing global warming theory, including *Climate of Change, An Inconve-*

nient Truth, An Inconvenient Sequel, Last Call at the Oasis, and *Merchants of Doubt.*

It also produced the documentary *99%: The Occupy Wall Street Collaborative Film* about the radical left-wing protests in 2011 that produced a lot of violence, filth, and sexual assaults on female participants. "The film situates Occupy within the recent emergence of decentralized resistance movements that are challenging the top-down structures of corporate and governmental hierarchy," according to Participant's description of the film.[19] Not focused on were the aforementioned violence, filth, and sexual assaults.

It has produced the anti–Second Amendment *American Gun,* which is described as "a powerful series of interwoven storylines that bring to light how the proliferation of guns in America dramatically affect and shape the everyday lives of its citizens."[20]

It made the anti–George W. Bush movie *Fair Game,* which perpetuates the myth that CIA employee Valerie Plame was a covert operative whose career was destroyed by a vindictive White House when her husband refused to back up the administration's plans for war in Iraq. Participant's website explains its "social action campaign" for the movie as an attempt to "explore the issues of nuclear nonproliferation and emphasize the importance of the participation of women in politics. Through strategic local events, and a two-day summit on lobbying and educating on the nuclear issue, the campaign will mobilize women from all over the country to take the lead in advocating for Senate ratification of the New START treaty."[21]

It has also produced several movies extolling the virtues of journalism. Films such as *The Fifth Estate,* a flattering look at WikiLeaks founder Julian Assange; *Good Night, and Good Luck,* which lionizes Edward R. Murrow for standing against the hunt for communists in the US government; *Page One,* a documentary about the *New York Times;* and *Spotlight,* about the reporting that exposed the Catholic Church's complicity in covering up child molestation by priests.

It also produced *Charlie Wilson's War*, which sought to minimize President Ronald Reagan's role in defeating communism, as well as the antifracking flop *Promised Land*, which had a production budget of $15 million,[22] and starred Matt Damon, and took in only $8 million worldwide.[23]

No liberal cause is off limits, and most of the company's movies include a digital campaign with websites and activist handbooks to further push its messages.

The audience thinks they're going to a movie to be entertained for ninety minutes, but they're really being subtly manipulated, to one degree or another.

Most of Participant's movies are not box office gold, as its reach is usually limited to people who are already convinced. Preaching to the choir has its place and its market, but it's not a fast track to getting rich. Luckily for the company, it's already rich, so tossing away $15 million on a bad Matt Damon movie is like not reaching under the couch cushions to dig out the change you heard fall out of your pockets.

But the audience, particularly the unsuspecting people who eventually see the movie on cable or Netflix, are infected with propaganda without knowing it. Then, should whatever the topic is come up in conversation with friends, they're armed with half-truths or outright lies to spread as fact because they saw them in a movie or documentary.

Propaganda spreads like a cold on a plane, without anyone noticing at the time. It's a brilliant strategy, if completely deceptive.

Participant isn't alone. When George W. Bush was elected president in 2000, movies and TV shows mocking a sitting president were extremely rare, outside of shows such as *Saturday Night Live* and late-night talk shows.

And for a short while after the September 11, 2001, terrorist attacks, there was a lull in the "Bush is a moron" commentary and pop culture references. But it didn't hold.

Hollywood went full-bore antiwar after a while, producing a string of high-profile box office flops in an attempt to damage Bush's re-election chances in 2004.

The highest-profile attempt, however, was not a flop. Michael Moore's *Fahrenheit 9/11* made Moore a fortune, but it didn't make him an electoral force. Bush easily won reelection.

Hollywood pressed on, producing antiwar movies about the Iraq and Afghanistan wars while the wars were still raging. And each did worse than the last one.

In one year, 2007, Hollywood produced ten antiwar movies that flopped, including:

Grace Is Gone, which cost $2 million to produce[24] and took in only $50,000 domestically, $1 million worldwide[25]

Lions for Lambs, which cost $35 million to produce[26] and took in only $15 million domestically, $63 million worldwide[27]

In the Valley of Elah, which cost $23 million to produce[28] and took in only $6 million domestically, $29 million worldwide[29]

Redacted, which cost $5 million to produce[30] and took in only $65,000 domestically, $716,000 worldwide[31]

Rendition, which cost $27 million to produce[32] and took in only $9 million domestically, $27 million worldwide[33]

Huge flops, all of them, yet they were cranked out because they sent a message liberal Hollywood wanted to send: that George W. Bush was evil.

As soon as George W. Bush was sworn into office, Hollywood came running to get him. In 2001, Comedy Central produced *That's My Bush!* at a cost of $700,000 per episode. It was canceled after only eight episodes because "the cost per ratings point was just too expensive."[34]

Although producers always want to make a difference, they also sometimes need to make a profit.

But "on the nose" TV shows and movies are not the only ways in which Hollywood seeks to influence people's lives and thoughts.

Liberals are like demographically awakened bouncers at a club worried about going over capacity and being fined for violating the fire code. They stand at the door of everything with a counter, clicking up the numbers each time someone of any group enters. And they are absolutely ruled by how many of each flavor of human being is inside.

Should the number of some type of person fall under whatever they determine the lowest acceptable number for that type of person, outrage is fomented.

In 2016, all twenty of the acting nominees for Oscars were white people. That caused outrage among the liberal Hollywood set and spawned the social media campaign #OscarsSoWhite. Missing from the outrage was any argument about who should have been nominated over the people who were nominated; there was just outrage that nonwhite people weren't nominated.

But the nominations are made by Hollywood itself, which is, again, a very liberal group of people. So where was the racism?

There wasn't any, of course, but that didn't stop the Academy of Motion Picture Arts and Sciences from "addressing the problem." Not the problem of bad movies being made or agenda-driven pap being foisted on the public or even the lack of good movies with predominantly minority casts being produced—nope. Membership in the Academy itself was to be altered.

Its goal was "doubling the number of women and minorities" in the "hopes that women will compose 48% and diverse groups more than 14% of the total membership."[35]

There was no commitment to making better movies for or offering better parts to minorities, just getting more voting members into the Academy. And if the problem was a lack of minority nominees, why focus on increasing the number of women? They have their own categories and aren't "underrepresented" in nominations.

We've seen over and over again that entertainment is more successful when it's good than when it's politically driven. Some viewers may say they want political barriers broken down, but when no one is looking, they binge on *Cupcake Wars* and *Real Housewives*.

Though it still produces "white shows" and "black shows," Hollywood has been in the forefront of gay rights. As with the race issue, most Americans couldn't give a damn about whether a character on TV is gay or not. They just want to be left alone to live their lives without being beaten about the head with a political agenda. But the beaters of the heads aren't interested in what people want; they have an agenda.

When not producing antimilitary or anti-Republican propaganda, they are producing pro-gay propaganda. There's nothing wrong with it, they can produce whatever they want to, but there isn't an audience for being politically preached to.

Will and Grace, for example, wasn't a hit show because it featured gay characters, it was a hit show that happened to feature gay characters. Since that time there has been a major upswing in the number of "gay-themed" TV shows and movies, but they haven't been hits and quickly went away. The ones such as *Modern Family* are clever, well-written shows that happen to have gay characters; the ones such as *The New Normal* were produced to be about gay characters and quickly failed. The failed shows forgot, or ignored, the most important aspect of any show or product: it must be good.

Doubt, a drama on CBS that lasted only two episodes, was showered with praise for being "groundbreaking" because it cast a transgender woman, Laverne Cox, known for her work in a supporting role on *Orange Is the New Black*, as a transgender woman on the show. It was during the height of the transgender bathroom debates across the country, so the topic was very hot with liberals.

Hollywood saw an opportunity for some publicity and cast Cox, who is at best an average actor, and was showered with praise for the move,[36] if not the show. Audiences weren't interested, with ratings falling in half from the first episode to the second, from an already bad 0.8 in the coveted 18-to-49 demographic to an abysmal 0.4.[37] People didn't tune in for the novelty, and those who did tune in quickly tuned out because the show, though the recipient of a lot of publicity, was bad.

Hollywood is often guilty of jumping on the bandwagon of whatever the "hot" progressive political issue of the day is, but it rarely translates to success.

CBS was predictably slammed for the timing of the cancellation. "Neither will those who may benefit from seeing a smart, successful trans woman on television. As celebrities, public figures, and businesses proclaimed 'protect trans kids' this week, a tone-deaf CBS pulled a show that might help protect them. Ratings aside, there is no doubt the move is a missed opportunity to be on the right side of history," declared *The Advocate*.[38]

Cox, however, took her rolling wave of positive press to ABC as she was immediately cast in a new drama called *The Trustee*. While the series was written up extensively in nearly every entertainment news outlet for the act of having cast Cox, the show must not have been that good, because it didn't make it past the pilot stage.[39] Whether or not it was any good or would be successful didn't really matter; it was sure to get a lot of publicity either way.[40]

That seems to be the pattern for the denizens of Hollywood: to produce moneymakers the general public actually wants to see so it can use some of the profits it doesn't spend on hookers and blow to churn out unpopular products so it can be seen as caring.

Each failure is presented not as a failure to produce a good product but as evidence that the American people "aren't ready" for whatever they aren't interested in or that there is some sort of -phobia or -ism that is at the very root of our country, especially among conservatives.

Nothing could be farther from the truth. Conservatives, like most Americans, aren't interested in being preached to in their entertainment. Someone who labels himself or herself a "conservative" something or other is not automatically granted success by conservatives. He or she actually has to be good.

In 2012, the band Madison Rising billed itself as a "conservative rock band," even showing up to the largest annual conference for conservatives in the country, the Conservative Political Action Conference (CPAC). It was exposed to more than 10,000 attendees, as well as millions more people when it appeared on Fox News.

None of that translated into success for the band because . . . it sucked.

Its members wrote songs about conservative causes and issues, but they were shitty songs. They forgot the first rule of anything that must attract an audience: it has to be good.

Liberals will accept crap from their ideological soul mates, even shower it with praise such as "they speak truth to power" while preaching to the choir. How else to explain the continued employment of people such as the unfunny comics Tig Notaro, Chelsea Handler, and Chris Gethard? People in the rest of the country just want to be entertained. If they want to be preached to, they can go to church or their in-laws' house.

None of this will stop Hollywood from producing politically biased garbage people don't want to see so it can congratulate itself on being "awakened." None of it will stop the faux outrage over perceived slights while actual ones go unnoticed.

The only thing that will change is the year on the fat checks they write to each other.

I hope you weren't surprised when *The President Show* premiered on Comedy Central, starring a Donald Trump impersonator mocking the forty-fifth president and the half of the country who voted for him.[41] Or by the fact that the 2017 MTV Video Music Awards got its lowest ratings ever[42] because it was turned into a three-hour-long Republican-bashing festival by drunk and high millionaires complaining about how unfair everything in the country has become in eight short months.[43]

The problem is not just that the entertainment industry is a bastion of liberalism, it's that it is a cult of liberalism. At one point it was acceptable to keep your political opinions to yourself; witness the old adage that you don't discuss politics or religion over dinner. Not anymore.

Perhaps the most popular singer/actress (though she's much more popular and successful as a singer) is Taylor Swift. Her sugary and sour songs about love and heartbreak have sold untold millions to teenagers, starting when she was a teenager.

But just entertaining people isn't good enough for liberals, who believe that everyone is either with them or against them. And if you have an audience, you absolutely must be with them.

"Taylor Swift's Silence on Politics Fuels Speculation That She Secretly Voted for Trump" read a headline in the New York *Daily News* because that's news, right?

The piece, taken from an interview of a friend of hers by Yahoo! News, begins, "Taylor Swift has remained notoriously tight-lipped on her political leanings, but her friend and back-up dancer Todrick Hall says that anyone who takes her silence as evidence she voted for Donald Trump is making a 'huge assumption.'"[44]

Of course, the entire story was a "huge assumption" and not news in any way, shape, or form, but that didn't stop a major metropolitan newspaper from making it such and splashing it across its pages.

The idea that someone might have an opinion different from theirs—or worse, might not have an opinion at all—is too much for devoted leftists to bear.

Swift faced criticism throughout the election season for remaining mum and not following in the footsteps of her fellow pop stars, who expressed their support for Hillary Clinton and disdain for Donald Trump. Her sole foray into the world of politics was an apolitical Instagram post on election day, telling her followers to "go out and VOTE." But according to Hall, who has been friends with the "Look What You Made Me Do" singer for years, nothing about

Swift leads him to believe that she's set on making America great again.[45]

The horror.

As if they were a kicked beehive, the media swarmed around the idea that someone in the entertainment industry might not despise a Republican president.

Here's a sampling of some of the headlines this one story led to:

Entertainment Weekly: "Todrick Hall Defends Taylor Swift Against 'Huge Assumption' She Voted for Trump"

Huffington Post: "Taylor Swift's Close Friend Todrick Hall Defends Her Election Silence"

Teen Vogue: "Todrick Hall Addressed Rumors That Taylor Swift Voted for Trump"

It could be that Swift isn't a rabid left-winger, or it could be that she's simply too busy living her life to bother. Whatever the case, there are people on her case because they, not the world, need to know.

That wasn't the first time witch-hunters set out after Swift's political scalp. During the 2016 election they were after her, too.

The Daily Beast, for example, speculated wildly that Swift could be a Trump supporter:

Here's some more irony for you: Despite her stated support for women's causes, Swift has yet to publicly endorse Hillary Clinton's presidential campaign. As two white feminists with more than a handful of racial blind spots between them, Swift and Clinton seem like a match made in second wave feminist heaven.[46]

The Beast praised Katy Perry for going all-in for Hillary:

In contrast, Katy Perry has proven herself to be very much With Her. Back when hip stars were feeling the Bern, Perry remained fire-resistant, campaigning alongside Clinton in a series of increasingly patriotic outfits. When Hillary clinched the Democratic nomination in June, Perry was among the first celebs to congratulate her, tweeting, "A lot of little girls are in bed right now dreaming for the first time, without limits." That's exactly the sort of vaguely political, girl power sentiment that we've come to expect from Taylor Swift's PR team.[47]

Then, in a rage-fueled speculation spiral, the piece delved into conspiracy theories about how one of Swift's friends, the model Karlie Kloss, was dating the brother of Donald Trump's son-in-law: "It's hard to say if Kloss's relationship with the other Kushner brother has anything to do with Swift's reticence to enter the political fray. But if that is the case, it's pretty unfortunate."[48]

It could just be that Swift doesn't care, but in Hollywood you're not allowed not to care; you have to care and in a very specific way.

None of the media obsession with Swift's lack of politics appears to have put a dent in her popularity. Her "Look What You Made Me Do" video broke YouTube's record for most-watched video on its debut day.[49]

Still, because she refused to get into line with the political Left, BuzzFeed "News" smeared her for her lack of outspoken politics, saying her image was "willowy, blonde, and aggressively white. Perhaps, in an awkward corner close by, are the white supremacist fans who've claimed her as a figurehead. In any blank space, you'll find her political silence and her idiosyncratic ways of communicating with the public."[50]

Marie Claire magazine declared Swift's declining to go political as one of the things she "should have addressed" on her album *Reputation*. "Fall of 2016 saw a slew of celebrities become outspokenly involved in the political process, **as they should have**," the magazine wrote (emphasis added).[51]

But, as it noted, even though Swift posted a picture of herself standing in line wearing a sweater at her polling place, *some people interpreted her sweater as confirmation that she was casting a vote for Hillary Clinton (see this post by Lena Dunham for explanation of the theory), but was it really enough? Taylor is not required to be vocal about her politics (obviously, every American has the right to keep their vote private), but it's also fair to side-eye and question her decision to remain silent—and said silence certainly contributed to her rep.*[52]

Because she hasn't condemned or endorsed any politician or cause (read: liberal politician or cause), everything about the singer is fair game to the liberal media. "Taylor was on the receiving end of criticism for being something of a poster child for white feminism. For years, feminist critiques of Taylor have been mounting, taking aim at everything from her music videos to her mostly tall/white/thin girl squad."[53] There have been no speculator pieces attacking the race of the "squads" of any other pop singers, no deep dives into the racial makeup of Beyoncé's crew or Fink's inner circle. Everyone knows where those two stand politically—firmly on the Left—so whatever they do is just fine. Swift, on the other hand, is an implied racist because, well, just because.

Haters gonna hate, hate, hate, hate . . .

Unlike Swift, celebrities in good political standing continue to churn out projects designed to portray the United States as a bedsheet sale away from turning into a Klan rally, even though estimates by left-wing groups themselves put the total of KKK members in the country around 6,500.[54]

One of Hollywood's favorite topics is movies about how racist the country is. They don't attract audiences, but maybe they help with the liberal guilt of nominating so many white people for Oscars. It's tough to know for sure since the people who make them live in gated communities, so they aren't available for questioning.

George Clooney, who has a longer history of liberal activism than he does of making movies large audiences want to see, was inspired by the 2016 election to make a movie about how racist everything is called: *Suburbicon*.

While looking for a project to make, he said he "was watching a lot of speeches on the campaign trail about building fences and scapegoating minorities and I started looking around at other times in our history when we've unfortunately fallen back into these things."[55] He based the idea he ultimately decided to make on an incident from 1957, because 1957 is just like 2017 to a liberal.

The movie stars Matt Damon as a man who goes on a killing spree after his wife is murdered, but all the mayhem he causes is blamed on a black family that moved into the neighborhood because that's what happens in the minds of liberals. "It's kind of the definition of white privilege when you're riding around your neighborhood on a bicycle covered in blood murdering people and the African American family is getting blamed for it," Damon said. He continued, "We couldn't have predicted obviously when we were filming these race riots, that we would have something like Charlottesville. It does speak to the fact that these issues have not and are not going away until there's an honest reckoning in our country."[56]

Two of the richest actors in Hollywood said the country was racist and blamed it on the fact that Donald Trump succeeded Barack Obama, a black man twice elected president, which is weird for a country in which Damon says there hasn't been "an honest reckoning" on race and liberals continually say was founded on white supremacy. But somehow just a few months of Trump in the White House has boiled to the surface something everyone allegedly ignored for decades.

The movie, by the way, bombed.

Of course racism still exists. Not only are there 330 million people in the country, there are 7 billion people on the planet, and math dictates that there be hundreds of millions of morons out there. Racism will always exist, just as there will always be people who believe Bigfoot is real and the moon landing was faked. But it's not prevalent, dominant, or even very common. You'd never know that, though, if you lived in the heads of multimillionaire actors.

It's not that Hollywood actors can't learn, they just don't want to. And they don't have to. There's too much money in lecturing the public about their need to lower their carbon footprint from a Gulfstream jet on the way to a warehouse-sized mansion in Ibiza or about the dangers of income inequality from the safety of their mansions.

To say they're hypocrites is to give a bad name to parents with a Marlboro hanging out of their mouths while lecturing their kids about the dangers of smoking. No, Hollywood has its own level of duplicity. It not only does its preaching overtly, it has mastered the covert, too.

Even ABC's reboot of *Roseanne* will have a nine-year-old "gender creative" grandson, because why not?[57] Everything is political, even rehashed sitcoms.

On why the world needed a return of a once popular show about a blue-collar family, star Sara Gilbert said, "That's a voice that's not been spoken for enough in this country and we feel hopefully that we can be a uniting force in that way."[58] Because who knows what working-class Americans need more than rich, pampered Hollywood types?

You should take the popcorn Hollywood dishes out not only with a grain of salt but with a salt lick. Because you're being manipulated.

Chapter 12

Famous for Being Infamous

Lindsey Stone had a job at a nonprofit in Massachusetts and was sent to Washington, DC, for work. While visiting Arlington National Cemetery, she posed for a joke picture near the Tomb of the Unknown Soldier, next to a sign reading SILENCE AND RESPECT. Stone was flipping her middle finger while posing as if she were yelling. She was not, it was just for the picture, but none of that mattered when the picture was discovered on her Facebook page.

"Outrage After Woman Flashes Middle Finger at Arlington National Cemetery and Posts Photo to Facebook to Brag About It" declared the headline in the UK *Daily Mail*.[1] The "outrage" it was referencing was limited to a few people on Facebook until the *Mail*'s story came out.

Huffington Post piled on with "Lindsey Stone, Plymouth Woman, Takes Photo at Arlington National Cemetery, Causes Facebook Fury."[2]

She apologized, her mother told the press. "She is very, very sorry for what she did, and she never meant it to be disrespectful to anybody." Her father had to defend her, saying, "I don't think she was reacting to the site [Arlington Cemetery], she was reacting to the sign." He added, "I'm appalled myself."[3]

Stone was placed on unpaid leave by her employer, Living Independently Forever (LIFE), over the joke picture.[4]

Soon after, and unsurprisingly, she was fired, as was the co-worker who had taken the picture. The media attention and social media outrage became so deafening that her employer let her go.

Stone became the target of death and rape threats and "refused to leave the house" for a year.[5]

The lesson? You're allowed to have only approved fun; cross an invisible line, and it's game on.

A movie star can check into rehab, hire a PR team, and set up fluffy interviews with a complicit media more interested in access than journalism. But if a "real person" steps over that ever-changing line, well, hell hath no fury than a clickbait liberal media bored.

Celebrities used to be the objects of admiration for their accomplishments and talents; now talent no longer matters.

Vladimir Lenin spoke of "useful idiots," people duped into believing communist propaganda who spread Russia's message around the world without question. Many of those idiots had press credentials.

Though there are still many idiots in public life and in the media, they're using their influence to elevate other idiots to celebrity status to influence the culture, advance their politics, pass time, and manipulate the masses. Celebrity ain't what it used to be; television is full of shows with people who are desperate for attention and looking for the shortest, easiest path to get there.

Fame is the real societal opiate, our true heroin, and we're all addicted to it. And the media are the biggest dealers on the block. Sometimes they use their power to advance a liberal political agenda or champion someone they'd otherwise ignore because they're on the "right side" of a cause; other times they destroy out of boredom or worse. The ability to elevate or obliterate is a prominent part of what journalism has become, making the modern press a mockery of what it once was and what it still claims to be.

The opinions of celebrities, both real and manufactured, are as valid as your average "man on the street" interview, only they get attention.

When the actress Jennifer Lawrence implied that the hurricanes of 2017 were "Mother Nature's rage, or wrath" for the United States' electing Donald Trump president, she was roundly mocked. But she was also protected.

The "fact-checking" website Snopes declared the accusation against her to be "false."[6] Here is the transcript of the exchange; judge for yourself:

INTERVIEWER: When the director was asked about the film, why it was so dark, he said, "It's a mad time to be alive." And there's certainly a sort of end-of-days feeling about it. For many people in America who would say perhaps it's truer there at the moment than anywhere else. I mean what are your thoughts about the changes that have happened in your own country over the last year or so?

LAWRENCE: It's scary, you know, it's this new language that's forming. I don't even recognize it. It's also scary to know— it's been proven through science that human activity—that climate change is due to human activity and we continue to ignore it and the only voice that we really have is through voting. Um, so . . .

INTERVIEWER: And you have voted . . .

LAWRENCE: And we voted, and it was really startling. You know, you're watching these hurricanes now, and it's really— it's hard, especially while promoting this movie not to feel Mother Nature's rage, or wrath.

Did Jennifer Lawrence say, "These hurricanes are all the fault of Donald Trump"? Clearly not. Did she imply that they were "Mother Nature's rage, or wrath" for the voters having elected him? Of course she did, it's right there.

Granted, the statement is muddled in a pile of incoherent rambling and hippie-speak, but it's there.

In a much more articulate statement, Lawrence (probably her publicist because it is coherent) declared her innocence: "My remarks were taken grossly out of context. Obviously I never claimed that President Trump was responsible for these tragic hurricanes. That is a silly and preposterous headline that is unfortunate, because it detracts from the millions of lives that are being impacted by these devastating storms and the recent earthquake."[7]

An exhaustive search of the Internet could find no record of Lawrence studying meteorology or weather or even studying beyond high school, so why was she asked anything political in the first place? Because she, like most celebrities, is reliably liberal. And journalists are keen to introduce politics into everything, even an interview with an actress publicizing a movie.

More important, she knows that raging against climate change these days is as safe as helping puppies and orphans. She knows that everyone around her will applaud—or be forced to applaud—what used to be a pretty liberal opinion.

You can see the transformation in the career of Michael Moore, who went from rabble-rousing outsider to feted genius.

Take his publicity stunt after a performance of his Broadway show to protest Trump. Moore and special guest Mark Ruffalo told their audience "that 200 of them would be driven the few blocks uptown on double-decker buses to Trump Tower, where President Donald Trump is staying during his brief visit (Moore encouraged the rest of the audience to walk over as well). The demonstration—which doubled as a candlelight vigil for Charlottesville, Va., victim Heather Heyer—followed the rally that took place the day before, when Trump first arrived in NYC."[8]

Heyer had been killed a few days earlier as she participated in a protest against white nationalists in Charlottesville when one of the opponents drove his car into a crowd.

There was no criticism of the duo for doubling up their protest with a vigil for Heyer sort of as an addendum or afterthought. The event was simply covered.

Moore has been a media darling since his first "documentary," *Roger & Me*, about his attempt to get answers from Roger Smith, then the CEO of General Motors, about the company's impact on

Flint, Michigan. Throughout the movie Moore is seen attempting to talk with Smith but being thwarted by a CEO indifferent about the plight of the struggling city.

Years later, a documentary about Moore called *Manufacturing Dissent* claimed:

> *We started to discover things about his films that we never knew, the most startling being that Moore had got rather more access to Roger Smith than he let on in* Roger & Me.
>
> *We spoke to a man called Jim Musselman, a former activist for Nader, who was organizing the community of Flint to fight back against General Motors, and claims that Moore did question Smith for 15 minutes during a General Motors expo at the Waldorf Astoria in New York.*
>
> *"He sat there and answered questions for about 10 or 15 minutes," said Musselman, who told us that he had watched the footage himself, in the* Roger & Me *edit suite. "It was great footage because it was Smith answering questions one-on-one from Michael."*
>
> *Then I found an article from a 1990 issue of* Premiere *magazine in which several people, including Nader, assert that Moore had also filmed an exchange with Smith at a 1987 General Motors shareholders' meeting; that was reportedly left out of the film, too.*[9]

Moore denied the allegation, obviously, because it would have made the entire reason he's a celebrity in the first place a fraud.[10]

But Moore really kind of is a fraud. He's a vocal union supporter but refused to hire a union stagehand crew to work on his movie *Capitalism: A Love Story.*[11] In addition, the "champion of the little guy" did not provide medical insurance to those nonunion employees.[12]

In spite of the fact that Moore has carefully constructed a celebrity image of being a hero of the workers, the reality doesn't always mesh with that image. When he had his *TV Nation* TV show, "His employees expected him to be the ideal boss—after all, he was the defender of the little guy," because that was his public image.[13] Only that didn't turn out to be the case.

After a time on his show, Moore started to change. "Little by little, he began to alienate people. He disliked sharing credit with his writers. He would often come in late. He didn't yell at people: if someone said something he didn't like, he wouldn't argue; he would simply not invite that person to the next meeting, or the person would be fired," the *New Yorker* reported.[14]

Demonstrating hypocrisy that would've been fatal to a nonliberal or noncelebrity, Moore once again showed his antiunion vein—when it could impact his bottom line:

> *One day during production on the first season of the show, Moore called two of his writers into his office. It was, for both of them, their first job in television, and they had been hired with the title of associate producer. They were not members of the Writers' Guild, the powerful union for writers in movies and TV, and thus were not receiving health benefits, and would not qualify later for a percentage of video and rerun sales. "Michael said, 'I'm getting a lot of heat from the union to call you guys writers and pay you under the union rules,'" Eric Zicklin, one of the associate producers, says. "'I don't have the budget for that. But if they keep coming down on me that'll mean I'll only be able to afford one of you and the other one's gotta go.'"*
>
> *Moore appeared to have surmised (incorrectly) that the two writers had been appealing to the union behind his back. (Moore says that he doesn't remember this and that he insisted that "TV Nation" be a union show.) "He wanted to let us know that this would hurt us if it continued," Zicklin says. "We were scared out of our minds. It was like a theme from 'Roger & Me.'" Of course, no one would have thought twice about a meeting like that with any other boss—but this was Michael Moore.*
>
> *One by one, his employees stopped believing in the Cause. The job became just a job, and Moore became just another boss in a business that had an almost limitless tolerance for bad behavior. But, because they had once believed in him, their disappointment was painful. "I have let go of Michael," the former "TV Nation"*

*employee says, in the shakily resolute tone of a reforming alcoholic.
"I have not seen one of his products, his movies, his TV shows, his
books. I'm sure they're all good. I'm sure they're spreading the message and enraging all the right people. But I can't accept him as
a political person. I can't buy into this thing of Michael Moore is
on your side—it's like trying to believe that Justin Timberlake is a
soulful guy. It's a media product: he's just selling me something.*[15]

Being a hypocritical jackass has its benefits. And being a celebrity—a celebrity with the correct politics—has insulated Moore, and
all the other Moores out there who are still protected, from charges
of hypocrisy.

The late film critic Roger Ebert, himself a dedicated leftist, wrote
a column defending Moore from charges of other manipulations
in *Roger & Me.*

About the allegations that Moore took liberties with the facts in
his movie, Ebert wrote, "Did I care? No. Was I offended at this manipulation of reality, this twisting of the facts to suit Moore's the-
sis? No. I thought it was obvious what he was doing. He was taking
the liberties that satirists and ironists have taken with material for
generations, and he was making his point with sarcasm and deft
timing."[16]

Ebert's article was entitled "Attacks on 'Roger & Me' Completely
Miss the Point of the Film." The problem wasn't that Moore was
creative with facts, it's that the film was sold as a documentary.
Documentaries, at least at the time, filmed or "documented" things
that happened without making judgments about them.

The idea that a documentarian would engage in "manipulation
of reality" and take "liberties" with the truth is the antithesis of
what a documentarian is supposed to do. Yet here was Ebert, the
preeminent film critic of his time, absolving Moore as though he
were the pope blessing the crowd in St. Peter's Square.

Why would Ebert, a film lover, absolve Moore of his deception?
Because he liked the movie. More important, he agreed with the
message of the movie. "I liked it because it felt like Michael Moore

was getting away with something. He was thumbing his nose at GM, he was taking cheap shots, he knew it, we knew it, and it was about time," he wrote.[17]

One fat white man lets another off the hook for betraying the genre that made him. Talk about white privilege.

But politics has always had a weird way of causing people to look the other way when it helps their team. They just don't normally, and so blatantly, admit it in public.

The "everyman" Moore still presents himself as just a schlub from Michigan, a blue-collar guy who's fighting for the little guy. But the only thing little about Moore is his final helping at the Old Country Buffet when the staff is trying to close and the only food left out is vegetables.

Fighting for the little guy, for the poor, has been very good to Moore. When he and his wife divorced, it was revealed that he had a net worth of $50 million.[18] Who knew helping the poor was so profitable?

———————————

While the media spotlight is warmly shone on liberals who earn it and those who simply seek it through reality shows or making spectacles of themselves, it is sometimes focused on those who do not seek it but simply find themselves on the business end of a slow news day and ambitious liberal reporters looking to score a scalp out of boredom.

Does the name Justine Sacco ring a bell? For a few days in 2013, she was at the center of the biggest story in the world. It wasn't an important story, it wasn't really a story at all, but young, progressive journalists started nibbling on a social media post on a slow news day and a feeding frenzy ensued. When it was done, her life was in tatters.

Sacco's crime? An attempted joke on Twitter. A bad joke, a dumb joke, an offensive joke, but a joke nonetheless. And even if it wasn't a joke, even if she was serious, who cares? She was an anonymous nobody, what does it matter if she said something people found offensive? If a tree falls over in the woods after a Polack joke and no one is around to be offended by it, was it really offensive?

So what was Justine's joke? On her Twitter page, where she had only 170 followers, she wrote, "Going to Africa. Hope I don't get AIDS. Just kidding. I'm white!"

It was dumb, someone could undoubtedly easily be offended by it, and if you didn't know she was trying to make a stupid joke, you could see how it would be seen as racist. But honestly, who gives a shit?

She was about to board a flight from London to South Africa, and the flight had no Wi-Fi. During the eleven-hour trip, she had no idea that her twelve words had become an obsession that would ultimately cost her her job as, ironically, a public relations executive, and send her life into turmoil.

By the time she landed, she'd been written up by nearly every news outlet in the Western world. The firing by her employer, InterActiveCorp (IAC), of this woman, who had been completely anonymous less than a half day earlier, was splashed everywhere.

CNN: "The 'tweet heard round the world' was followed by the sound of a slamming door Saturday. Media company IAC has 'parted ways' with company PR executive Justine Sacco over her tweet."[19]

New York *Daily News*: "Sacco has been sacked. Justine Sacco, the New York PR executive who sparked a global firestorm for her wildly insensitive tweet on AIDS, was fired Saturday by her bosses at media conglomerate IAC."[20]

ABC News: "The communications director for the Internet giant that owns popular websites like Match.com, Dictionary .com, and Vimeo has been fired over 'hateful statements' in a tweet that came from her account. The tweet Friday from the account of Justine Sacco read: 'Going to Africa. Hope I don't get AIDS. Just kidding. I'm white!'

"InterActive Corp, Sacco's employer, issued a statement to ABC News this afternoon distancing itself from the tweet and saying the employee was fired."[21]

Variety: "IAC said it has parted ways with Justine Sacco, who had been its senior director of corporate communications, after she posted a racially loaded message Friday on Twitter joking about AIDS in Africa."[22]

The Huffington Post: "Justine Sacco's Tweet About AIDS, Africa Is the Craziest Thing You'll See Today."[23]

That is just a sampling. A search for "Justine Sacco" for just December 21, 2013, returns more than 150 separate results in multiple languages.

Imagine waking up to find the world suddenly obsessing about a lame joke you thought you'd told a few friends who follow you on Twitter.

The hashtag "#HasJustineLandedYet" trended worldwide; celebrities piled on. Lizz Winstead, a cocreator of *The Daily Show*, tweeted, "Hey Justine, Maybe Paula Deen is looking for a communications director. #HasJustineLandedYet." The actress Kerry Washington, who plays the political fixer Olivia Pope on *Scandal*, retweeted someone saying "Olivia Pope: 'Gurl, you're on your own with this one' #HasJustineLandedYet" and added an "LOL" of her own.[24]

"I cried out my body weight in the first 24 hours. It was incredibly traumatic. You don't sleep. You wake up in the middle of the night forgetting where you are," Justine recounted when she reemerged in 2015.[25]

Justine eventually got her life back together and some semblance of anonymity and landed another job after eight months of unemployment.[26] But it never should have happened. A dumb joke would normally just fall flat and be forgotten, but that dumb joke was politically incorrect and, being politically incorrect, was no longer allowed.

None other than Jerry Seinfeld, in an interview on ESPN Radio, said, "I don't play colleges, but I hear a lot of people tell me don't go near colleges—they're so PC [politically correct]."[27]

That goes double for rank amateurs on social media.

Seinfeld added, "[The younger generation] just want to use these words: 'that's racist, that's sexist, that's prejudice.' They don't even know what they're talking about."[28] That goes triple for modern journalists when it comes to slow news days and a willingness to destroy to gain Web traffic and self-satisfaction.

But the mob doesn't exist only online, sometimes it's your co-workers.

A Google engineer, James Damore, wrote a post on an internal company message board about the idea of diversity; then his life was turned upside down.

The ideas expressed in the Damore memo, as it has come to be known, was that rather than focusing exclusively on skin color and gender in corporate recruiting, Google might want to consider some ideological diversity as well. This was code for "Hey, maybe having different colors of like-minded drones doesn't really represent the full spectrum of diversity."

This line of thinking—that diversity should encompass all aspects of human existence, not just the superficial—was met with a resounding thud. More than a thud, actually; anger and even threats from coworkers ensued.[29]

Hostile coworkers weren't disciplined, however; it was Damore who was fired.

The cause? Google fired him for "perpetuating gender stereo-types" because he wrote that there might be many reasons, including some biological, for why there are more male computer engineers than female.[30]

His positing this question sent employees of the largest search engine in the world into a panic, scrambling for "safe spaces." Some employees were so upset, NPR reported, that they felt "uncomfortable going back to work."[31]

Google hastily scheduled an all-staff meeting to discuss what

Damore had written but canceled it because employees were "concerned about their safety and worried they may be 'outed' publicly for asking a question in the Town Hall," because they faced online criticism for attacking Damore.[32]

All of that was over words, words strung together not to make a threat but to express an opinion; to ask questions. But those questions were questioning liberal orthodoxy, and that is not allowed, especially from Prius-driving leftists with CELEBRATE DIVERSITY bumper stickers.

As for Damore, his treatment by the media went according to the script. This anonymous engineer was described as writing an "anti-diversity screed" and being a "hero" of the "alt-right."[33,34]

What did Damore write that was so awful? Was his post about how women need to accept that they simply can't write computer code and should kick off their shoes, get pregnant, and run back to the kitchen? Of course not.

"I value diversity and inclusion, am not denying that sexism exists, and don't endorse using stereotypes. When addressing the gap in representation in the population, we need to look at population-level differences in distributions. If we can't have an honest discussion about this, then we can never truly solve the problem," the memo began.[35]

Damore then explored different possibilities to explain why more women aren't entering the field. It was harmless questioning and cited various studies. That it became national news, a feeding frenzy described as sexist, is more a testament to media bias than an accurate recounting of anything Damore wrote.

Where he really got into trouble was here:

STOP ALIENATING CONSERVATIVES.

> Viewpoint diversity is arguably the most important type of diversity and political orientation is one of the most fundamental and significant ways in which people view things differently.

> In highly progressive environments, conservatives are a minority that feel like they need to stay in the closet to avoid open hostility. We should empower those with different ideologies to be able to express themselves.

> Alienating conservatives is both noninclusive and generally bad business because conservatives tend to be higher in conscientiousness, which is require [sic] for much of the drudgery and maintenance work characteristic of a mature company.[36]

He also recommended that the company "Confront Google's biases" and "Stop restricting programs and classes to certain genders or races" because it is alienating.[37]

Not exactly *Mein Kampf.*

Still, when Damore sued Google as part of a class action case for ideological discrimination, the lede paragraph in the NBC News story read, "A former engineer who wrote a sexist manifesto disparaging Google's efforts to close the gender gap is now suing, claiming the search giant discriminates against conservative white men."[38]

Narrative protection was in full effect.

Fame is one hell of a drug. Some people will do anything to get it; others have it thrust upon them. The "dealers" of fame are the media, and they decide who basks in its warm glow and who burns up in it. And the decision as to who falls into which category, more often than not, is based on the political agenda of the Left.

Conclusion: So What Now?

There are few professions that celebrate themselves more than journalism. It's not uncommon for offices in newsrooms across the country to be littered with plaques, trophies, certificates, and laser-etched Lucite blocks marking their "wins" in various categories of reporting. If you have a byline and haven't been declared the winner of some sort of award, you're either in the wrong profession or a conservative.

Hollywood, while being on par with journalism for self-love, has its own problems. Well, not all of them are unique to Hollywood—the men there seem to share a predilection for sexually harassing women—but the American people have lately been less interested in their product.

With journalism's popularity waning and scandals raging, journalists have never been more interested in the political opinions of "stars." While the idea of a reporter caring what they think about matters beyond what it was like to work with some other actor or director, this wading by the make-believe set has begun to impact its bottom lines. "Stars" are asked to weigh in, to speak out on everything, and fewer and fewer people want to hear it. It's a business model straight out of a Monty Python skit.

As for science, the once-pure pursuit of truth is now just reduced to yet another arrow in the left-wing quiver, a cudgel to be used to beat those who won't conform about the head and neck until they submit or are chased from the public square. The modern Left is the Catholic Church of the modern age; heresy is punishable by excommunication.

That said, the power of science and Hollywood, to be effective, must travel through the portal of journalism. And journalism . . . is dead.

Okay, maybe it's not dead, but it's certainly dying, ready to turn into a zombie.

Forgive me as I break the fourth wall here and make this first person, but that is not a good thing. For all the problems I have with modern journalism, journalism itself is incredibly important. Or at least it should be. And you won't find many people who love movies more than I do or are a bigger supporter of the pursuit of truth.

That last part, the pursuit of truth, permeates everything else. Without it, nothing has meaning, nothing matters. If the truth is Play-Doh, then it can be molded and bastardized to fit whatever the holder of it wants it to. That includes a lot of things, but it's not truth.

The United States, or any other free people, needs access to accurate, truthful information. Without it we're serfs making decisions based on lies told to us by those in power. When you make decisions based on lies, you are under the control of those feeding you the lies.

But not all lies are obvious and innocuous, "No, those jeans don't make your butt look big" type of lies. What you've just read about are the ways lies and liberal agenda items are the unsuspected dash of salt in a stew: you might not have noticed them before, but now you're acutely aware of them.

It's not my desire that you stop consuming news, it's my hope that you will consume more of it, from as many sources as you can, from all sides. No one has a monopoly on truth-telling, no matter what his motto is, how earnestly he proclaims it, or how much you agree with what he says.

And certainly do not shut yourself off from pop culture. Too many conservatives dismiss something as stupid or worthless simply because it's blatantly liberal. So what? Funny is funny, regardless of the politics. And drama is drama, and romance is . . . well, okay, you might want to check into what the plot of the movie is if it's being sold as a romance. But everything else stands.

You can't win the culture war by refusing to engage in it; you can only lose it.

Still, I'd recommend you not be afraid to leave your comfort zone every now and then. Liberals are attempting to craft safe spaces where their views and opinions won't be challenged. Don't accept that. People don't require a refuge from things they're confident of. The snowflakes on college campuses need the coloring books and the external affirmation; don't be afraid to inspire the cracking open of a few Crayola boxes. Be confident in the truth, don't be afraid to seek it, and question it even if you cause everyone around you to shove their fingers into their ears and hum.

Not to get all *X-Files*-y, but the truth is out there. Not "your truth," as some like to say, but *the* truth. There is no "your truth," there's only your opinion about the truth. The actual truth is not dependent upon your belief in it, it just is. It's people who pervert it.

So go see movies, watch some TV, Lord knows we can all use some distractions from life. If you enjoy Neil deGrasse Tyson or Bill Nye's shows, keep watching them. Just recognize what they are beyond entertainment and do what liberals fear most: question.

Question assumptions, question absolutes, question yourself; everything. Just when you think you've got it is when you're most likely to lose your grip.

The American people have never been more misinformed by the media, but they've also never had access to more information. The house of cards that is the mainstream media will either fall or be forced to change completely. Until that happens, it's up to you to not only be informed but to inform others.

However, and for the love of God, have some fun. Politics is important, certainly, but living beats it in a walk.

Acknowledgments

First, I want to thank my wife, Heather, for her patience. Having a newborn baby and writing a book at the same time generally don't go together, or at least I can't imagine they do. Yet she afforded me all the time needed for research and writing while working full-time and being a first-time mother. I don't know where she hides her "SuperWife" cape, but she wears it well.

Next, my daughter, Quinn. Sure, she's not even a year old, and she's our first child, but I couldn't imagine a more well-behaved baby. That she slept through the night from the start was more helpful than the Internet.

Then there's Eric Nelson at HarperCollins. When I got an email out of the blue asking if I had a literary agent, I first thought it was spam, the new "Nigerian Price" hoping to get me to supply some personal information so that he could steal my identity. But he was real, and crazy enough to think I should write a book. His patience with me as I fumbled through the process and his understanding of family issues and the discussions over the title are something I'll be forever grateful for. Thanks, Eric.

Everyone who ever helped me with writing: Mark Tapscott, Paul Gallagher, Jim Weidman, Rich Tucker, and Brian McNicoll, who, when I worked at the Heritage Foundation, taught me to write and edited me into coherence. And additional thanks to Brian for making sure my columns made sense long after it was his job to.

The team at Townhall.com. When I got an email in 2011 from

Jonathan Garthwaite, the honcho over there, inviting me to lunch to discuss the prospect of writing something for them, I again thought it was a mistake. I immediately agreed because it was a free lunch. He and Kevin Glass then offered me their platform for whatever I felt like writing about, just to see how it went. Seven years and two columns per week later, it is my longest professional relationship. I still think they're crazy for doing it, but I'm eternally grateful. Additional thanks go to the editors there, led by Leah Barkoukis, for making sure my typos don't see the light of day.

Tucker Carlson and Neil Patel. I was the first person they hired back when the Daily Caller was a vague idea hatched by two high school friends. How they found me is too long a story to recount here, but I am so lucky they did.

To anyone who's ever given me a job, and having had nearly seventy (so far), that's a lot people. A special shout-out to those who fired me. While I deserved each of them, they still motivated me.

Finally, and most importantly, my parents. Two better role models I could not have asked for. They not only made me, but made me who I am. Their love and encouragement throughout my life have enabled me to exceed my abilities in all that I've done. My mother passed away with her whole family by her side as I was finishing this book, but to the end, she and my father were always insistent that I work on it, no matter how bad it got and how much I didn't want to. Through fifty-seven years of marriage they loved each other in a way that set an example for me and all my siblings to aspire to. My brother and sisters and I all love one another, get along, love our parents, and speak to and see each other as often as possible. And we all love our parents deeply. There is no better measure for success as people, which easily makes Carol and Doug Hunter the most successful people I've ever known. Thank you, and I love you.

Notes

Introduction

1. Nicholas St. Fluer, "Scientists, Feeling Under Siege. March Against Trump Policies," *New York Times*, April 22, 2017, https://www.nytimes.com/2017/04/22/science/march-for-science.html.
2. Ibid.
3. Anousha Sakoui, "Hollywood Had a Terrible 2017," Bloomberg, January 2, 2018, https://www.bloomberg.com/news/articles/2018-01-02/hollywood-s-2017-is-a-bomb-as-moviegoing-slumps-to-25-year-low.

Chapter 1: The Crazy Factory

1. "A Life Saver Called 'Plumpynut,'" *60 Minutes*, October 19, 2007, https://www.cbsnews.com/news/a-life-saver-called-plumpynut/3/.
2. "Microaggression," Merriam-Webster.com.
3. "Award Abstract #1420168," National Science Foundation, https://www.nsf.gov/awardsearch/showAward?AWD_ID=1420168&HistoricalAwards=false.
4. "Award Abstract #1661279," National Science Foundation, https://www.nsf.gov/awardsearch/showAward?AWD_ID=1661279&HistoricalAwards=false.
5. Ibid.
6. Ibid.
7. "What Is Critical Race Theory?" UCLA School of Public Affairs, https://spacrs.wordpress.com/what-is-critical-race-theory/.
8. "Intersectionality," Wikipedia, https://en.wikipedia.org/wiki/Intersectionality.
9. "Tuition and Fees and Room and Board over Time," College Board, November 14, 2017, https://trends.collegeboard.org/college-pricing/figures-tables/tuition-fees-room-and-board-over-time.
10. Ibid.
11. Emily Tate, "Graduation Rates and Race," Inside Higher Ed, April 26, 2017, https://www.insidehighered.com/news/2017/04/26/college-completion-rates-vary-race-and-ethnicity-report-finds.
12. Christine DiGangi, "The Average Student Loan Debt in Every State," *USA Today*, April 28, 2017, https://www.usatoday.com/story/money/personalfinance/2017/04/28/average-student-loan-debt-every-state/100893668/.

13. "Topics in Comparative Media: American Pro Wrestling," MIT Open Courseware, https://ocw.mit.edu/courses/comparative-media-studies-writing /cms-997-topics-in-comparative-media-american-pro-wrestling-spring-2007/.

14. "CAST 240: How to Win a Beauty Pageant: Race, Gender, Culture, and U.S. National Identity," Oberlin College, http://catalog.oberlin.edu/preview_course _nopop.php?catoid=32&coid=68043.

15. "Wasting Time on the Internet," Engl 111.301, University of Pennsylvania, https://www.english.upenn.edu/courses/undergraduate/2015/spring/engl111.301.

16. "PE 1657—Tree Climbing," Cornell University, http://courses.cornell.edu /preview_course_nopop.php?catoid=12&coid=95399.

17. "Message from the Interim Chair," UCLA Gender Studies Department, http://www.genderstudies.ucla.edu/message-from-the-chair.

18. Elizabeth Howell, "Guion Bluford: First African-American in Space," Space.com, February 8, 2017, https://www.space.com/25602-guion-bluford-biography.html.

19. Beth Dumbauld, "Which College Majors Have the Highest (and Lowest) Employment Rates," StraighterLine, February 26, 2016, https://www.straighter line.com/blog/which-college-majors-have-the-highest-and-lowest-employment -rates/.

20. Katherine Long, "Long-Simmering Discord led to the Evergreen State College's Viral Moment," Seattle Times, June 10, 2017, https://www.seattletimes .com/seattle-news/education/discord-at-evergreen-state-simmered-for-a-year -before-it-boiled-over/.

21. "Day of Absence & Day of Presence," Evergreen State College, https://ever green.edu/multicultural/day-of-absence-day-of-presence.

22. Ibid.

23. Walker Orenstein, "Read the Email Exchange That Sparked Protests Against an Evergreen Professor," News Tribune [Tacoma, WA], June 1, 2017, http://www .thenewstribune.com/news/politics-government/article153826039.html.

24. Katherine Long, "Evergreen Professor Who Questioned Day of Absence Event Plans to Sue College for $3.85 Million," Seattle Times, July 26, 2017, https:// www.seattletimes.com/seattle-news/education/evergreen-professor-plans-to -sue-college-for-385-million/.

25. Andy Thomason, "Evergreen State Will Pay $500,000 to Settle with Professor Who Criticized Handling of Protests," The Chronicle of Higher Education, September 16, 2017, http://www.chronicle.com/blogs/ticker/evergreen-state-will -pay-500000-to-settle-with-professor-who-criticized-handling-of-protests/120110.

26. George S. Bridges, The "The Evergreen State College President: In a Divided Country, Our Campus Will Remain United," Seattle Times, June 14, 2017, https://www.seattletimes.com/opinion/the-evergreen-state-college-president-in -a-divided-country-our-campus-will-remain-united/.

27. Charlotte Allen, "The Fallout Continues at Evergreen," The Weekly Standard, August 8, 2017, http://www.weeklystandard.com/the-fallout-continues-at-ever green/article/2009198.

28. Scott Jaschik, "Who Defines What Is Racist?," Inside Higher Ed, May 30, 2017, https://www.insidehighered.com/news/2017/05/30/escalating-debate-race -evergreen-state-students-demand-firing-professor.

29. Tom Banse, "Enrollment Drops at Evergreen State College, Hiring Freeze Coming," Northwest News Network, August 31, 2017, http://nwnewsnetwork .org/post/enrollment-drops-evergreen-state-college-hiring-freeze-coming.

30. Jennifer Kabbany, "Evergreen State College Faces $2.1M Budget Shortfall, Cites Enrollment Drop, Issues Layoff Notices," The College Fix, August 29, 2017, https://www.thecollegefix.com/post/36145/.

31. Susan Svrluga, "Students Accuse Yale SAE Fraternity Brother of Saying 'White Girls Only' at Party Door," Washington Post, November 2, 2015, https:// www.washingtonpost.com/news/grade-point/wp/2015/11/02/students-accuse -yale-sae-fraternity-brothers-of-having-a-white-girls-only-policy-at-their-party /?utm_term=.059e4f3a65f9.

32. Emily Shire, "Yale Finds No Evidence of Halloween Party Racism," Daily Beast, December 10, 2015, https://www.thedailybeast.com/yale-finds-no-evidence -of-halloween-party-racism.

33. Matt Henson, "No Charges in UND Fraternity Incident," WDAZ-TV, October 8, 2015, http://www.wdaz.com/news/north-dakota/3857144-no-charges-und-fra ternity-incident.

34. "Kean University's Kayla-Simone McKelvey Pleads Guilty to Sending Anonymous Racial Threats on Twitter, Independent, April 19, 2016, http://www .independent.co.uk/student/news/kean-university-s-kayla-simone-mckelvey -pleads-guilty-to-sending-anonymous-racial-threats-on-twitter-a6991841.html.

35. Jessica Remo, "Kean Twitter Threat: I Will Shoot Black Students at Kean University," NJ.com, November 18, 2015, http://www.nj.com/union/index.ssf /2015/11/twitter_account_threatens_to_kill_black_students_a.html.

36. Eric Owens, "JUSTICE: Judge Sends Black Activist to Jail for Hoax Death Threats to Black Students, Faculty," The Daily Caller, June 6, 2016, http://daily -caller.com/2016/06/19/justice-judge-sends-black-activist-to-jail-for-hoax-death -threats-to-black-students-faculty/.

37. Michael Pearson, "A Timeline of the University of Missouri Protests," CNN, November 10, 2015, http://www.cnn.com/2015/11/09/us/missouri-protest-time line/index.html.

38. Daniel Arkin, Alex Johnson, and Jon Schuppe, "University of Missouri President Tim Wolfe Resigns amid Racial Unrest," CNN, November 12, 2015, https://www.nbcnews.com/news/us-news/tim-wolfe-university-missouri-presi dent-says-hes-resigning-amid-racial-n459941.

39. Eric Owens, "AT LAST! Mizzou Has Officially Fired Both Employees Who Bullied Students During Mob Protests," The Daily Caller, July 25, 2017, http:// dailycaller.com/2017/07/25/at-last-mizzou-has-officially-fired-both-employees -who-bullied-students-during-mob-protests/.

40. Jessica Chasmar, "University of Missouri Student Body President Apolo-

gizes for Spreading False KKK Threat," *Washington Times*, November 12, 2015, https://www.washingtontimes.com/news/2015/nov/12/payton-head-mizzou-student-body-president-apologiz/.

41.   Ian Cummings, "Fired MU Professor Melissa Click Hired at Gonzaga University," *Kansas City Star*, September 2, 2016, http://www.kansascity.com/news/state/missouri/article99689332.html.

42.   "University of Missouri Enrollment Lowest Since 2008," *U.S. News & World Report*, September 21, 2017, https://www.usnews.com/news/best-states/missouri/articles/2017-09-21/university-of-missouri-enrollment-lowest-since-2008.

43.   Blake Neff, "Mizzou Closing Four Whole Dorms Because of Collapsing Enrollment," The Daily Caller, April 4, 2016, http://dailycaller.com/2016/04/12/mizzou-closing-four-whole-dorms-because-of-collapsing-enrollment/.

44.   Robby Soave, "Elite Campuses Offer Students Coloring Books, Puppies to Get Over Trump," Daily Beast, November 16, 2016, https://www.thedailybeast.com/elite-campuses-offer-students-coloring-books-puppies-to-get-over-trump.

45.   Briana Boyington, "See 20 Years of Tuition Growth at National Universities," *U.S. News & World Report*, September 20, 2017, https://www.usnews.com/education/best-colleges/paying-for-college/articles/2017-09-20/see-20-years-of-tuition-growth-at-national-universities.

Chapter 2: Who Checks the Fact-Checkers?

1.   Angie Drobnic Holan, "Lie of the Year: the Romney Campaign's Ad on Jeeps Made in China," PolitiFact, December 12, 2012, http://www.politifact.com/truth-o-meter/article/2012/dec/12/lie-year-2012-Romney-Jeeps-China/.

2.   Ibid.

3.   Paul Bedard, "Jeep, An Obama Favorite, Looks to Shift Production to China," *Washington Examiner*, October 25, 2012, http://www.washingtonexaminer.com/jeep-an-obama-favorite-looks-to-shift-production-to-china/article/2511703#.UL-XlmejhAN.

4.   Ibid.

5.   Stephen Jewkes and Stefano Rebaudo, "Fiat Sees at Least 100,000 Jeeps Made in China by 2014," Reuters, January 17, 2013, http://uk.reuters.com/article/uk-fiat-marchionne-china-idUKBRE90G0O620130117.

6.   Holan, "Lie of the Year: the Romney Campaign's Ad on Jeeps Made in China."

7.   Glenn Kessler, "4 Pinocchios for Mitt Romney's Misleading Ad on Chrysler and China," *Washington Post*, October 30, 2012, https://www.washingtonpost.com/blogs/fact-checker/post/4-pinocchios-for-mitt-romneys-misleading-ad-on-chrysler-and-china/2012/10/29/2a153a04-21d7-11e2-ac85-e669876c6a24_blog.html?utm_term=.d4ce8e6bd63b.

8.   Ibid.

9.   Ibid.

10.   Ibid.

11. Glenn Kessler, "Reaffirmed: 4 Pinocchios for a Misleading Mitt Romney Ad on Chrysler and China," *Washington Post*, January 25, 2013, https://www .washingtonpost.com/blogs/fact-checker/post/reaffirmed-4-pinocchios-for -a-misleading-mitt-romney-ad-on-chrysler-and-china/2013/01/24/095964a8 -667d-11e2-9e1b-07db1d2ccd5b_blog.html?utm_term=.bdc032651e58.

12. Angie Drobnic Holan, "Obama's Plan Expands Existing System," PolitiFact, October 9, 2008, http://www.politifact.com/truth-o-meter/statements/2008/oct /09/barack-obama/obamas-plan-expands-existing-system/.

13. Ibid.

14. Angie Drobnic Holan, "Barack Obama Promises You Can Keep Your Health Insurance, but There's No Guarantee," PolitiFact, August 11, 2009, http://www .politifact.com/truth-o-meter/statements/2009/aug/11/barack-obama/barack -obama-promises-you-can-keep-your-health-ins/.

15. Ibid.

16. Louis Jacobson, "Barack Obama Says That Under His Health Care Law, Those Who Have Health Insurance Will Keep It," PolitiFact June 29, 2012, http://www.politifact.com/truth-o-meter/statements/2012/jun/29/barack -obama/barack-obama-says-under-his-health-care-law-those-/.

17. Ibid.

18. David Rutz, "36 Times Obama Said You Can Keep Your Health Plan," *Washington Free Beacon*, November 5, 2013, http://freebeacon.com/issues/36-times -obama-said-you-can-keep-your-health-plan/.

19. Angie Drobnic Holan, "Lie of the Year: 'If You Like Your Health Care Plan, You Can Keep It,'" PolitiFact, December 13, 2013, http://www.politifact.com /truth-o-meter/article/2013/dec/12/lie-year-if-you-like-your-health-care-plan -keep-it/.

20. Lisa Meyers and Hannah Rappleye, "Obama Admin. Knew Millions Could Not Keep Their Health Insurance," NBC News, October 28, 2013, http://www .nbcnews.com/news/other/obama-admin-knew-millions-could-not-keep-their -health-insurance-f8C11484394.

21. Derek Hunter, "Bias: NBC Runs 6 'Fact Checks' During the Debate on Trump, None on Hillary," Daily Caller, October 10, 2016, http://dailycaller.com /2016/10/10/bias-nbc-news-runs-6-fact-checks-during-debate-on-trump-none -on-hillary/.

22. Azadeh Ansari and Rosa Flores, "Chicago's 762 homicides in 2016 is highest in 19 years," CNN, January 2, 2017, https://www.cnn.com/2017/01/01/us /chicago-murders-2016/index.html.

23. "Trump Cites Chicago Gun Laws and Crime Stats as Proof Gun Laws Don't Work. Not So Fast," NBC News, October 19, 2016, http://www.nbcnews.com /card/trump-cites-chicago-gun-laws-crime-stats-proof-gun-laws-n669506.

24. Ibid.

25. Mark Berman, "Chicago Has Tough Gun Laws, but People Can Still Buy Guns Elsewhere and Bring Them There," *Washington Post*, October 19, 2016,

https://www.washingtonpost.com/politics/2016/live-updates/general-election
/real-time-fact-checking-and-analysis-of-the-final-2016-presidential-debate
/chicago-has-tough-gun-laws-but-people-can-still-buy-guns-elsewhere-and
-bring-them-there/?utm_term=.29510ef0e084.

26. Emily Fuhrman, "Watch How Chicago Gets Flooded with Thousands of
Crime Guns," Mike Spies and The Trace, November 2, 2015, https://www.the
trace.org/2015/11/chicago-gun-laws-shootings-trafficking/.

27. Ibid.

28. "Trump Says Union That Endorsed Hillary Is 'All with Me,'" NBC News,
November 1, 2016, http://www.nbcnews.com/card/trump-says-union-endorsed
-clinton-all-me-n676536.

29. "ABC's Brian Ross Suspended for Erroneous Report on Flynn Plea Deal,"
BBC, December 3, 2017, http://www.bbc.com/news/world-us-canada-42214214.

30. Manu Raju and Jeremy Herb, "Email Pointed Trump Campaign to WikiLeaks
Documents," CNN, December 8, 2017, http://www.cnn.com/2017/12/08/politics
/email-effort-give-trump-campaign-wikileaks-documents/index.html.

31. Ibid.

32. Glenn Greenwald, "The U.S. Media Suffered Its Most Humiliating Debacle
in Ages and Now Refuses All Transparency over What Happened," The Intercept,
December 9, 2017, https://theintercept.com/2017/12/09/the-u-s-media-yesterday
-suffered-its-most-humiliating-debacle-in-ages-now-refuses-all-transparency
-over-what-happened/.

33. Ibid.

Chapter 3: Blind to the Truth

1. Joe Concha, "NY Times Mocked for Not Mentioning Embattled Senator
Is a Democrat," The Hill, September 9, 2017, http://thehill.com/homenews
/media/349198-ny-times-mocked-for-not-mentioning-embattled-senator-is-a
-democrat.

2. Mike Ciandella, "Study: CNN's Failure to Cover Democrat's Corruption
Trial," Newsbusters, November 7, 2017, https://www.newsbusters.org/blogs/nb
/mike-ciandella/2017/11/07/study-cnns-failure-cover-democrats-corruption-trial.

3. Ibid.

4. "CNN Loves to Cover Corruption Trials of Senators, Unless the Senator's
a Democrat," The Federalist, September 27, 2017, http://thefederalist.com
/2017/09/27/cnn-loves-to-cover-corruption-trials-of-senators-unless-senators
-a-democrat/.

5. "Sen. Ted Stevens' Conviction Set Aside," CNN, April 7, 2009, http://www
.cnn.com/2009/POLITICS/04/07/ted.stevens/.

6. Mike Ciandella, "CNN Ignores Menendez Trial, Barely Skipped a Day
for Ted Stevens in '08," Newsbusters, September 27, 2017, https://www.news
busters.org/blogs/nb/mike-ciandella/2017/09/27/cnn-ignores-menendez-trial
-barely-skipped-day-ted-stevens-08.

7.   Tim Graham, "Same Partisan Networks That Buried Us in Mark Foley News Utterly Skipping Tim Mahoney Sex Scandal," Newsbusters, October 17, 2008, https://www.newsbusters.org/blogs/nb/tim-graham/2008/10/17/same-partisan-networks-buried-us-mark-foley-news-utterly-skipping-tim.

8.   Emma Schwartz, Rhonda Schwartz, and Vic Walter, "Congressman's $121,000 Payoff to Alleged Mistress," ABC News, October 13, 2008, http://abcnews.go.com/Blotter/Politics/story?id=5997043&page=1.

9.   Graham, "Same Partisan Networks That Buried Us In Mark Foley News Utterly Skipping Tim Mahoney Sex Scandal."

10.   Colby Hall, "Andrew Brietbart to CNN: I Don't Trust Rep. Weiner's Lawyers to Exonerate Anyone," Mediaite, May 31, 2011, https://www.mediaite.com/tv/andrew-brietbart-to-cnn-i-dont-trust-rep-weiners-lawyers-to-exonerate-anyone/.

11.   Matt Schneider, "Jeffrey Toobin: 'Too Bad' Andrew Breitbart Was Allowed on CNN to Make 'Weinergate' Claims," Mediaite, May 31, 2011, https://www.mediaite.com/tv/jeffrey-toobin-too-bad-breitbart-was-allowed-on-cnn-to-make-weinergate-claims/.

12.   Melissa Russo, Tom Winter, and Erik Ortiz, "Anthony Weiner Pleads Guilty in Teen Sexting Case, Wife Huma Abedin Files for Divorce,' NBC News, May 19, 2017, https://www.nbcnews.com/news/us-news/anthony-weiner-plead-guilty-sexting-case-teen-sources-n762036.

13.   Doree Lewak and Heather Hauswirth, "Anthony Weiner Looking for Pen Pals While in Prison," New York Post, November 9, 2017, http://nypost.com/2017/11/09/anthony-weiner-cant-text-in-prison-so-he-wants-snail-mail-instead/.

14.   "Chris Matthews: Trump's Inaugural Address Had a 'Hitlerian Background to It,'" Fox News, January 20, 2017, http://insider.foxnews.com/2017/01/20/chris-matthews-trumps-inaugural-address-had-hitlerian-background-it.

15.   Bernie Sanders, Twitter, January 12, 2017, https://twitter.com/SenSanders/status/819590552576491520.

16.   David Himmelstein and Steffie Woolhandler, "Repealing the Affordable Care Act Will Kill More than 43,000 People Annually," Washington Post, January 23, 2017, https://www.washingtonpost.com/posteverything/wp/2017/01/23/repealing-the-affordable-care-act-will-kill-more-than-43000-people-annually/?utm_term=.5a5fa2305a62.

17.   Fedja Buric, "Trump's Not Hitler, he's Mussolini: How GOP Anti-intellectualism Created a Modern Fascist Movement in America," Salon, March 16, 2017, https://www.salon.com/2016/03/11/trumps_not_hitler_hes_mussolini_how_gop_anti_intellectualism_created_a_modern_fascist_movement_in_america/.

18.   Julia Belluz, "The GOP Plan for Obamacare Could Kill More People Each Year than Gun Homicides," News, June 26, 2017, https://www.vox.com/policy-and-politics/2017/3/14/14921962/ahca-mortality-gun-homicides.

19.   Elizabeth Warren, Twitter, June 22, 2017, https://twitter.com/SenWarren/status/877995366049828866/video/1.

20. Charles M. Blow, "Trump Isn't Hitler. But the Lying . . . ," *New York Times*, October 19, 2017, https://www.nytimes.com/2017/10/19/opinion/trump-isnt -hitler-but-the-lying.html.

21. Robert Barnes, "Gorsuch's Speeches Raise Questions of Independence, Critics Say," *Washington Post*, September 27, 2017, https://www.washingtonpost .com/politics/courts_law/gorsuchs-speeches-raise-questions-of-independence -critics-say/2017/09/27/5accdb3c-a230-11e7-b14f-f41773cd5a14_story.html?utm _term=.cdc8605ad85f.

22. Tom Rogan, "Media Bias? Just Look at Today's Healthcare Headlines," *Washington Examiner*, June 22, 2017, http://www.washingtonexaminer.com /media-bias-just-look-at-todays-healthcare-headlines/article/2626821.

23. Scott Wong, "Top Conservative Calls for Ban on Device Used by Vegas Shooter," The Hill, October 4, 2017, http://thehill.com/homenews/house/353881 -top-conservative-calls-for-ban-on-device-used-by-vegas-shooter.

24. The Hill, Twitter, October 4, 2017, https://twitter.com/thehill/status /915646230159593473.

25. The Hill, Twitter, September 21, 2017, https://twitter.com/thehill/status /910912527822934017.

26. Avery Anapol, "DeVos Flies on Her Own Private Jet for Work-Related Travel," The Hill, September 21, 2017, http://thehill.com/blogs/blog-briefing -room/news/351755-devos-flies-on-private-jet-for-work-related-travel.

27. Peter Baker, "Biden's Speech Likely to Spotlight Strengths, or Foibles," *New York Times*, September 5, 2012, http://www.nytimes.com/2012/09/06/us/politics /bidens-speech-likely-to-highlight-strengths-or-foibles.html?mtrref=www .google.com.

28. "Obama Is the SMARTEST Prez Ever According to Prez Historian," https:// www.youtube.com/watch?v=c50JUQohYwY.

Chapter 4: Bias by Proxy

1. Melissa Locker, "John Oliver Compares Republicans' Health Care Cover-age to Your Dad in a Thong," *Time*, February 26, 2017, http://time.com/4683418 /john-oliver-health-care-republicans-obamacare/.

2. "Federal Subsidies for Health Insurance Coverage for People Under Age 65: 2016 to 2026," Congressional Budget Office, March 2016, https://www.cbo.gov /sites/default/files/114th-congress-2015-2016/reports/51385-healthinsurance baselineonecol.pdf, 19.

3. Peter Ubel, "Why Many Physicians Are Reluctant to See Medicaid Patients," *Forbes*, November 17, 2013, https://www.forbes.com/sites/peterubel/2013/11/07 /why-many-physicians-are-reluctant-to-see-medicaid-patients/#2448fa331045.

4. Betsy McCaughey, "Another 25 Million Obamacare Victims," *New York Post*, January 14, 2014, http://nypost.com/2014/01/14/another-25-million-obama care-victims/.

5. Melissa Locker, "John Oliver Takes Out More Ads to Explain the Health

Care Bill to Trump," *Time*, March 13, 2017, http://time.com/4699225/john-oliver-fox-health-care-bill-trump/.

6. Melissa Locker, "John Oliver Tackles Reality Itself in the Wake of Trump's Presidency," *Time*, February 12, 2017, http://time.com/4668566/john-oliver-trump-president-lies/.

7. Sam Dorman, "ABC Spends 2x More Time on 'Brangelina' than U.S. Economy," Newsbusters, October 11, 2016, http://www.newsbusters.org/blogs/business/sam-dorman/2016/10/11/abc-spends-2x-more-time-brangelina-us-economy.

8. Sam Dorman, "ABC Spends 2x More Time on Elderly Cheerleader than U.S. Economy in October," Newsbusters, November 4, 2016. http://www.newsbusters.org/blogs/business/sam-dorman/2016/11/04/abc-spends-2x-more-time-elderly-cheerleader-us-economy-october.

9. Kate Dwyer "Chrissy Teigen Has the 'Utmost Respect' for Working and Single Mothers," *Time*, March 2, 2017, http://motto.time.com/4689616/chrissy-teigen-does-it-all-help/.

10. Kate Samuelson, "Chrissy Teigen Had the Perfect Reaction to Beyonce's Grammy Performance," *Time*, February 13, 2017, http://motto.time.com/4668787/chrissy-teigen-beyonce-grammys/.

11. Cady Lang, "Beyoncé Posted a Snapchat Photo and the Internet Can't Handle It," *Time*, February 24, 2017, http://time.com/4681768/beyonce-snapchat-internet-reactions/.

12. Ibid.

13. Samantha Cooney, "Chrissy Teigen's Latest Tweet to President Trump Is Epic," *Time*, February 6, 2017, http://time.com/4661009/chrissy-teigen-donald-trump-tweet/.

14. Cady Lang, "Beyoncé Supports LGBTQ Youth After Trump Rolls Back Guidelines Protecting Transgender Students," *Time*, February 23, 2017, http://time.com/4680826/beyonce-trans-youth-bathroom-laws/.

15. Cady Lang, "10 Celebrities Who Lost It When Beyoncé Announced She Was Pregnant with Twins," *Time*, February 2, 2017, https://www.yahoo.com/news/10-celebrities-lost-beyonc-announced-174455340.html.

16. "What Nicki Minaj & Taylor Swift's Feud Says About Feminism," *The Melissa Harris-Perry Show*, July 26, 2015, http://www.msnbc.com/melissa-harris-perry/watch/what-nicki-minaj---taylor-swifts-feud-says-about-feminism-491482691967.

17. "Kanye West Visits Donald Trump," *The O'Reilly Factor*, December 13, 2017, http://video.foxnews.com/v/5246977147001/?#sp=show-clips.

Chapter 5: As Seen on TV

1. Peter Wade, "An Impassioned Bill Nye Gave a Rousing Speech at the DC March for Science," *Esquire* April 22, 2017, http://www.esquire.com/news-politics/news/a54688/bill-nye-march-for-science/.

2.   Ted Johnson, "Bill Nye Joins March for Science amid Threat of Trump Budget Cuts," *Variety*, April 22, 2017, http://variety.com/2017/biz/news/bill-nye -march-for-science-president-trump-1202392989/.

3.   Laura Smith-Spark and Jason Hanna, "March for Science: Protesters Gather Worldwide to Support 'Evidence,'" CNN, April 22, 2017, http://www.cnn .com/2017/04/22/health/global-march-for-science/index.html.

4.   Joel Achenbach, Ben Guarino, and Sarah Kaplan, "Why Scientists Are Marching on Washington and More than 600 Other Cities," *Washington Post*, April 21, 2017, https://www.washingtonpost.com/news/speaking-of-science/wp /2017/04/20/why-scientists-are-marching-on-washington-and-more-than-400 -other-cities/?utm_term=.234fb3c3d9ad.

5.   Eliza Barclay, "Tens of Thousands Marched for Science in More than 600 Cities on 6 Continents," Vox, April 23, 2017, https://www.vox.com/2017/4/23/15395786 /march-for-science-world.

6.   Steven Greenhouse and Jana Kasperkevic, "Fight for $15 Swells into Largest Protest by Low-Wage Workers in US History," *The Guardian* [UK], April 15, 2015, https://www.theguardian.com/us-news/2015/apr/15/fight-for-15-minimum -wage-protests-new-york-los-angeles-atlanta-boston.

7.   Mark Guarino, "Minimum Wage Fight Hits the Streets of Nearly 200 U.S. Cities," Reuters, December 4, 2014, http://www.reuters.com/article/us-usa-fast food-protests/minimum-wage-fight-hits-the-streets-of-nearly-200-u-s-cities -idUSKCN0JI10M20141204.

8.   "Fast-Food Workers Strike in 200 Cities," Daily Beast, https://www.thedaily beast.com/fast-food-workers-strike-in-200-cities.

9.   Steven Greenhouse, "Movement to Increase McDonald's Minimum Wage Broadens Its Tactics," *New York Times*, March 30, 2015, https://www.nytimes .com/2015/03/31/business/movement-to-increase-mcdonalds-minimum-wage -broadens-its-tactics.html.

10.   John Podhoretz, "The Actual Pauline Kael Quote—Not as Bad, and Worse," *Commentary*, February 27, 2011, https://www.commentarymagazine.com/culture -civilization/the-actual-pauline-kael-quote—not-as-bad-and-worse/.

11.   Caitlin Gibson, "The March for Science Was a Moment Made for Bill Nye," *Washington Post*, April 23, 2017, https://www.washingtonpost.com/lifestyle/style /the-march-for-science-was-a-moment-made-for-bill-nye/2017/04/23/bc9429ae -282f-11e7-a616-d7c8a68c1a66_story.html?utm_term=.2e0cfc6e9285.

12.   Ibid.

13.   David Freeman, "Bill Nye Has a Brilliant Idea to Transform NASCAR," Huffington Post, January 29, 2016, https://www.huffingtonpost.com/entry/bill-nye -nascar_us_56ab9303e4b0010e80e9c6fc.

14.   Ibid.

15.   Cristen Conger, "Are Batteries Bad for the Environment?," NBC News, September 16, 2010, http://www.nbcnews.com/id/39214032/ns/technology_and _science-science/t/are-batteries-bad-environment/#.Wf343baZNp8.

16. David Biel, "Electric Cars Are Not Necessarily Clean," *Scientific American*, May 11, 2016, https://www.scientificamerican.com/article/electric-cars -are-not-necessarily-clean/.

17. "Neil De Grasse Tyson: Sexiest Astrophysicist," *People*, November 13, 2000, http://people.com/archive/neil-de-grasse-tyson-sexiest-astrophysicist-vol-54 -no-20/.

18. "Closer to Truth, Full Cast & Crew," IMDb, http://www.imdb.com/title /tt0337541/fullcredits?ref_=tt_cl_sm#cast.

19. "Neil deGrasse Tyson,' IMDb, http://www.imdb.com/name/nm1183205/.

20. Rebecca Shapiro, "Neil deGrasse Tyson Has No Time for Climate Change Deniers Marveling at the Eclipse," Huffington Post, August 29, 2017, https:// www.huffingtonpost.com/entry/neil-degrasse-tyson-climate-change-deniers -eclipse_us_59a5213fe4bc41393a204021.

21. Ibid.

22. "Definition of the NHC Track Forecast Cone," National Oceanic and Atmo-spheric Administration, http://www.nhc.noaa.gov/aboutcone.shtml.

23. Brett Clarkson, "How Hurricane Matthew's Last-Minute Wobble Spared South Florida," *Miami Sun-Sentinel*, October 14, 2016, http://www.sun-sentinel .com/news/weather/hurricane/fl-matthew-after-the-storm-20161013-story.html.

24. Alexandra King, "Neil deGrasse Tyson Says It Might Be 'Too Late' to Re-cover from Climate Change," CNN, September 18, 2017, http://www.cnn.com /2017/09/17/us/neil-degrasse-tyson-on-climate-change-cnntv/index.html ?sr=twCNN091717neil-degrasse-tyson-on-climate-change-cnntv0558PMVODtop.

25. Ibid.

26. Marlow Stern, "Neil deGrasse Tyson Defends Scientology—and the Bush Administration's Science Record," Daily Beast, March 31, 2015, https://www.the dailybeast.com/neil-degrasse-tyson-defends-scientologyand-the-bush-adminis trations-science-record.

27. Ibid.

28. Sean Davis, "Super Scientist Neil deGrasse Tyson Doesn't Understand Sta-tistics," The Federalist, September 10, 2014, http://thefederalist.com/2014/09/10 /super-scientist-neil-degrasse-tyson-doesnt-understand-statistics/.

29. Ibid.

30. Sean Davis, "Another Day, Another Quote Fabricated by Neil deGrasse Ty-son," The Federalist, September 16, 2014, http://thefederalist.com/2014/09/16 /another-day-another-quote-fabricated-by-neil-degrasse-tyson/.

31. "Like Reagan Before Him, Bush Mourns Shuttle Loss," NPR, February 1, 2003, http://www.npr.org/news/specials/shuttle/reagan_bush/.

32. Davis, "Another Day, Another Quote Fabricated by Neil deGrasse Tyson."

33. Maya Rhodan, "Here's How Neil deGrasse Tyson Tried to Completely Ruin *Star Wars*," *Time*, December 21, 2015, http://time.com/4157409/star-wars-neil -degrasse-tyson-force-awakens/.

34. Keith Wagstaff, "Neil deGrasse Tyson Debunks 'Star Wars' Science on Twit-

ter," NBC News, December 21, 2015, https://www.nbcnews.com/tech/tech-news /neil-degrasse-tyson-debunks-star-wars-science-twitter-n483991.

35. Henry Hanks, "Neil deGrasse Tyson Got This Wrong About Sex: 5 Internet brouhahas," CNN, March 13, 2016, http://www.cnn.com/2016/03/13/tech/neil -degrasse-tyson-wrong-sex-twitter/index.html.

36. Patt Morrison, "Bill Nye on the Terrifying Ascendancy of American 'Ding-batitude,'" *Los Angeles Times*, July 19, 2017, http://www.latimes.com/opinion /op-ed/la-ol-patt-morrison-bill-nye-science-20170719-htmlstory.html.

37. Jim Haddadin, "Bill Nye's Guy: Popular TV Show Scientist Throws Support Behind President Obama," Fosters.com, July 19, 2012, http://www.fosters.com /article/20120719/GJNEWS_01/707199689.

38. David Weigel, Ed O'Keefe, and Alex Horton, "Congressman: John Kelly is a 'disgrace to the uniform' and should resign over DACA decision," *Washington Post*, September 5, 2017, https://www.washingtonpost.com/news/powerpost /wp/2017/09/06/congressman-wont-apologize-for-calling-kelly-a-disgrace-to -the-uniform/?utm_term=.691a852619e8.

39. "Anti-war mom glad she didn't meet Bush," NBC News, August 31, 2005, http://www.nbcnews.com/id/9137815/ns/us_news/t/anti-war-mom-glad-she -didnt-meet-bush/#.Wf6MibaZNp8.

40. Mike Allen, "Refusal to See Sheehan Is Second-Guessed," *Washington Post*, August 21, 2005, http://www.washingtonpost.com/wp-dyn/content/article /2005/08/20/AR2005082001046.html.

41. Michael A. Fletcher, "Cindy Sheehan's Pitched Battle," *Washington Post*, August 13, 2005, http://www.washingtonpost.com/wp-dyn/content/article/2005 /08/12/AR2005081201816.html.

Chapter 6: The Doomsday Cult

1. Peter Gwynne, "The Cooling World," *Newsweek*, April 28, 1975, http://www .denisdutton.com/newsweek_coolingworld.pdf.

2. Betty Friedan, "The Coming Ice Age: A True Scientific Detective Story," *Harper's Magazine*, September 1958, https://harpers.org/archive/1958/09/the -coming-ice-age/.

3. Gwynne, "The Cooling World."

4. Ibid.

5. Ibid.

6. "How Al Gore Amassed a $200-Million Fortune After Presidential Defeat," Financial Post, May 6, 2013, http://business.financialpost.com/news/how-al -gore-amassed-a-200-million-fortune-after-presidential-defeat.

7. Jaclyn Schiff, "2006: Al Gore Does Sundance," Associated Press, January 26, 2006, https://www.cbsnews.com/news/2006-al-gore-does-sundance/.

8. Andrea Thompson, "Lightning May Increase with Global Warming," *Scientific American*, November 13, 2014, https://www.scientificamerican.com/article /lightning-may-increase-with-global-warming/.

9. Robert Wilder and Daniel M. Kammen, "Exposed: The Climate Fallacy of 2100," *Scientific American*, October 19, 2016, https://blogs.scientificamerican .com/guest-blog/exposed-the-climate-fallacy-of-2100/.

10. Aly Nielsen and Joseph Rossell, "Katrina Anniversary: Media's 10 Most Outlandish Hurricane Predictions Full of Hot Air," Newsbusters, August 26, 2015, https://www.newsbusters.org/blogs/business/alatheia-nielsen/2015/08/26 /katrina-anniversary-medias-10-most-outlandish-hurricane.

11. Michael E. Mann, Facebook, August 27, 2017, https://www.facebook.com /MichaelMannScientist/posts/1515449771844553.

12. Porter Fox, "The End of Snow?," *New York Times*, February 7, 2014, https://www.nytimes.com/2014/02/08/opinion/sunday/the-end-of-snow .html?mcubz=3.

13. Jon Erdman, "New England Record Snow Tracker: Boston Breaks All Time Seasonal Snow Record in 2014–2015," Weather Channel, https://weather.com /news/news/new-england-boston-record-snow-tracker.

14. Jason Samenow and Ian Livingston, "Snowzilla, Biggest Snow on Record in Baltimore, Top 5 in D.C., Has Ended," *Washington Post*, January 23, 2016, https:// www.washingtonpost.com/news/capital-weather-gang/wp/2016/01/23/blizzard -warning-updates-heavy-snow-and-wind-for-storms-closing-phase/?utm_term =.7bbe8599f1a8.

15. Chris Mooney, "The Surprising Way That Climate Change Could Worsen East Coast Blizzards," January 25, 2016, https://www.washingtonpost.com/news /energy-environment/wp/2016/01/25/climate-scientist-why-a-changing-ocean -circulation-could-worsen-east-coast-blizzards/?utm_term= f734f562f7bb.

16. Roy W. Spencer, "95% of Climate Models Agree: The Observations Must Be Wrong," February 7, 2014, http://www.drroyspencer.com/2014/02/95-of -climate-models-agree-the-observations-must-be-wrong/.

17. Ibid.

18. Larry Bell, "ClimateGate Star Michael Mann Courts Legal Disaster," *Forbes*, September 18, 2012, https://www.forbes.com/sites/larrybell/2012/09/18/climate gate-star-michael-mann-courts-legal-disaster/#6a3ab4c6118c.

19. Hans von Spakovsky, "16 Democrat Ags Begin Inquisition Against 'Climate Change Disbelievers,'" The Daily Signal, April 4, 2016, http://dailysignal .com/2016/04/04/16-democrat-ags-begin-inquisition-against-climate-change-dis believers/.

20. Melanie Arter, "AG Lynch: DOJ Has Discussed Whether to Pursue Civil Action Against Climate Change Deniers," CNS News, March 9, 2016, https:// www.cnsnews.com/news/article/melanie-hunter/ag-lynch-doj-has-discussed -whether-pursue-legal-action-against-climate.

21. Valerie Richardson, "California Senate Sidelines Bill to Prosecute Climate Change Skeptics," *Washington Times*, June 2, 2016, http://www.washingtontimes .com/news/2016/jun/2/calif-bill-prosecutes-climate-change-skeptics/.

22. Marc Morano, "Bill Nye, 'The Jail-the-Skeptics Guy!': Nye Entertains Idea

of Jailing Climate Skeptics for 'Affecting My Quality of Life' (Exclusive Video)," Climate Depot, April 14, 2016, http://www.climatedepot.com/2016/04/14/bill -nye-the-jail-the-skeptics-guy-nye-entertains-idea-of-jailing-climate-skeptics-for -affecting-my-quality-of-life-exclusive-video/.

23. Larry Bell, "That Scientific Global Warming Consensus . . . Not!," *Forbes*, July 17, 2012, https://www.forbes.com/sites/larrybell/2012/07/17/that-scientific -global-warming-consensus-not/#2c6eb7383bb3.

24. Christopher Cadelago, "World Needs 'Brain Washing' on Climate Change, Jerry Brown Says at Vatican," *Sacramento Bee*, November 4, 2017, http://www .sacbee.com/news/politics-government/capitol-alert/article182789821.html.

25. Graham Readfearn, "Global Warming Scientists Learn Lessons from the Pause That Never Was," *The Guardian* [UK], May 3, 2017, https://www.theguard ian.com/environment/planet-oz/2017/may/04/global-warming-scientists-learn -lessons-from-the-pause-that-never-was.

26. Matt McGrath, "Climate Change: Fresh Doubt over Global Warming 'Pause,'" BBC, January 5, 2017, http://www.bbc.com/news/science-environment-38513740.

27. Ibid.

28. Tim Collins, "The Chance of 'Catastrophic' Climate Change Completely Wiping Out Humanity by 2100 Is Now 1-in-20," *Daily Mail* [UK], September 15, 2017, http://www.dailymail.co.uk/sciencetech/article-4888574/1-20-chance-climate -change-wipe-humanity.html.

29. Ibid.

30. "Mass Extinction," http://www.dictionary.com/browse/mass-extinction.

31. Tim Collins, "Earth Will Face a SIXTH Mass Extinction by 2100 Thanks to Global Warming, Predicts Mathematician," *Daily Mail* [UK], September 21, 2017, http://www.dailymail.co.uk/sciencetech/article-4899512/Mathematics-predicts -sixth-mass-extinction-2100.html#ixzz52nudW6Dv.

32. Paul Cassell, "The physical evidence in the Michael Brown case supported the officer [updated with DNA evidence]," *Washington Post*, November 28, 2014, https://www.washingtonpost.com/news/volokh-conspiracy/wp/2014/11/28 /the-physical-evidence-in-the-michael-brown-case-supported-the-officer/?utm _term=.b58c0b53bb75.

33. Ibid.

34. Laura Geggel, "US in Longest 'Hurricane Drought' in Recorded History," Live Science, May 4, 2015, https://www.livescience.com/50704-hurricane-drought .html.

35. Erica Staehling and Ryan Truchelut, "With Harvey and Irma, America's Luckiest Streak of Low Hurricane Activity Is Over," *Washington Post*, September 14, 2017, https://www.washingtonpost.com/news/capital-weather-gang/wp /2017/09/14/with-harvey-and-irma-americas-luckiest-ever-streak-of-low-hurri cane-activity-is-over/?utm_term=.93c5a1118b8f.

36. Ibid.

37. Alexandra King, "Neil deGrasse Tyson Says It Might Be 'Too Late' to Recover from Climate Change," CNN, September 18, 2017, http://www.cnn
.com/2017/09/17/us/neil-degrasse-tyson-on-climate-change-cnntv/index.html.
38. Ibid.

Chapter 7: The Party of Science!

1. Russell Goldman, "Here's a List of 58 Gender Options for Facebook Users,"
ABC News, February 13, 2014, http://abcnews.go.com/blogs/headlines/2014/02
/heres-a-list-of-58-gender-options-for-facebook-users/.
2. Rhiannon Williams, "Facebook's 71 Gender Options Come to UK Users,"
Daily Telegraph [UK], June 27, 2014, http://www.telegraph.co.uk/technology
/facebook/10930654/Facebooks-71-gender-options-come-to-UK-users.html.
3. "Pangender," Dictionary.com, http://www.dictionary.com/browse/pangender.
4. "Gender Nonconformity," Merriam-Webster, https://www.merriam-webster
.com/dictionary/gender%20nonconformity.
5. "Nonbinary Gender or Non-binary Gender," Dictionary.com, http://www
.dictionary.com/meaning/nonbinary-gender.
6. Mary Bowerman, "Siri Corrects Bruce Jenner Questions to Caitlyn Jenner,"
USA Today, July 16, 2015, https://www.usatoday.com/story/tech/2015/07/16/siri
-bruce-jenner-caitlyn-jenner-espn-award/30231421/.
7. Meg Wagner, "Caitlyn Jenner Won't Face Felony Charges for Fatal Crash:
Report," *Daily News* [New York], July 13, 2013, http://www.nydailynews.com
/entertainment/gossip/caitlyn-jenner-won-face-felony-charges-crash-report-arti
cle-1.2290313.
8. Justin Wm. Moyer, "Way Some Critics Don't Think Caitlyn Jenner Deserved the Arthur Ashe Courage Award," *Washington Post*, July 16, 2015, https://
www.washingtonpost.com/news/morning-mix/wp/2015/07/16/why-some-crit
ics-dont-think-caitlyn-jenner-deserved-the-arthur-ashe-courage-award/?utm
_term=.cd6ee484bed9.
9. Julie Tate and Ernesto Londoño, "Judge Finds Manning Not Guilty of Aiding
the Enemy, Guilty of Espionage," *Washington Post*, July 30, 2013, https://www
.washingtonpost.com/world/national-security/2013/07/29/e894a75c-f897-11e2
-afc1-c850c6ee5af8_story.html?utm_term=.06174a7859f8.
10. Aaron Blake and Julie Tate, "Bradley Manning Comes Out as Transgendered: 'I Am a Female,'" *Washington Post*, August 22, 2013, https://www
.washingtonpost.com/world/national-security/bradley-manning-comes-out
-as-transgendered-i-am-a-female/2013/08/22/0ae67750-0b25-11e3-8974-f9
7ab3b3c677_story.html?utm_term=.cd319321bdb7.
11. "San Francisco Gay Pride Rescinds Honour for Bradley Manning," *The
Guardian* [UK], April 27, 2013, https://www.theguardian.com/world/2013/apr/27
/san-francisco-gay-pride-bradley-manning.
12. Ibid.

13. Lucas Grindley, "San Francisco Pride Apologizes, Honors Chelsea Manning," *The Advocate*, April 13, 2014, https://www.advocate.com/pride/2014/04/13/san-francisco-pride-apologizes-honors-chelsea-manning.

14. Ibid.

15. Nancy Coleman, "Transgender Man Gives Birth to a Boy," CNN, August 1, 2017, http://www.cnn.com/2017/07/31/health/trans-man-pregnancy-dad-trnd/index.html.

16. Stephanie Haney, "Modern Family: Mom, Dad, 11-Year-Old Son and Daughter, 13, ALL Identify as Transgender," *Daily Mail* [UK], December 15, 2017, http://www.dailymail.co.uk/news/article-5185209/An-entire-family-four-transgender.html.

17. Max Margan, "'I'm Just Not Sure That I Am a Girl'": Teen Who Began Gender Transition at 12 Reveals WHY He Changed His Mind and Wanted to Go Back to Being a Boy," *Daily Mail* [UK], September 10, 2017, http://www.dailymail.co.uk/news/article-4870974/Boy-began-gender-transition-changed-mind.html.

18. Tristin Hopper, "Why CBC Cancelled a BBC Documentary That Activists Claimed Was 'Transphobic,'" *National Post* [Canada], December 13, 2017, http://nationalpost.com/news/cbc-orders-last-minute-cancellation-of-bbc-documentary-that-activists-say-is-transphobic.

19. Ibid.

20. "100M Men," Rio de Janeiro Olympics, 2016, https://www.olympic.org/rio-2016/athletics/100m-men.

21. Alan Murphy, "Exclusive: Fallon Fox's Latest Opponent Opens Up to #WHOATV," #WHOATV, September 17, 2014, http://whoatv.com/exclusive-fallon-foxs-latest-opponent-opens-up-to-whoatv/.

22. "Teen Transgender Wrestler—A Reluctant Symbol of a Nation Divided," *All Things Considered*, NPR, February 26, 2017, https://www.npr.org/2017/02/26/517394108/teen-transgender-wrestler-a-reluctant-symbol-of-a-nation-divided.

23. Kent Babb, "Transgender Wrestler Mack Beggs Identifies as a Male. He Just Won the Texas State Girls Title," *Washington Post*, February 25, 2017, https://www.washingtonpost.com/sports/highschools/meet-the-texas-wrestler-who-won-a-girls-state-title-his-name-is-mack/2017/02/25/982bd61c-fb6f-11e6-be05-1a3817ac21a5_story.html?utm_term=.c426ef475a7b.

24. Scott Gleeson, "Transgender Wrestler Reluctantly Thrust into Spotlight," *USA Today*, March 2, 2017, https://www.usatoday.com/story/sports/2017/03/02/mack-beggs-transgender-rights-high-school-wrestling-trump-administration/98592436/.

25. Joe Tacopino, "Not Using Transgender Pronouns Could Get You Fined," *New York Post*, May 19, 2016, http://nypost.com/2016/05/19/city-issues-new-guidelines-on-transgender-pronouns/.

26. Anders Hagstrom, "California Can Now Jail People for Misusing Gender Pronouns," The Daily Caller, October 6, 2017, http://dailycaller.com/2017/10/06/california-can-now-jail-people-for-misusing-gender-pronouns/.

27. Ibid.

28. Lindsey Bever, "Students Were Told to Select Gender Pronouns. One Chose 'His Majesty' to Protest 'Absurdity,'" *Washington Post,* October 7, 2016, https://www.washingtonpost.com/news/education/wp/2016/10/07/a-university-told -students-to-select-their-gender-pronouns-one-chose-his-majesty/?utm_term =.0e35d9f9afbf.

29. Zainab Hamid, "Yale Formalizes Freshman to First Year Change," *Yale Daily News,* September 16, 2017, http://yaledailynews.com/blog/2017/09/15/yale -formalizes-freshman-to-first-year-change/.

Chapter 8: Survey Says

1. Max Greenwood, "Support for Stricter Gun Laws Hits All-Time High in Poll," The Hill, October 12, 2017, http://thehill.com/blogs/blog-briefing-room /news/355154-poll-support-for-stricter-gun-laws-hits-all-time-high.

2. Ibid.

3. Tim Graham, "NBC Skips Own Poll Results on Gun Rights, Hillary's Toxic Unpopularity (Worse than Trump)," Newsbusters, September 18, 2017, https://www.newsbusters.org/blogs/nb/tim-graham/2017/09/18/nbc-skips-own-poll -results-gun-rights-hillarys-toxic-unpopularity.

4. "NBC Ignores Own Poll Showing 54 Percent of Americans Disapprove of Obama Job Performance," Media Research Center, August 2014, https://www .mrc.org/biasalerts/nbc-ignores-own-poll-showing-54-percent-americans-disap prove-obama-job-performance.

5. "NBC Ignores Obama Disapproval at 54% in Own Poll, Yet Declares Americans 'Fed Up with Washington,'" Media Research Center, August 2014, https://www.mrc.org/biasalerts/nbc-ignores-obama-disapproval-54-own-poll-yet-de clares-americans-fed-washington.

6. John Eligon and Michael Schwirtz, "Senate Candidate Provokes Ire with 'Legitimate Rape' Comment," *New York Times,* August 19, 2012, http://www.ny times.com/2012/08/20/us/politics/todd-akin-provokes-ire-with-legitimate-rape -comment.html?mtrref=www.google.com.

7. Nia-Malika Henderson and Paul Kane, "Todd Akin Should Drop Out of Senate Race, Romney Says," *Washington Post,* August 21, 2012, https://www.washington post.com/politics/gop-eye-tuesday-deadline-for-akin/2012/08/21/fcf695a2-eb8c -11e1-9ddc-340d5efb1e9c_story.html?utm_term=.ed65ac69a8d6.

8. Bill Schneider, "Why Akin Hurts Romney," Politico, August 27, 2012, https://www.politico.com/story/2012/08/why-akin-hurts-romney-080163.

9. Rebecca Berg, "Biden Warns Romney Policies Would Put Crowd 'Back in Chains,'" *New York Times,* August 14, 2012, https://thecaucus.blogs.nytimes.com /2012/08/14/biden-warns-romney-policies-would-put-crowd-back-in-chains/?m trref=www.google.com

10. Ibid.

11. Mackenzie Weiger, "GOP Slams Biden 'Chains' Remark," Politico, August 14, 2012, https://www.politico.com/story/2012/08/gop-lashes-biden-chains-remark-079717.

12. "Joe Biden 'Chains' Remark Seized Upon by Mitt Romney's Campaign," Huffington Post, August 14, 2012, https://www.huffingtonpost.com/2012/08/14/joe-biden-chains-remark_n_1776463.html.

13. Eligon and Schwirtz, "Senate Candidate Provokes Ire with 'Legitimate Rape' Comment."

14. Jonathan Weisman, "Indiana Senate Candidate Draws Fire for Rape Comments," New York Times, October 23, 2012, https://thecaucus.blogs.nytimes.com/2012/10/23/indiana-senate-candidate-draws-fire-for-rape-comments/.

15. Ibid.

16. Josh Katz, "Who Will Be President?," New York Times, November 8, 2016, https://www.nytimes.com/interactive/2016/upshot/presidential-polls-forecast.html.

17. Natalie Jackson and Adam Hooper, "Election 2016 Forecast," Huffington Post, November 8, 2016, http://elections.huffingtonpost.com/2016/forecast/president.

18. "Who Will Win the Presidency?," FiveThirtyEight, November 8, 2016, https://projects.fivethirtyeight.com/2016-election-forecast/.

19. "Scientist Predicts 99% Chance of Clinton Win," The Last Word with Lawrence O'Donnell, MSNBC, November 4, 2016, https://www.nbcnews.com/video/scientist-predicts-99-chance-of-clinton-win-801634371744.

20. Rob Crilly, "Newsweek Recalls 125,000 Copies of Its Souvenir Madam President Issue," The Telegraph [UK], November 10. 2016, http://www.telegraph.co.uk/news/2016/11/10/newsweek-recalls-125000-copies-of-its-souvenir-madam-president-i/.

21. Katz, "Who Will Be President?"

22. Natalie Jackson, "Why HuffPost's Presidential Forecast Didn't See a Donald Trump Win Coming," Huffington Post, November 10, 2012, https://www.huffingtonpost.com/entry/pollster-forecast-donald-trump-wrong_us_5823e1e5e4b0e80b02ceca15.

23. Ibid.

24. Victor Davis Hanson, "Apocalyptic Progressivism," National Review, April 20, 2017, http://www.nationalreview.com/article/446837/rahm-emanuel-californias-drought-progressives-agenda-more-government.

25. Tory Newmyer, "No Law Could Have Prevented Vegas Shooting, Feinstein Says," Washington Post, October 8, 2017, https://www.washingtonpost.com/news/post-politics/wp/2017/10/08/no-law-could-have-prevented-vegas-shooting-feinstein-says/?utm_term=.df100d444288.

26. Sarah D. Wire, "Sen. Dianne Feinstein Reintroduces Assault Weapons Ban Legislation," Los Angeles Times, November 8, 2017. http://www.latimes.com/politics/essential/la-pol-ca-essential-politics-updates-sen-dianne-feinstein-reintroduces-1510159003-htmlstory.html.

27. Bernie Sanders, "Health Care Is a Right, Not a Privilege," Huffington Post, July 9, 2009, https://www.huffingtonpost.com/rep-bernie-sanders/health-care-is-a-right-no_b_212770.html.

28. Mollie Reilly, "Bernie Sanders: 'Higher Education Should Be a Right,'" Huffington Post, April 4, 2015, https://www.huffingtonpost.com/2015/04/08/bernie-sanders-higher-education_n_7026884.html.

29. Maren Machles, "House Democrats Introduce Children's Bill of Rights," Scripps Howard Foundation Wire, October 9, 2015, http://www.shfwire.com/house-democrats-introduce-childrens-bill-rights/.

Chapter 9: The Hate Crime Hoax

1. Penny Star, "Domestic Terror Attack on Family Research Council in New Exhibit at National Crime Museum," CNS News, March 20, 2015, https://www.cnsnews.com/news/article/penny-starr/domestic-terror-attack-family-research-council-new-exhibit-national-crime.

2. Carol Cratty, "25-year Sentence in Family Research Council Shooting, "CNN, September 19, 2013, http://www.cnn.com/2013/09/19/justice/dc-family-research-council-shooting/index.html.

3. "Southern Poverty Law Center Report: Ku Klux Klan," https://www.splcenter.org/fighting-hate/extremist-files/ideology/ku-klux-klan.

4. "WNBA's Record-Breaking Season Scores Highest Attendance in Five Years," WNBA press release September 21, 2016, http://www.wnba.com/news/record-breaking-attendance-five-years-digital-social-retail/.

5. Paul Krugman, "Assassination Attempt in Arizona," New York Times, January 8, 2011, https://krugman.blogs.nytimes.com/2011/01/08/assassination-attempt-in-arizona/?mcubz=3.

6. Dan Berry, "Looking Behind the Mug-Shot Grin," New York Times, Jan 15, 2011, http://www.nytimes.com/2011/01/16/us/16loughner.html?mcubz=3.

7. The Editorial Board, "America's Lethal Politics," New York Times, June 14, 2017, https://www.nytimes.com/2017/06/14/opinion/steve-scalise-congress-shot-alexandria-virginia.html?_r=0.

8. Ibid.

9. Alexander Burns, "Shooting Is Latest Eruption in a Grim Ritual of Rage and Blame," New York Times, June 14, 2017, https://www.nytimes.com/2017/06/14/us/baseball-shooting-is-latest-eruption-in-a-grim-ritual-of-rage-and-blame.html?smprod=nytcore-iphone&smid=nytcore-iphone-share.

10. The Editorial Board, "America's Lethal Politics."

11. "SPLC Has Seen Rise in Hate Crime, Domestic Terrorism Attacks," All Things Considered, May 27, 2017, http://www.npr.org/2017/05/27/530393081/splc-has-seen-rise-in-hate-crime-domestic-terrorism-attacks.

12. Derek Hunter, "Portland Killer Is an Anti-Circumcision, Bernie Sanders Supporter," The Daily Caller, May 5, 2017, http://dailycaller.com/2017/05/28/portland-killer-is-an-anti-circumcision-bernie-sanders-supporter/.

13. "SPLC Has Seen Rise in Hate Crime, Domestic Terrorism Attacks."

14. Hunter, "Portland Killer Is an Anti-Circumcision, Bernie Sanders Supporter."

15. Ibid.

16. "SPLC Has Seen Rise in Hate Crime, Domestic Terrorism Attacks."

17. Phil Davis and Rachael Pacella, "No Hate Crime Charges for Severna Park Man in University of Maryland Stabbing," *Capital Gazette*, July 14, 2017, http://www.capitalgazette.com/news/for_the_record/ph-ac-cn-sean-urbanski-indictment-0714-20170713-story.html.

18. Dan Rather, "Dear President Trump," Facebook, May 28, 2017, https://www.facebook.com/theDanRather/posts/10158743532925716.

19. Kyle Griffin, Twitter, May 28, 2017, https://twitter.com/kylegriffin1/status/868987396137922560.

20. Olivia Nuzzi, Twitter, May 28, 2017, https://twitter.com/Olivianuzzi/status/868987320908861440.

21. Brad Jaffy, Twitter, May 28, 2017, https://twitter.com/BraddJaffy/status/868989086874423296.

22. "Identifying and Responding to Bias Incidents," Southern Poverty Law Center, https://www.tolerance.org/professional-development/identifying-and-responding-to-bias-incidents.

23. "Documenting Hate," ProPublica, https://projects.propublica.org/graphics/hatecrimes.

24. "Post-Election Bias Incidents Up to 1,372; New Collaboration with Pro-Publica," SPLC Hate Watch, February 10, 2017, https://www.splcenter.org/hatewatch/2017/02/10/post-election-bias-incidents-1372-new-collaboration-propublica.

25. Ibid.

26. Oren Liebermann, "CC Bomb Threats: Teen Suspect Arrested in Israel," CNN, March 23, 2017, http://www.cnn.com/2017/03/23/middleeast/israeli-american-teen-arrested-jcc-bomb-threats/index.html.

27. Mark Berman and Matt Zapotosky, "Former Journalist Arrested, Charged with Threats Against Jewish Facilities," *Washington Post*, March 3, 2017, https://www.washingtonpost.com/news/post-nation/wp/2017/03/03/missouri-man-arrested-charged-with-threats-against-jewish-facilities/?utm_term=.1f1fadec1a93.

28. Anna North, "This Week in Hate: A High School Defaced with 'Trump' and Swastikas," *New York Times*, January 25, 2017, https://www.nytimes.com/2017/01/25/opinion/a-high-school-defaced-with-trump-and-swastikas.html.

29. Ibid.

30. The Editorial Board, "This Week In Hate: A Muslim Police Officer Attacked in Brooklyn," *New York Times*, December 6, 2016, https://www.nytimes.com/2016/12/06/opinion/a-muslim-police-officer-attacked-in-brooklyn.html?rref=collection%2Fcolumn%2Fthis-week-in-hate&action=click&contentCollection=opinion&region=stream&module=stream_unit&version=latest&contentPlacement=10&pgtype=collection.

31. John Counts, "Ann Arbor Woman Pleads Guilty to Making Up Hate Crime,"

MLive, March 7, 2017, http://www.mlive.com/news/ann-arbor/index.ssf/2017/03/ann_arbor_woman_pleads_guilty_1.html.

32. Elizabeth Choi, "Brown Co. Church Member Charged in Staged Hate Crime," WISH-TV, May 3, 2017, http://wishtv.com/2017/05/03/church-organist-charged-after-post-election-vandalization-to-church/.

33. "ISU Professor Arrested, Accused of Making Up Threats and Attack," *Tribune-Star* [Terre Haute, IN], April 21, 2017, http://www.tribstar.com/news/isu-professor-arrested-accused-of-making-up-threats-and-attack/article_c7ca5b60-26d9-11e7-a35a-0f3c7868f652.html.

34. "St. Olaf: Report of Racist Note on Black Student's Windshield Was 'Fabricated,'" Jennifer Brooks and Paul Walsh, *Star Tribune* [Minneapolis], May 11, 2017, http://www.startribune.com/st-olaf-report-of-racist-note-on-black-students-windshield-was-fabricated/421912763/.

Chapter 10: Millionaire Victims

1. Steve Wyche, "Colin Kaepernick Explains Why He Sat During National Anthem," NFL.com, August 27, 2016, http://www.nfl.com/news/story/0ap3000000691077/article/colin-kaepernick-explains-why-he-sat-during-national-anthem.

2. "Fatal Force," *Washington Post*, https://www.washingtonpost.com/graphics/national/police-shootings-2017/.

3. Jackson Connor, "CNN Hosts Under Fire for Putting 'Hands Up' on Air, Critics Claim Bias," Huffington Post, December 15, 2014, http://www.huffingtonpost.com/2014/12/15/cnn-hands-up-host-under-fire-critics-claim-bias_n_6327546.html.

4. Michelle Ye Hee Lee, "'Hands Up, Don't Shoot' Did Not Happen in Ferguson," *Washington Post*, March 19, 2014, https://www.washingtonpost.com/news/fact-checker/wp/2015/03/19/hands-up-dont-shoot-did-not-happen-in-ferguson/?utm_term=3628c2e2a13e.

5. Ibid.

6. Charlene A. Carruthers, "Every 28 Hours . . . ," Huffington Post, December 1, 2014, http://www.huffingtonpost.com/charlene-carruthers/every-28-hours_b_6226490.html.

7. Michelle Ye Hee Lee, "The Viral Claim That a Black Person Is Killed by Police 'Every 28 Hours,'" *Washington Post*, December 24, 2014, https://www.washingtonpost.com/news/fact-checker/wp/2014/12/24/the-viral-claim-that-a-black-person-is-killed-by-police-every-28-hours/?utm_term=.93badb02a243.

8. Emanuella Grinberg, "Why 'Hands Up, Don't Shoot' Resonates Regardless of Evidence," CNN, January 11, 2015, http://www.cnn.com/2015/01/10/us/ferguson-evidence-hands-up/index.html.

9. Josh Levin, "He Doesn't Fit the System," Slate, August 31, 2107, http://www.slate.com/articles/sports/sports_nut/2017/08/kaepernick_isn_t_getting_blackballed_nfl_execs_say_they_re_just_racist.html.

10. Sean Wagner-McGough, "Ray Lewis: Ravens Refused to Sign Colin Kaeper-

nick Because of Girlfriend's Tweet," CBS Sports, September 6, 2017, https://www.cbssports.com/nfl/news/ray-lewis-ravens-refused-to-sign-colin-kaepernick-because-of-girlfriends-tweet/.

11. AJ Willingham, "The #TakeAKnee Protests Have Always Been About Race. Period," CNN, September 27, 2017, http://www.cnn.com/2017/09/27/us/nfl-anthem-protest-race-trump-trnd/index.html.

12. German Lopez, "Trump's Tweets About the NFL Protests Miss the Point Entirely," Vox, September 25, 2017, https://www.vox.com/identities/2017/9/25/16361258/trump-nfl-protests-racism.

13. "Electoral History of John Conyers," Wikipedia, https://en.wikipedia.org/wiki/Electoral_history_of_John_Conyers.

14. Mallory Shelbourne, "Conyers Attorney: Congressman Won't Pay Settlement Back Because It Was 'Cleared,'" The Hill, December 5, 2017, http://thehill.com/homenews/house/363376-conyers-attorney-congressman-wont-pay-settlement-back-because-it-was-cleared.

15. Kelsey Tamborrino, "Pelosi Defends Conyers as 'an Icon,'" Politico, November 26, 2017, https://www.politico.com/story/2017/11/26/pelosi-conyers-icon-harassment-259832

16. Jennifer Hansler, "Michelle Obama: 'Any Woman Who Voted Against Hillary Clinton Voted Against Their Own Voice,'" CNN, September 27, 2017, http://www.cnn.com/2017/09/27/politics/michelle-obama-women-voters/index.html.

17. Nicholas Fondacar, "ABC/NBC Smear Trump, Claim Racially Coded Rhetoric on Kneeling," Newsbusters, September 24, 2017, https://www.newsbusters.org/blogs/nb/nicholas-fondacaro/2017/09/24/abcnbc-smear-trump-claim-racially-coded-rhetoric-kneeling.

18. Paul Bedard, "Mainstream Media Scream: NBC Guest Calls National Anthem 'White Supremacist,'" Washington Examiner, September 25, 2017, http://www.washingtonexaminer.com/mainstream-media-scream-nbc-guest-calls-national-anthem-white-supremacist/article/2635522.

19. Jesse Benn, "White Athletes Still Standing for the Anthem Are Standing for White Supremacy," Huffington Post, September 25, 2017, http://www.huffingtonpost.com/entry/white-athletes-still-standing-for-the-anthem-are-standing_us_59c8acbbe4b0f2df5e83afcd.

20. "Ku Klux Klan," Encyclopaedia Britannica, https://www.britannica.com/topic/Ku-Klux-Klan.

21. "Historical National Population Estimates," US Census Bureau, June 28, 2000, https://www.census.gov/population/estimates/nation/popclockest.txt.

22. Alex Griswold, "House Democratic Caucus Vice Chair: 'I Think It's Time' for Pelosi to Step Down from Leadership," Washington Free Beacon, October 5, 2017, http://freebeacon.com/politics/house-democratic-caucus-vice-chair-time-pelosi-step-down-leadership/.

23. Paul Crookston, "Dem Rep: Criticism of Pelosi 'Really Reflects the Sexism That Still Exists in Politics,'" Washington Free Beacon, October 5, 2017, http://

freebeacon.com/politics/dem-rep-criticism-pelosi-really-reflects-sexism-still
-exists-politics/.

24. "Take Back America Conference 2004," Fair Vote America, http://archive
.fairvote.org/?page=251.

25. "The Real Dope on the TAKE BACK AMERICA Conference," Daily Kos,
June 14, 2006, https://www.dailykos.com/stories/2006/6/14/218715/-.

26. "Arianna Speaking at the 2008 Take Back America Conference," HuffTV,
Huffington Post, March 3, 2008, https://www.huffingtonpost.com/huff-tv/ari
anna-speaking-at-the-2_2_b_92476.html.

27. "'Countdown with Keith Olbermann' for June 19," transcript, NBC News,
June 19, 2007, http://www.nbcnews.com/id/19330534/ns/msnbc-countdown
_with_keith_olbermann/t/countdown-keith-olbermann-june/#.Wdj5WkyZPUo.

28. Chris Cillizza and Shailagh Murray, "'Take Back America' Conference Is a
Chance for Democrats to Highlight Progressive Politics," Washington Post, March
16, 2008, http://www.washingtonpost.com/wp-dyn/content/article/2008/03/15
/AR2008031501958.html.

29. Cheryl K. Chumley, "Eric Holder: 'Racial Animus' Fuels Opposition to
Obama and Me," Washington Times, July 14, 2014, http://www.washingtontimes
.com/news/2014/jul/14/eric-holder-racial-animus-fuels-opposition-obama-a/.

30. Kenneth T. Walsh, "Obama Says Race a Key Component in Tea Party Protests," U.S. News & World Report, March 2, 2011, https://www.usnews.com/news
/articles/2011/03/02/obama-says-race-a-key-component-in-tea-party-protests
?page=3.

31. Tim Graham, "Newsweek Editor Promotes Obama View That Opponents
Are 'Afraid of the Future,' and Oppose Greater 'Understanding,'" Newsbusters,
April 8, 2010, https://www.newsbusters.org/blogs/nb/tim-graham/2010/04/08
/newsweek-editor-promotes-obama-view-opponents-are-afraid-future-and.

32. "'Hardball with Chris Matthews' for Monday, April 5th. 2010," transcript,
NBC News, http://www.nbcnews.com/id/36194089/ns/msnbc-hardball_with_chris
_matthews/t/hardball-chris-matthews-monday-april-th/#.Wdk3vUyZPUo.

33. "'Hardball with Chris Matthews' for June 20," transcript, NBC News, June
21, 2007, http://www.nbcnews.com/id/19351912/ns/msnbc-hardball_with_chris
_matthews/t/hardball-chris-matthews-june/#.WdkD9UyZPUo.

34. Damon Young, "Polite White People Are Useless," The Root, August 8, 2017,
https://verysmartbrothas.theroot.com/polite-white-people-are-useless-17985
46057.

35. Kareem Abdul-Jabbar, "Cornrows and Cultural Appropriation: The Truth
About Racial Identity Theft," Time, August 26, 2015, http://time.com/4011171
/cornrows-and-cultural-appropriation-the-truth-about-racial-identity-theft/.

36. Ibid.

37. Katie Rogers, "Oberlin Students Take Culture War to the Dining Hall," New
York Times, December 21, 2015, https://www.nytimes.com/2015/12/22/us/oberlin
-takes-culture-war-to-the-dining-hall.html.

38. Meredith Simons, "100 Times a White Actor Played Someone Who Wasn't White," *Washington Post*, January 28, 2016, https://www.washingtonpost.com /posteverything/wp/2016/01/28/100-times-a-white-actor-played-someone-who -wasnt-white/?utm_term=.dd215e1bcb33.

39. Reihan Salam, "The Sum of All PC," Slate, May 28, 2002, http://www.slate .com/articles/arts/culturebox/2002/05/the_sum_of_all_pc.html.

40. Alanna Bennett and Krutika Mallikarjuna, "The Head of Marvel TV Says Iron Fist Is White Because It's Important Danny Be an Outsider," Buzzfeed, October 11, 2016, https://www.buzzfeed.com/alannabennett/so-outsidery?utm _term=.imxJzRWeY#.uv47egMjA.

41. Rod Norland, "Lionel Shriver's Address on Cultural Appropriation Roils a Writers Festival," *New York Times*, September 12, 2016, https://www.nytimes .com/2016/09/13/books/lionel-shriver-cultural-appropriation-brisbane-writers -festival.html.

42. Kaitlyn Greenidge, "Who Gets to Write What?," *New York Times*, September 24, 2016, https://www.nytimes.com/2016/09/25/opinion/sunday/who-gets-to-write -what.html?_r=0.

43. Viet Thanh Nguyen, "Arguments over the Appropriation of Culture Have Deep Roots," *Los Angeles Times*, September 26, 2016, http://www.latimes.com /books/jacketcopy/la-ca-jc-appropriation-culture-20160926-snap-story.html.

44. Ayana Byrd, "How to Donate Money and Other Aid to Communities of Color in Houston," ColorLines, August 29, 2017, http://www.colorlines.com/articles /how-donate-money-and-other-aid-communities-color-houston.

45. "About Us, Race Forward: The Center for Racial Justice Innovation," https:// www.raceforward.org/about.

46. Ibid.

47. Ibid.

Chapter 11: They're Making a Movie About It

1. Kelly Lawler, "Chris Evans Is Not Apologizing for Speaking Out About Politics," *USA Today*, March 15, 2017, https://www.usatoday.com/story/life/entertain -this/2017/03/15/chris-evans-politics-twitter-trump-esquire-profile/99203768/.

2. "Wyclef Jean's Haiti Charity a 'Cesspool of Fraud and Broken Promises' That Has Collapsed Under Mountain of Debt," *Daily Mail* [UK], October 12, 2012, http://www.dailymail.co.uk/news/article-2217090/Wyclef-Jeans-Haiti-charity -cesspool-fraud-broken-promises-collapsed-mountain-debt.html.

3. Deborah Sontag, "In Haiti, Little Can Be Found of a Hip-Hop Artist's Charity," *New York Times*, October 11, 2012, http://www.nytimes.com/2012/10/12/world /americas/quake-hit-haiti-gains-little-as-wyclef-jean-charity-spends-much.html.

4. Gary Baum, "Leonardo DiCaprio, the Malaysian Money Scandal and His 'Unusual' Foundation," *Hollywood Reporter*, August 17, 2016, https://www.holly woodreporter.com/features/leonardo-dicaprio-malaysian-money-scandal-920199.

5. Ibid.

6. Ibid.

7. Ibid.

8. "The Truth About Celebrity Giving," *Forbes*, November 24, 2008, https://www.forbes.com/2008/11/24/oprah-philanthropy-celebrity-biz-media-cz_dkr_1124charitycelebs.html#67c127845dbf.

9. Isabel Vincent, "Charity Watchdog: Clinton Foundation a 'Slush Fund,'" *New York Post*, April 26, 2015, https://nypost.com/2015/04/26/charity-watchdog-clinton-foundation-a-slush-fund/.

10. Cristina Alesci and Laurie Frankel, "Clinton Foundation Takes Steps to Be Rated by Charity Watchdog," CNN Money, May 12, 2016, http://money.cnn.com/2016/05/12/news/economy/clinton-foundation-charity-navigator/index.html.

11. Richard Johnson, "MSNBC Fires Baldwin over Anti-Gay Slurs," *New York Post*, November 26, 2013, http://pagesix.com/2013/11/26/msnbc-fires-alec-baldwin/.

12. Stephen M. Silverman, "Did Zach Galifianakis Want Mel Gibson's *Hangover 2* Cameo Canceled?," *People*, October 22, 2010, http://people.com/movies/zach-galifianakis-protests-mel-gibson-in-the-hangover-2/.

13. "Guardians of the Galaxy Vol. 2," IMDb, http://www.imdb.com/title/tt3896198/?ref_=nv_sr_1.

14. "Moonlight," IMDb, http://www.imdb.com/title/tt4975722/.

15. Ibid.

16. David Rutz, "Sandra Bullock Attached to Star in Movie Dramatizing Wendy Davis Abortion Filibuster," Washington Free Beacon, November 10, 2017, http://freebeacon.com/culture/sandra-bullock-attached-to-star-in-movie-dramatizing-wendy-davis-abortion-filibuster/.

17. "Deepwater Horizon," Box Office Mojo, http://www.boxofficemojo.com/movies/?id=deepwaterhorizon.htm.

18. Dana Harris, "Skoll Toasts New Shingle," *Variety*, June 16, 2004, http://variety.com/2004/film/markets-festivals/skoll-toasts-new-shingle-1117906598/.

19. "99%: The Occupy Wall Street Collaborative Film," Participant Media, https://www.participantmedia.com/film/99-occupy-wall-street-collaborative-film.

20. "American Gun," Participant Media, https://www.participantmedia.com/film/american-gun.

21. "Fair Game," Participant Media, https://www.participantmedia.com/film/fair-game.

22. "Promised Land," IMDb, http://www.imdb.com/title/tt2091473/?ref_=nv_sr_1.

23. "Promised Land," Box Office Mojo, http://www.boxofficemojo.com/movies/?id=promisedland2012.htm.

24. "Grace Is Gone," IMDb, http://www.imdb.com/title/tt0772168/?ref_=nv_sr_1.

25. "Grace Is Gone," Box Office Mojo, http://www.boxofficemojo.com/movies/?id=graceisgone.htm.

26. "Lions for Lambs," IMDb, http://www.imdb.com/title/tt0891527/?ref_=nv _sr_1.

27. "Lions for Lambs," Box Office Mojo, http://www.boxofficemojo.com/movies /?id=lionsforlambs.htm.

28. "In the Valley of Elah," Wikipedia, https://en.wikipedia.org/wiki/In_the _Valley_of_Elah.

29. "In the Valley of Elah," Box Office Mojo, http://www.boxofficemojo.com /movies/?id=inthevalleyofelah.htm.

30. "Redacted," IMDb, http://www.imdb.com/title/tt0937237/?ref_=nv_sr_1.

31. "Redacted," Box Office Mojo, http://www.boxofficemojo.com/movies/?id =redacted.htm.

32. "Rendition," IMDb, http://www.imdb.com/title/tt0804522/?ref_=nv_sr_1.

33. "Rendition," Box Office Mojo, http://www.boxofficemojo.com/movies/?id =rendition.htm.

34. Dylan, "Lil' Bush: Prepubescent Prez Part of New Comedy Central Cartoon," *Adweek*, June 5, 2007, http://www.adweek.com/digital/lil-bush-prepubescent -prez-part-of-new-comedy-central-cartoon/.

35. Rebecca Keegan, "Kicking It into 'High Gear,' Academy President Says Oscar Changes Are 'the Right Thing to Do,'" *Los Angeles Times*, January 22, 2016, http://www.latimes.com/entertainment/envelope/la-et-mn-oscars-reform -20160123-story.html.

36. Nellie Andreeva, "Legal Drama 'Doubt' Co-starring Laverne Cox Picked Up to Series by CBS, Breaks New Ground for Transgender Actors," Deadline Hollywood, May 14, 2016, http://deadline.com/2016/05/doubt-cbs-series-laverne -cox-katherine-heigl-transgender-actors-1201756155/.

37. "22 LGBT TV Shows Killed by Low Ratings," *The Advocate*, https://www .advocate.com/television/2017/3/15/22-lgbt-tv-shows-killed-low-ratings#slide-0.

38. Daniel Reynolds, "*Doubt*'s Cancellation Is a Cruel and Ill-Timed Blow to Trans Visibility," *The Advocate*, February 25, 2017, https://www.advocate.com/commen tary/2017/2/25/doubts-cancelation-cruel-and-ill-timed-blow-trans-visibility.

39. Greg Hernandez, "Laverne Cox pilot The Trustee will not be a series on ABC," Gay Star News, May 16, 2017, https://www.gaystarnews.com/article/laverne -cox-pilot-the-trustee-will-not-be-a-series-on-abc/.

40. Nellie Andreeva, "Laverne Cox to Star in ABC Pilot 'The Trustee' Pro- duced by Elizabeth Banks," Deadline Hollywood, March 7, 2017, http://deadline .com/2017/03/laverne-cox-star-the-trustee-abc-pilot-elizabeth-banks-1202038279/.

41. Megan Garber, "'Donald Trump' Gets a Comedy Central Series," *The Atlan- tic*, April 3, 2017, https://www.theatlantic.com/entertainment/archive/2017/04/ donald-trump-impression-gets-a-comedy-central-show/521718/.

42. Peter A. Berry, "2017 MTV Video Music Awards Had Lowest Ratings of All Time," XXL, August 30, 2017, http://www.xxlmag.com/news/2017/08/2017-mtv -video-music-awards-lowest-viewership-of-all-time/?trackback=tsmclip.

43. Heather Hunter, "What a Surprise: Another Hollywood Award Show Goes Political," Lifezette, August 28, 2017, https://www.lifezette.com/popzette/yet-an other-hollywood-award-show-goes-political/.

44. Rachel Desantis, "Taylor Swift's Silence on Politics Fuels Speculation That She Secretly Voted for Trump," Daily News [New York], September 3, 2017, http://www.nydailynews.com/entertainment/taylor-swift-political-silence-sparks -belief-voted-trump-article-1.3465716.

45. Ibid.

46. Amy Zimmerman, "Taylor Swift's Loud Election Silence—and Connection to Donald Trump," Daily Beast, July 20, 2016, http://www.thedailybeast.com /taylor-swifts-loud-election-silenceand-connection-to-donald-trump.

47. Ibid.

48. Ibid.

49. Hugh McIntyre, "Taylor Swift's 'Look What You Made Me Do' Video Has Shattered YouTube Records," Forbes, August 29, 2017, https://www.forbes.com /sites/hughmcintyre/2017/08/29/taylor-swifts-look-what-you-made-me-do-video -has-shattered-youtube-records/#7ac5d2c212a6.

50. Alanna Bennett, "Taylor Swift's Persona Is Not Built for 2017," Buzzfeed News, November 10, 2017, https://www.buzzfeed.com/alannabennett/taylor-swift -persona-2017-reputation?bftw&utm_term=.jvvBrGVQO#.rkJ9LV4wX.

51. Kayleigh Roberts, "5 Things Taylor Swift *Should* Have Addressed on 'Rep utation' but Didn't," Marie Claire, November 14, 2017, http://www.marieclaire .com/celebrity/music/a13527003/taylor-swift-reputation-should-have-addressed/.

52. Ibid.

53. Ibid.

54. "Ku Klux Klan," Southern Poverty Law Center, https://www.splcenter.org /fighting-hate/extremist-files/ideology/ku-klux-klan.

55. Nick Vivarelli, "George Clooney: 'There's a Dark Cloud Hanging over Our Country,'" New York Post, September 2, 2017, http://pagesix.com/2017/09/02 /george-clooney-theres-a-dark-cloud-hanging-over-our-country/?utm_campaign =SocialFlow&utm_source=NYPTwitter&utm_medium=SocialFlow&sr_share =twitter.

56. Hillary Hughes, "Matt Damon Explains How Suburbicon Shows the 'Defini tion of White Privilege' at Work," MTV News, September 2, 2017, http://www.mtv .com/news/3034190/matt-damon-george-clooney-suburbicon-white-privilege/.

57. Roger Friedman, "Exclusive: 'Roseanne' Revival Will Feature 'Gender Cre ative' 9 Year Old Son of Darlene and David," Showbiz 411, July 31, 2017, http:// www.showbiz411.com/2017/07/31/exclusive-roseanne-revival-will-feature-gen der-creative-9-year-old-son-of-darlene-and-david.

58. Ruth Kinane, "Roseanne Reboot Casts Darlene and David's Son," Entertain ment Weekly, September 7, 2017, http://ew.com/tv/2017/09/07/roseanne-reboot -casts-darlene-david-son/.

Chapter 12: Famous for Being Infamous

1. Leslie Larson, "Outrage After Woman Flashes Middle Finger at Arlington National Cemetery and Posts Photo to Facebook to Brag About It," *Daily Mail* [UK], November 20, 2012, http://www.dailymail.co.uk/news/article-2236012/Lindsey-Stone-flashes-middle-finger-Arlington-National-Cemetery-posts-photo-Facebook-brag-it.html.

2. Cavan Sieczkowski, "Lindsey Stone, Plymouth Woman, Takes Photo at Arlington National Cemetery, Causes Facebook Fury," Huffington Post, November 20, 2012, http://www.huffingtonpost.com/2012/11/20/lindsey-stone-facebook-photo-arlington-national-cemetery-unpaid-leave_n_2166842.html.

3. "Facebook Photo of Plymouth Woman at Tomb of the Unknowns Sparks Outrage," CBS Boston, November 20, 2012, http://boston.cbslocal.com/2012/11/20/facebook-photo-of-plymouth-woman-at-tomb-of-the-unknowns-sparks-outrage/.

4. Rheana Murray, "Woman on Unpaid Leave After Taking Disrespectful Photo Next to Soldier's Grave During Work Trip," *Daily News* [New York], November 21, 2012, http://www.nydailynews.com/news/national/vulgar-facebook-pic-woman-canned-article-1.1205609.

5. Pete D'Amato, "Non-profit Worker Who Provoked Fury with Disrespectful Arlington Photo Tells How She Lost Her Job, Can't Date and Now Lives in Fear," *Daily Mail* [UK], February 22, 2015, http://www.dailymail.co.uk/news/article-2964489/I-really-obsessed-reading-Woman-fired-photo-giving-middle-finger-Arlington-National-Cemetery-says-finally-Google-without-fear.html.

6. "Did Jennifer Lawrence Say Hurricanes Are 'Nature's Wrath' Against Trump?," Snopes, http://www.snopes.com/jennifer-lawrence-hurricanes-trump/.

7. Ibid.

8. Ashley Lee, "Michael Moore, Mark Ruffalo Lead Trump Tower Protest After Broadway Play," *Hollywood Reporter*, August 15, 2017, http://www.hollywoodreporter.com/news/michael-moore-leads-trump-tower-protest-mark-ruffalo-broadway-play-1029906.

9. Debbie Melnyk, "Taking On the Big Man," *The Telegraph* [UK], April 15, 2007, http://www.telegraph.co.uk/culture/3664554/Taking-on-the-big-man.html.

10. "Moore: No Manufacturing in Roger & Me," *Globe and Mail* [Toronto], June 18, 2007, https://beta.theglobeandmail.com/arts/moore-no-manufacturing-in-roger-me/article687822/?ref=http://www.theglobeandmail.com&reqid=%257B%257Brequest_id%257D%257D.

11. Russell Goldman, "Michael Moore Snubs Union Workers in Making 'Capitalism: A Love Story,'" ABC News, October 1, 2009, http://abcnews.go.com/Business/michael-moore-snubs-union-workers-making-capitalism-love/story?id=8715559.

12. Ibid.

13. Larissa MacFarquhar, "The Populist," *The New Yorker*, February 16, 2004, https://www.newyorker.com/magazine/2004/02/16/the-populist.

14. Ibid.

15. Ibid.

16. Roger Ebert, "Attacks on 'Roger & Me' Completely Miss the Point of the Film," February 11, 1990, http://www.rogerebert.com/rogers-journal/attacks-on -roger-and-me-completely-miss-point-of-film.

17. Ibid.

18. "Michael Moore's Lavish Property Empire Is Revealed in Court Documents as He and Wife of 22 Years Divorce," *Daily Mail* [UK], July 24, 2014, http://www .dailymail.co.uk/news/article-2705149/Michael-Moores-lavish-property-empire -revealed-court-documents-wife-22-years-divorce.html#ixzz4u8Sku3bo.

19. Brian Stelter, "Company Parts Ways with PR Exec After AIDS in Africa Tweet," CNN, December 21, 2013, http://www.cnn.com/2013/12/21/us/sacco-of fensive-tweet/index.html.

20. Beth Stebner, "IAC Fires PR Exec Justine Sacco over 'Racist' Tweet over AIDS," *Daily News* [New York], December 21, 2013, http://www.nydailynews.com /news/national/pr-exec-justine-sacco-tweet-sparks-aids-donations-article -1.1554932.

21. Kami Dimitriva, "Woman Fired After Tweet on AIDS in Africa Sparks In ternet Outrage," ABC News, December 21, 2013, http://abcnews.go.com/Interna tional/woman-fired-tweet-aids-africa-sparks-internet-outrage/story?id=21298519.

22. Todd Spangler, "IAC Fires PR Chief Justine Sacco After Firestorm over AIDS Tweet," *Variety*, December 21, 2013, http://variety.com/2013/biz/exec-shuffle -people-news/iac-fires-pr-chief-justine-sacco-after-firestorm-over-aids-tweet -1200984675/.

23. Hunter Stuart, "Justine Sacco's Tweet About AIDS, Africa Is the Craziest Thing You'll See Today," Huffington Post, December 21, 2013, http://www.huff ingtonpost.com/2013/12/20/justine-sacco-tweet-iac-aids-africa_n_4482502.html.

24. Ali Vingiano, "This Is How a Woman's Offensive Tweet Became the World's Top Story," Buzzfeed, December 21, 2013. https://www.buzzfeed.com/alison vingiano/this-is-how-a-womans-offensive-tweet-became-the-worlds-top-s?utm _term=.jeyZoRWy3#.ffqQZVO9j.

25. Lucy Waterlow, "'I Lost My Job, My Reputation and I'm Not Able to Date Anymore': Former PR Worker Reveals How She Destroyed Her Life One Year After Sending 'Racist' Tweet Before Trip to Africa," *Daily Mail* [UK], February 16, 2015, http://www.dailymail.co.uk/femail/article-2955322/Justine-Sacco-reveals -destroyed-life-racist-tweet-trip-Africa.html.

26. Justine Sacco, LinkedIn profile, https://www.linkedin.com/in/justinesacco.

27. Michael Schramm, "Jerry Seinfeld Says Comedians Avoid College Gigs, Students Are 'So PC,'" USA Today College, June 8, 2015, http://college.usatoday .com/2015/06/08/jerry-seinfeld-espn-college-campuses-politically-correct/.

28. Ibid.

29. David French, "James Damore's Lawsuit Exposes Google's Culture of Ignorant Intolerance," *National Review*, January 9, 2017, http://www.nationalreview.com /article/455288/james-damores-google-lawsuit-exposes-companys-intolerance.

30. David Ingram and Ishita Palli, "Google Fires Employee Behind Anti-diversity Memo," Reuters, August 7, 2017, https://www.reuters.com/article/us-google -diversity/google-fires-employee-behind-anti-diversity-memo-idUSKBN1AO088.
31. Bill Chappell and Laura Sydell, "Google Reportedly Fires Employee Who Slammed Diversity Efforts," NPR, August 7, 2017, https://www.npr.org/sections /thetwo-way/2017/08/07/542020041/google-grapples-with-fallout-after-employee -slams-diversity-efforts.
32. Hamza Shaban, "Google Canceled All-Hands Meeting After Employees Were Harassed Online," *Washington Post*, August 11, 2017, https://www.washing tonpost.com/news/the-switch/wp/2017/08/11/google-canceled-all-hands-meet ing-after-employees-were-harassed-online/?utm_term=.89e8f97d253f.
33. Kate Conger, "Exclusive: Here's the Full 10-Page Anti-Diversity Screed Circulating Internally at Google [Updated]," Gizmodo, August 5, 2017, https://giz modo.com/exclusive-heres-the-full-10-page-anti-diversity-screed-1797564320.
34. Abby Ohlheiser, "How James Damore Went from Google Employee to Right-Wing Internet Hero," *Washington Post*, August 12, 2017, https://www.washington post.com/news/the-intersect/wp/2017/08/12/how-james-damore-went-from -google-employee-to-right-wing-internet-hero/?utm_term=.dd52930234f2.
35. Conger, "Exclusive: Here's the Full 10-Page Anti-Diversity Screed Circulating Internally at Google [Updated]."
36. Ibid.
37. Ibid.
38. Elizabeth Chuck, "James Damore, Google Engineer Fired for Writing Manifesto on Women's 'Neuroticism,' Sues Company," NBC News, January 8, 2018, https://www.nbcnews.com/news/us-news/google-engineer-fired-writing-mani festo-women-s-neuroticism-sues-company-n835836.

Index

About the Author

Derek Hunter is a writer, radio host, columnist, and political consultant. He has worked at the Heritage Foundation as a health policy analyst; was federal affairs manager at Americans for Tax Reform, focusing on tech, education, and judicial policy; and was a cofounder of the Daily Caller. He lives in Washington, DC.